PARISH THE THOUGHT

PARISH
THE THOUGHT

An Inspirational Memoir of Growing Up Catholic in the 1960s

JOHN BERNARD RUANE

POCKET BOOKS
NEW YORK   LONDON   TORONTO   SYDNEY

Pocket Books
A Division of Simon & Schuster, Inc.
1230 Avenue of the Americas
New York, NY 10020

First Pocket Books trade paperback edition October 2008

POCKET and colophon are registered trademarks of Simon & Schuster, Inc.

For information about special discounts for bulk purchases,
please contact Simon & Schuster Special Sales at
1-800-456-6798 or business@simonandschuster.com.

Manufactured in the United States of America

10 9 8 7 6 5 4 3 2 1

ISBN-13: 978-1-4165-8949-5
ISBN-10:   1-4165-8949-X

This book is dedicated to the memory of
Bernard and Therese Ruane

Author's Note

Parish the Thought *is a true story. The Ruane family and relatives, as well as the names of the priests and teachers from St. Bede the Venerable, are accurate. The other names mentioned in this book have been changed to protect the privacy of those individuals.*

Acknowledgments

I would like to thank the following people for their memories and insights about the experiences shared with them in the 1960s and early '70s. Their input allowed me to accurately expand on the details of these memoirs. Maureen Gibbons, Kathy Savory, Dan Ruane, Margaret Sedlak, Charlotte Ruane, Brother Robert Ruane, James Conoboy, Ann Conoboy, Sheila Madjecki, Patricia Karnick, JoAnne Nealon, Edward Haggerty, Malachy Mannion, Martin and Patricia Durkin, Marty Durkin, Edward Crane, Glen Leonard, Mike Hannigan, Kevin Wolf, William Matevich, Mike Rourke, Charles Naso, Jamie Corso, Anne O'Malley, Wally Bruckner, Tom O'Halleran, Keith Marciano, Leo Miklius, Tom McKeague, Dan Lemmonier, James Muting Sr., Robert Kostolanski, and Richard Kawczynski.

In addition, I thank the following people and organizations for the historical documentation required to accurately relate the stories in this book: Father Marion Soprych, Marianne Cook, Marion Schmitz, Joan Sclusnik, and Richard Guerin of St. Bede the Venerable; Julie Sackett of the Archdiocese of Chicago's Cardinal Bernadin Archives; and the Chicago Public Library.

I would also like to thank my editor, Ken Paxson, and designer, John Vieceli, for their wonderful work on this book. They are two very talented professionals, and I was blessed to have their support on this project. Also, thanks to Mark Vancil for his guidance.

And I thank my wife, Charlotte, and children, Megan, Sean, Maggie, and Kelly, for their support as I dedicated a great deal of time to this book over the past three years.

Contents

Introduction

We are all born into this world with no choice for the circumstances and environment we enter. A good number of us are born into poor families; many others into the middle class; and a far smaller percentage are placed into the cradle with a silver spoon.

When we open our eyes, we may be lucky enough to see a loving mother and father; or perhaps just one loving parent; or maybe even the ceiling of an orphanage. Our first birthday celebration is a surprise party, and the present is the life into which God has delivered us.

If we are lucky enough to have one or both parents, we will be raised according to the choices those parents make on our behalf. That doesn't mean those choices are right or wrong, good or bad, just merely decisions parents are called upon to make.

Religion is one of those choices. I could have been born into a Jewish, Protestant, or Muslim family. Or, my God, even an atheist family! But no matter what faith we receive, our parents are there to guide us. How they conduct themselves within that faith will affect our own personal view about religion and eventually how we conduct ourselves. We are all products of our parents.

As we grow older, we begin to break away from our parents' views and start making our own religious assessments. We begin forming our own opinions, which may or may not be in agreement with those of our parents. By the time we are in our midteens, we pretty much know it all and are eager to let our parents and anyone else who will listen know it.

I was born into a hard-working, blue-collar, middle-class, Irish-Catholic family in St. Bede the Venerable Parish on the Southwest Side of Chicago. This was a typical neighborhood, but upon meeting new people and being asked "Where you from?" the initial answer was always "Bede's." Our home was our parish and anyone blurting out "Bede's" or "Dennis" or "Redeemer" understood who you were and where you lived. And if they wanted to pinpoint the location, "84th and Kostner, right down the street from the church." This quick oral exchange was more efficient than today's MapQuest.

My father, Bernard Joseph Ruane, emigrated from Galway, Ireland, in 1948 at the age of twenty-one. He was born and raised Roman Catholic, as are most in Ireland. My mother grew up on the West Side of Chicago and was a devout Catholic who gave serious consideration to becoming a nun. My parents met on New Year's Eve 1953, were married in Resurrection Church, and, like the good Catholics they were, proceeded to have five children.

When they moved to St. Bede's in 1958, my mother found a new home only one block away from the new church, the perfect location—just down the block from God's house. I was brought to His house every Sunday beginning from as early as I can remember, age four. Soon I was enrolled in St. Bede's Catholic School.

Reflecting on my days at St. Bede's, I realize what a wonderful place it was: a great neighborhood with a good family environment. But when I was growing up, like all kids, I had no perspective. I thought everyone in America grew up in a Catholic parish, with their mom at home and father at work.

Parish the Thought is a nostalgic look at growing up Catholic in America in the 1960s, most certainly a unique though shared experience for many baby boomers. As we age, many of us struggle to gain perspective on our lives during those formative years. It's amazing how many lost memories I found through thoughtful concentration and rummaging through family memorabilia, as well as through discussions and interviews with family and friends.

This book is an honest account of how this altar boy thought, felt, and acted during that time. I tell of the good and bad times the Ruanes of South Kostner Avenue enjoyed and endured during the chaotic '60s, including a fire that nearly destroyed our home and my mother's battle with cancer.

I recount some funny and challenging episodes at St. Bede's School, where my favorite teacher—a beautiful miniskirted blonde who introduced all the boys in our class to the forbidden land of lust—was fired in 1968 for protesting the Vietnam War. I share the story of my first love and how she broke my heart.

I detail my experience as an altar boy at St. Bede's Church, surviving the impatience of a drunken, flatulent priest and money-hungry pastor, as well as a heaven-sent guitar-playing tenor in black cassock and white Roman collar who showed us the light.

I relate anecdotes from my neighborhood: summer days of bounce-or-fly off the porch steps and baseball at Durkin Park, standing up to my first bully, building forts and quarreling brothers.

I chronicle how the Vietnam War was ever present with the brass nameplates listing the parish soldiers on the large wooden board hung on the church wall, as well as the sight of the blue service stars in the windows of the homes along my paper route.

My story is just one among the millions of American Catholics growing up in the 1960s. I hope my experiences will take you back to that time and place in your own life, allowing you to relive those days of youth.

Thank you for taking the time to read *Parish the Thought*. I hope you enjoy reading it as much as I enjoyed writing it.

Chapter One

HOLY FATHER GRIFFIN

I always will remember the first time I saw Father John Griffin, the pastor of St. Bede the Venerable Catholic Church. It was May of 1963 and I was a six-year-old first-grader at John Crerar School, the public school I attended because St. Bede's Grammar School didn't offer kindergarten or first grade at the time.

On this memorable spring Saturday afternoon, I was sitting in the big, brand-new beautiful church that would open officially a few months later when Auxiliary Bishop Raymond Hillinger would dedicate it formally. I was sitting at the end of a pew about halfway down the east wall next to one of the two wooden confessionals recessed into the wall. Waiting for my mother to come out of the confessional, I couldn't understand what was taking her so long. I mean, what did she have to say in that tiny room that took so long? My mom didn't do anything wrong. All she had to say was "Bless me, Father, for I have not sinned. When will I be up for sainthood?"

As I looked around the church, there were lines of penitents, awaiting their turns to cleanse their souls. There must have been a lot of sinning going on during the previous week. Then, through the two glass doors at the back of the church, I saw a tall figure entering. He was dressed in the standard long black priest's cassock with a black belt, or cincture, tied around his middle and the white Roman collar across his neck indicating he, indeed, was a priest. He walked down the main aisle to my right. I could see he wasn't fat, wasn't skinny, that he wore glasses and his brown hair was graying.

His walk got my attention: perfect posture with his head tilted slightly to the right, looking down at the green rug in front of him as he made his way to the altar. For whatever reason, when he walked, he placed his left hand on his left side, just above the cincture as if he was holding his stomach. His right hand swung with each long step, giving him a dignified gait. As he passed me, I could see his face was stern, determined. He looked and walked like he was in charge, reminding me of John Wayne in priestly garb. Later, I learned he was in charge. I watched him walk up the plush, red-carpeted steps of the altar, crossing to the right side where the folding light brown door led to the sacristy.

When my mother came out of the confessional, she entered the pew.

"Move down, Johnny," she directed me.

I slid over as she pulled down the brown foam-padded kneeler and began praying.

"Mom, did you do something wrong?" I asked, wondering why she was praying after Confession.

"Shhhhh!" She held her right index finger across her red-lipsticked-sealed kisser. I decided to kneel down and ask God why my mother was praying.

No answer.

As we walked out of the church that Saturday, I told her I had seen the priest. She had me describe him, and knew immediately it was Father Griffin.

"He's a very holy man, Johnny, very holy," Mom said, taking me by the hand and leading me out the glass doors at the back of the church. "He worked very hard to have this church built so everyone in the parish could go to Mass here. Remember when we had to go to Mass in the church next to the school?"

"The gymnasium?"

"Yes, the gym. Well, Father Griffin knew this parish was growing and deserved a big, beautiful church—one that the Emperor Constantine himself would be proud of. So he asked everyone in the parish to donate as much as they could to help build it. Your father and I gave $400."

Now today, $400 doesn't sound like much money, but in 1961 it seemed a fortune. My mother's priorities—which of course became my father's whether he liked it or not—were her family and God, which meant the Church. And if the holy Father Griffin with the John Wayne walk asked for $400, she was going to find the money somehow. One thing I vividly remember growing up was the constant reference to that $400 donation.

From that point on, Father Griffin represented St. Bede's to me. It seemed he celebrated almost every Mass I attended. This was before Vatican II, so we would sit in the church and basically watch the priest and the altar boys perform the Mass. Mom, my sister Maureen, and I were the only ones attending Mass each Sunday because Dad was at home watching sister Kathy and our new baby brother, Danny, both of whom were still too young for church.

At six, I had no appreciation at all for the Mass. We didn't say anything, didn't do anything. We just sat, knelt, and stood when instructed, folding our hands in prayer. Every so often, the organist played a song and we joined in. The only time the priest addressed us directly was in the homily after the Gospel. Father Griffin usually talked about Jesus and why He sacrificed so much for us. There was something about his mannerisms and speech that indicated he was a holy man. But I couldn't help thinking of him as John Wayne in vestments.

And every so often after he finished talking about Jesus, he called on the parishioners to please give enough in the church offering to cover the expenses of the parish. He talked about the many bills he had to pay and prayed that everyone in the parish would do their part. Well, I knew my parents did their part. Mom turned in our family donation envelope every Sunday to help with the bills, just as Father Griffin had asked.

No one really got to know any of the priests very well in those days. They didn't stand out at the front of the church after Mass to greet their flock. The final procession took them right back to the sacristy. In the early 1960s, the priest seemed a dignified and somewhat aloof figure whom everyone in the parish admired and respected for the dedication and commitment he made to the church. I believe this is why so many mothers wanted at least one son to become a priest, so they could talk about how admired and respected their son the somewhat-aloof priest is among the parishioners. With so many good Catholic families following the teachings of the Church and practicing the Vatican-approved rhythm method of birth control, five or six children was common. And of the five or six, two or three boys was fairly common, which meant the mothers wanted one of them to make her proud and become a priest.

I'm sure that's why Father Griffin became a priest. His mother probably watched him walk around and said, "John Griffin, you walk around like you are in charge and remind me a little of John Wayne with that strut. I think you should become a priest, because everyone will think you are holy and will admire and respect you and tell me what a great son I have."

Most kids I knew in those days would agree quite quickly that Mass was the most boring thing they were forced to do each Sunday. And if we complained about it . . .

"You be quiet, young man. You sit and kneel and fold your hands in prayer and ask God to forgive you for complaining about Mass. You are lucky to be at Mass in a country where they allow you to do this freely. People have died for the right to be at Mass. They have been tortured and killed because they believed in Jesus Christ and wanted to celebrate their faith through the re-creation of the Last Supper, which is the Mass and the receiving of Communion, which is Christ's Body. Do you understand?"

At six, I didn't have any idea of what my mother was talking about, but I clearly knew one thing: If I complained about Mass, she got angry. And when she got angry, she yelled at me. And when she yelled at me, I felt bad. So to avoid feeling bad, I chose the boredom that was the Mass of the early 1960s starring the holy Father Griffin with his John Wayne walk.

Little did I know back in first grade how big a role Father John Wayne would play during my grammar-school years. I watched him at that time thinking him such a holy man, such a good man—just as my mother had told me. When he held his hands together in prayer, they were pointed perfectly toward Heaven. I thought that was pretty good, because everyone knows that your fingers have to be pointed toward Heaven for your prayers to reach God. Oh sure, this priest was boring, but I figured I was just a stupid little kid and didn't understand the significance of his homilies about Jesus. Maybe someday when I grew older, I would understand why the parents sat in the church with eyes gazing straight at Father Griffin, appreciating every word and action on the sacred altar. My mother looked like she was watching John Glenn's space capsule orbit the Earth on television. She was enamored with the entire ritual.

"Mom, don't you think this is boring?" I asked.

"Shhhhh," she sternly directed me with the right index finger over the red-lipsticked kisser signal. And shush, I did.

Even though I was only six, there were portions of the Mass that I looked forward to each Sunday. I could always count on the ushers to keep things interesting. The army of men in dark suits, smelling of Old Spice, marched down the aisles every week after the homily. Each was armed with a woven-straw collection basket attached to a six-foot-long wooden handle. These guys were experts at shooting that basket handle through their left hand while holding it with their right to reach those in the middle of the pew. No one could evade the collection basket.

I liked to watch the people's faces as they reached in their pockets for their weekly envelope. With each pew collection, as the usher shot the basket to the middle of the pew and began pulling it back toward him like a fisherman of the religious treasury, he would give each parishioner ample time to drop the envelope into the church's kitty. When someone didn't seem to be reaching in their pocket for an envelope, the usher held that basket in front of them just a few seconds longer, so everyone in the area could see and stare daggers at the uncharitable person who sat in Father's Griffin's church.

And people did watch!

When someone didn't give, the eyes grew wide and the heads turned to the neighbors to make sure they were aware of the stingy Catholic. This had to be embarrassing for anyone who didn't drop at least some money into the basket. I wondered why anyone would expose themselves to that shame.

Geez, throw an empty envelope in there, I thought.

Anything!

But why shame yourself in front of so many during a service where you're supposed to elevate your spirit, not have it torn down by the usher with the basket and his band of wide-eyed finger-pointers.

And everyone knew who was the most feared usher at St. Bede's. I used to call him Mr. Chubs, a rotund usher with about four chins who sweated profusely all over his Sunday's best whether it was winter or summer. Each week, he made his way up the aisle with his basket, shooting it down each pew and bringing it back slowly expecting an envelope, cash, or coin from every single adult. Anyone who didn't fork over some type of donation was admonished by Chubs with a loud "Ayhem!" clearing his throat and directing his growing wide-eyed stare at the non-donator.

The "Ayhem!" was the worst torture one could receive at St. Bede's. Not only did it draw the attention from those around the victim, but on one occasion Father Griffin, upon hearing Mr. Chubs clear his throat several times in succession, glanced down from the altar to view the disturbance. The entire congregation at the 10:00 A.M. Mass that Sunday was amazed. The elderly, balding white-haired man with a stubble-beard face, tattered gray suit, and worn-out brown shoes was so embarrassed, he stood up and stumbled his way over the others in his pew to escape. As he reached the main aisle, he looked up at the grinning Mr. Chubs. Then he glanced at Father Griffin and shook his head in disbelief before limping down the main aisle and out of the church. It must have been a long, painful walk as he made his way from the third row. When he reached the glass doors, he turned around and left with a sad and disappointed expression across his face.

I had never seen him before. Maybe he was new to the parish and just didn't realize what he was walking into. Maybe he didn't have any money, although that excuse wouldn't wash with my mother. She never had the money, but she found it somehow, even if it meant going into debt.

Money was always an issue at St. Bede's, and somehow the Gospel messages didn't reflect the actions or words of Father Griffin, who would stand up at the pulpit and tell us how money wasn't important to Jesus. "Give unto Caesar the things that are Caesar's and to God the things that are God's," the priest quoted from Matthew, Chapter 22: 15–22. Money may not have been important to Jesus, but it sure was a priority for Father John Wayne telling his flock to fork it over to his ambassador of embarrassment, Mr. Chubs. I never saw that old man in church again.

The other segment of the Mass that always was interesting was Communion. I would sit in the first row watching all of the blessed make their way up to the white marble altar rail, where they knelt and waited for one of the priests to arrive in front of them with the consecrated hosts. The altar boy then placed a six-inch wooden-handled golden round platter, called a paten, under each communicant's chin.

I liked to watch the way each person received the host. It was like watching a parade of the religious, semireligious, and those forced to be there. The way each person dressed, walked, and acted during Communion said so much about them. These Catholics were not taken from a cookie-cutter mold. No, each was different, walking up to the white marble altar rail and kneeling down.

One fairly tall teenage boy with unruly hair and dressed in jeans and a white T-shirt reacted to the priest's "Body of Christ" as if the entire ceremony was an infringement on his time. He stuck out his tongue with a look on his face that said "C'mon, let's get this over with." As he stood up and walked back to his pew with hands in his pockets, he began to chew the host as if he were eating breakfast at Denny's.

The midfortyish woman next to him, wearing a nice blue ankle-length dress and looking as though she had just come from the beauty parlor presenting the Jackie Kennedy look of the day, received the host on her tongue in a very solemn manner, as if Jesus Himself was giving her the blessed bread. Then she closed her mouth just as respectfully, slowly made the Sign of the Cross, rose and walked back to her pew with hands pointed toward Heaven. It must have been her daughter next to her, because this grammar-school girl with the curled brown hair and a light blue knee-high dress looked like a carbon copy of her mother, so respectful in her walk and manner. This went on with each person approaching the holy process a little differently than the person before.

I looked around to see if others were watching. They certainly were. It made for great religious theater—still does to this day.

At the end of Mass, I always looked around to see who had eaten and run. Depending on the Mass, sometimes I would see only a few open spaces in the pews. The later the Mass, the more people would be gone after Communion, especially during football season when the Bears were playing.

Ducking out after Communion was not as risky as stiffing Mr. Chubs, but it did take some strategy to pull it off. Those who did it regularly were like professional church-escape artists. They usually sat in one of the side pew sections near the exit or toward the back of the church, also close to the escape doors. Those in the side pew areas received Communion and made their way back down the aisle toward their pew, looking like they were just walking back to their seats. But as they passed by the exit doors, they quickly made a left turn and were out the doors before the wide-eyed finger-pointers could record the early departure. Those in the back of the church understood that by the time they were returning to their seats, the few parishioners in the rows behind them most likely would have been headed down the main aisle in the Communion line. So they had a clear getaway.

After all had received Communion and Father Griffin was finished cleaning and organizing the chalices, patens, and extra hosts with the altar boys, he would sit back down on his throne behind the altar table while the lector read the weekly announcements. As I grew older, I understood how important these announcements were for us. After all, how else could you find out when basketball tryouts would be held? Oh sure, those announcements were printed in the weekly bulletin, but that would require reading—not for me.

Once the lector was finished, Father Griffin would stand and mosey back around the altar table to the middle of the altar, where he would peruse the crowd to see how many had ditched the final blessing. He would say his final prayer, bow toward the crucifix, and then follow the procession of two altar boys back down the steps and left around the white marble rail and through the two heavy brown wooden doors.

This was not the last time I would see Father Griffin come in and out of those brown doors. No, it was just the beginning.

Chapter Two

FIRST COMMUNION

I t seemed like we practiced for First Communion nearly every afternoon in May of 1964. The first time we were brought over to the basement of St. Bede's Church for that first practice session left quite an impression on me. The church was new, having opened only a year earlier, and the basement seemed gigantic, dark, and cold. From front to back, it seemed the green and beige checkered tile floor ran forever toward the back stucco wall, which was really difficult to see under the few lights that had been illuminated in the drop ceiling. This was the kind of place no second-grader ever would want to be left in alone; very scary.

As we stood there in that cold, dark basement at the first rehearsal, Sister Mary and the four other second-grade teachers talked in somewhat of a huddle, trying to determine how they would organize this procession of young Catholics. The nuns looked like five sets of black drapes, bobbing and weaving as they talked. Their shadows bounced off the stucco walls, which made them look like giant nuns—a scary thought indeed.

In 1964, the nuns wore the traditional religious habits familiar to most baby boomer alumni of Catholic schools. From top to bottom, the Sisters of St. Joseph of Carondelet wore black head veils that came down past their shoulders;

stiff white coifs across their foreheads; long black tunics with white chest bibs known as wimples just below their necks; and black leather belts tied around the waist.

It was easy to see from the group of talking drapes that I most definitely had the nicest nun. Sister Mary was always smiling and was probably a pretty lady underneath her hood. But with that black contraption on, there was really no telling what she looked like, except she had a friendly face.

When the huddle broke, an older nun with a loud voice took control.

"All right, we want you to form two lines—boys on the left and girls on the right," bellowed Sister Old Yeller, her voice echoing ominously across the length of the church basement. She emphasized the direction she wanted us to go with her hands and arms, looking much like a football referee signaling a first down.

"Now I want you to line up shoulder to shoulder so we can place you in order," she said.

Seemed simple enough. As everyone shuffled around, trying to make their way into the line as instructed, the nuns didn't wait to see where the height line would begin and end.

"You!" boomed Old Yeller at me. "You come down here. You'll be first."

I'll be first? Wow, how did I get that honor? Then as I stood in the front of the line and watched the nuns move each child, it quickly became apparent what they were doing. Shortest went up front, tallest in the back. The five nuns moved around taking children by the arms and leading them to the correct place. I knew I was easily the youngest kid in the second grade, but I was certainly as tall as five other boys. Nonetheless, I was first.

I looked over to the girls' side to see my partner. There stood Eileen Donnelly, staring right at me and smiling from ear to ear. Eileen was the cutest girl in the second grade; everyone knew it. There was no contest; it was just a well-known fact. Second-graders talk about the fastest kid, tallest kid, smelliest kid, fattest kid, skinniest kid, and, of course, the prettiest girl. And every kid in the second grade knew the prettiest girl was Eileen.

This young beauty was slim—not too skinny—and just a bit shorter than this boy, which was just fine by me. She had pretty brown eyes, beautiful straight brown hair that ran to her shoulders, a beautiful face highlighted by her bright white smile, and a beautiful olive complexion. But her best attribute was her positive, energetic personality. This was a happy girl and her personality was electric. It was easy to see why all the girls wanted to be her friend and all the boys wished they were standing next to her, instead of me. Luck of the draw!

"Okay, hands together in prayer with head and eyes straight ahead," Sister Old

Yeller demanded. "Now I want the two lines to move closer together so you are side by side."

Side by side? What happens if we bump into each other? Then what?

Eileen came right up against my right arm. I felt a sensation run up my back and my face suddenly felt very warm. I slowly peeked over at her and saw her staring at me with that big smile. Boy, I liked her, but I had no idea why. I looked back to see if anyone noticed. The three girls behind her were all looking at me, giggling. I didn't dare look at the boys behind me.

Sister Mary walked to the side of the line to address everyone before going upstairs to the church.

"Now, children, I want you to understand the importance of your First Communion here at St. Bede the Venerable," she said warmly, very different in manner from Sister Old Yeller. "You are the first class to make your First Communion in this new church."

A loud gasp filled the basement. I guess none of us had thought of that. A few kids started to clap and then we all clapped. Sister Mary made us feel special and she looked thrilled at our reaction.

"All right! Settle down!" Sister Old Yeller barked, bringing St. Bede's second-grade class of 1964 back to order. "Let's walk in a perfect procession up to the church."

Eileen leaned in against my arm again, a touch to which I was quickly growing accustomed. By the second flight of steps, I realized I really liked her bumping against me. My head felt so hot, I thought it was going to pop off. I wondered if she could notice. I just stared down at the beige steps with small red speckles as we walked up the second and final flight of fifteen steps. I could hear someone tapping against the shiny silver handrail on the wall. No reprimand? Wow!

"Stop!" a nun shouted.

We did, right at the double-glass doors guarding the entrance to the church.

"Now, as we proceed to the altar, it is very important that we do it in a very honorable and dignified fashion," this intense nun said, determined to make this the most organized First Communion ceremony in the history of the Roman Catholic Church. "I want each boy and girl to take the first step with your right foot and then follow with your left. And your pace has to be perfect, not too fast, not too slow. Your head should be straight up, looking at the altar. Mr. Ruane and Miss Donnelly, you are first, so you have an important responsibility here. If you start the procession correctly, we will have a beautiful ceremony. If not, it will be a disaster. Do you understand?"

Ah, nothing like placing a little pressure on a couple of seven-year-olds!

"Each pair must wait until the pair in front of you has taken three full steps before you begin. Do you understand?"

"Yes, Sister," the group said in a whispering tone.

"Mr. Ruane and Miss Donnelly, when you get to the first pew, walk around the front and enter from the other side. Everyone else will do the same."

Eileen and I looked at each other. This was more than smiles and bumping. We were now in this thing together and had to lead the procession or Sister Old Yeller would not be happy. I nodded at Eileen. She wasn't smiling anymore. My face started feeling normal again, not so warm. We had a job to do. I think we both realized that not only were we in the first official First Communion class of the new St. Bede's, but we would be the first two kids in that class to receive Communion.

"Begin!"

Eileen glanced over and together we took our first right step together, then left. With heads straight, looking up at the altar, off we went in perfect unison down the long green carpet to the front pew. I turned left, she went right. We entered our pews from the opposite ends, turned, and walked to our respective pews toward each other. I looked straight into her eyes. We both smiled. We had done it right. When we reached our seats, we turned and looked straight ahead at the altar. A few seconds later, as the other students passed in front of me, I glanced over through the procession at Eileen. She was smiling again, right at me. My face felt warm.

Each day I looked forward to rehearsal and seeing Eileen's smiling face. All day I would look forward to seeing her, walking shoulder to shoulder with her and feeling her soft touch as she gently bumped against my arm all the way up the aisle.

Two weeks later, Sister Mary was in charge and she introduced all of us to the two altar boys who would lead the procession with Father John Griffin, pastor of St. Bede.

"This is Pete Hannon and Marty Donnelly," Sister Mary said calmly. "They will lead you up the aisle to Father Griffin. John and Eileen, just let them get three steps ahead of you before you begin."

This was different. We didn't feel threatened by the direction.

"Yes, Sister, we will," I said, and nodded at the smiling Eileen.

As Sister Mary organized all of the others into line, I watched the two altar boys who were much older than us. They both looked really tall, probably seventh- or eighth-graders. The Hannon boy just leaned against the wall, looking bored as he waited for the rehearsal to begin. Donnelly stood in front of me, watching Sister Mary get things in order. He was a cool-looking kid with thick brown hair, a James Dean look-alike to be sure. And like James Dean, the front of his hair wouldn't stay in place, a few locks continually falling down onto his forehead.

He had the coolest response to this problem, though. Every time his hair would tumble onto his forehead, he would blow it, sending it right back up in place. This was quite a trick, as he extended his bottom lip, allowing him to blast a shot of wind straight up past his nose, knocking his locks back up over his forehead. He did this every few minutes, it seemed. For a second-grader, it didn't get any cooler than this. He was without question the coolest kid I had ever seen. I wanted to be just like him, an altar boy who blew his hair back over his head. Problem for me was that I had a crew cut. It didn't matter. I went home and practiced it anyway, as if I did have hair that fell onto my forehead. My mother caught me doing it and asked me what was wrong. I said I was fine, but she took my temperature anyway.

As Sister Mary and the other nuns finished organizing everyone, I heard the Donnelly boy say to Eileen, "Hey, wait for me after rehearsal. I'll walk you home."

What? I'll walk you home? This kid was a seventh- or eighth-grader. Why was he offering to walk her home? Sure, he was cool. He could blow his disheveled hair back over his forehead with the best of them, but that didn't give him any right to . . .

"Okay," Eileen said. "Mom's taking me to Goldblatt's after school to shop for a dress."

Mom! Ah, of course, it was her brother. Why didn't I figure that out earlier? *Donnelly*! It just never clicked.

"Okay, let's all move upstairs to the glass door," Sister Mary said in a civil tone.

This was new. I liked instructions minus yelling. There was no doubt it had a certain appeal to the ear. I wonder what happened to Sister Old Yeller.

"Eileen, is that your brother?" I whispered.

She just nodded her head. Then she smiled. I needed a cold glass of water.

A few weeks later came the big day. We were told to report to the church at 8:30, the procession scheduled for 9:00 A.M. When I arrived, half the kids were already milling about the basement, but everyone looked different. All the boys were dressed in what looked like the same exact navy blue suit I was wearing, with the exact same navy blue tie. Goldblatt's must have had a run on blue suits and ties.

And the girls! They all looked so pretty with their white dresses. Each looked like she had been to the beauty parlor with her mother. There were shiny curls, special braids, and long flowing hair combed perfectly for the big occasion. Some of the girls probably wore curlers for two days, just to look as pretty as possible for the big day. A small white headband and veil had been placed perfectly over each girl's hair, making her look like a little First Communion princess. But when we lined up, there was no doubt in my mind that the prettiest princess was standing next to me.

Eileen Donnelly was a sight to behold. She was always beautiful, but in her white dress she looked incredible. I just stared at her as she talked with her brother, who was dressed in his altar boy uniform, with the white surplice over a long black cassock and white Converse sneakers. After a few seconds, his hair fell onto his forehead and, poof, he blew his dangling locks right back in place for all of a minute, maybe. Even in the altar boy garb, this was one cool cat.

"Okay, children, we need to line up," boomed Sister Old Yeller, who had really taken the name Sister Marie. She was sounding louder than normal. I guess her adrenaline was pumping extra hard on this spring morning. As we lined up, Eileen looked at me.

"You look very pretty, Eileen," I said before I could stop myself.

She smiled. My face flushed. The three girls behind her giggled.

"You look very handsome," she said to me so the giggling girls could hear.

That shut them up quickly as their eyes grew wide, and they looked at each other as if they had just heard the biggest news of the century. Eileen smiled, realizing she had put them in their place.

After leading us in the Our Father, Sister Mary led us up the stairs, just as we had done so many times before during practice. This was it. We couldn't make any mistakes. When we arrived at the glass doors, which were already opened, the entire feel of the church was different. It was packed. All of the mothers were in their finery with beauty-parlor hair, smiling so excitedly to see their second-grader walk up the aisle looking so nice, so holy, so happy. The dads were in dark suits with white hankies protruding from the front pockets. Brothers, sisters, aunts, uncles, and grandparents filled every seat in the church except for the first ten rows. Those were reserved for the nervous boys in the blue suits and curly-headed girls in the white dresses.

The organ in the choir loft directly above us boomed out an unfamiliar but inspirational tune, the music filling every square inch of this magnificent new church. Then the voices came up, revealing a full choir for this Mass. I didn't expect this much religious pageantry, but it sounded so beautiful—the voices, the reverent music. This was one thing they didn't prepare us for in practice, which was conducted in virtual silence.

I quickly glanced at Eileen. She looked nervous but determined. We were all business now, ready to lead the procession perfectly, as instructed by Sister Old Yeller. We could see Father Griffin enter from the right side, walking around the white marble altar rail and up the three red-carpeted steps of the altar. He turned and raised his arms, letting the altar boys know they should begin moving toward him. Hannon and Eileen's cool brother both looked back at us and nodded, then started up the aisle. Eileen and I both counted three steps, looked at each other, and, at the same time, stepped with our right, then left. Step right, then left, all the way down the aisle; just like at practice every Tuesday and Thursday afternoon for the past two weeks. As we walked down the aisle, I just looked straight ahead. I could feel the eyes of all the people in their seats.

"Johnny!"

I glanced to my left to see my mother in her pretty light yellow dress and dark black beehive, smiling and waving at the corner of her pew. A flashbulb went off and there was Dad, standing behind Mom, holding the family camera, a leather-covered Canon. I smiled but kept stride all the way down to the foot of the altar, where I looked up to see the stone-faced Father Griffin, whose hands were clasped together in prayer as he watched the procession in front of him. Turning left, I kept the same pace in front of the pew to the other side, then turned the corner and entered the row moving cautiously toward Eileen. She mirrored me and I just stared at her, momentarily forgetting everything that was going on around me.

Once at the corner of the pew, I turned toward the altar and looked straight ahead. The most difficult part was over. Now I could concentrate on the excitement of receiving my First Communion. Would it taste different from the unconsecrated host Sister Mary gave us at practice two days ago? Would I feel differently when I received it? It represented the Body and Blood of Jesus Christ, and I was supposed to let it dissolve in my mouth. I tried not to think about it.

But what about that smart-aleck fifth-grader who told us that if we received the host but had not told the priest all of our sins in Confession beforehand, our head would explode? We weren't that stupid. Okay, maybe we were, because every kid I knew said they told the priest every single sin they could ever remember. Either way, we would all be watching to see if anyone's head exploded.

As the Mass went on, the heat of the May day mixed with a crowded church began to take effect as the white ceiling fans whirred above us. Father Griffin looked like he was sweating a bit. Sister Mary and the other nuns must have felt horrible in their heavy black attire. I watched their faces. They looked solemn and really hot.

I took a quick view of the people behind me. Fathers were pulling white hankies from their pants pockets to wipe their foreheads. Those weren't the decorative hankies like the ones adorning their jackets, but the everyday useable face-wipers and nose-blowers. It seemed like all dads carried white hankies in those days.

Some mothers had little fans they waved in front of themselves to keep cool. There were few air-conditioned churches. When it was hot it was hot, and everyone dealt with it. But through it all, there was Marty Donnelly, the coolest altar boy on the face of the earth. He wasn't hot. No, he knelt there on his kneeler watching

Father Griffin during the consecration. When the priest raised the large host high, Marty reached down and rang the string of three bells until the pastor brought the host down to the altar. Marty set the bells down and returned upright. His hair was a bit messed from bending over. I knew what would happen next. I watched his lip curl up and, poof—there it was, his hair shot back over his head. Father Griffin lifted the chalice of wine up in the air, Marty rang the bells again. Down came the Blood of Christ. Up came Marty with his hair messed and, poof, right back in place.

Then came the big moment. Two ushers signaled for the children in my row and Eileen's row to stand. We stood and looked past the ushers at each other. She looked nervous, but she managed a slight smile. I grinned back, hoping to reassure her everything would be just fine.

The three other parish priests walked out of the sacristy to help distribute the Blessed Sacrament as the ushers each took a step back, indicating it was time for us to lead the procession toward the altar rail. I could feel the excitement as camera lights flashed and dads scurried up the side aisles for a better vantage point to take pictures of their children receiving Jesus for the first time.

Eileen and I walked directly toward each other, just like we had practiced. She was all business again, as was I. When we met in the middle, we both turned toward the altar and went up to the rail. Her dress brushed against me as we reached the foot of the altar. There was no bumping, no smiling. This was an important moment as I knelt to the left of the rail's opening and Eileen to the right. The other boys and girls then followed our lead.

We all held our hands in prayer and everything looked like it was going according to Sister Marie's direction under the adoring watch of our parents. Eileen looked almost angelic, her hands folded in prayer as she looked up at the cross. I knew the next time we saw each other we would be different, changed after receiving the Body of Christ.

I watched Father Griffin walk around the altar table toward the center steps leading right up to me and Eileen. Marty Donnelly, holding the gold paten, followed him. The pastor approached Eileen first, her brother placing the paten under her chin in case the host dropped. The priest reached into the chalice and pulled out the small round wafer. All eyes in the church were on Eileen, the first of our class to receive First Communion.

Even with the buzz in the air, I could hear Father Griffin say, "Body of Christ," holding the host a few inches in front of Eileen's eyes.

"Amen," she said, sticking out her tongue to receive the host. She closed her mouth and eyes and made the Sign of the Cross.

Then Father Griffin walked over to me. It was obvious that at the inaugural First Communion ceremony in the biggest church Father Griffin would build in his lifetime, he would be giving the first girl and boy their first Blessed Sacrament.

I felt the paten under my chin as Father Griffin reached into his chalice. He held the host in front of my face and said, "Body of Christ."

"Amen," I said, closing my eyes and sticking out my tongue. I felt the pressure of the host and brought the Blessed Eucharist into my mouth, closed it, and made the Sign of the Cross. As I stood to return to my pew, I concentrated on the host in my mouth. It didn't taste any different than the practice host Sister Mary gave to us, I think. I wasn't quite sure what it tasted like, but it seemed to taste the same. The difference was this host was Christ, the other just a piece of bread.

As I turned into my pew, Eileen was nearly at her seat. We both knelt and prayed.

"Dear God, thank You for letting me receive my First Communion today." I prayed with my hands together, pointing toward Heaven. "Please help me to be a good boy and a good Catholic. Please bless my mother, father, my sisters Maureen and Kathy and baby brother Danny."

I wanted to be sure God heard all of my most important prayers during the most important Communion of my life. I made the Sign of the Cross. I had done it. I knelt there trying to determine if I felt differently. I wasn't sure. But I knew from that point on, I could participate in the re-creation of the Last Supper. And that made me feel grown up, like I was finally a true member of the Roman Catholic Church. So I guess I did feel I was different, special just like all the others who are privileged to receive the Body and Blood of Jesus Christ.

I looked up at the statue of Jesus hanging on the wooden cross on the green marble wall behind the altar table. That's when it dawned on me. I realized what it was all about. That man gave His life for all of us, and we were now sharing His purpose in life by sharing His Body and Blood, just as He shared it with his Apostles at the Last Supper.

Kneeling there in the first seat in the first pew, I knew this place would always be special for me. I glanced over at Eileen, whose eyes were shut as she prayed. I hoped she felt the same thing. It was all sort of fun and games up until the moment when our lives changed. And from then on, every time I receive Communion I feel as though God has given me an opportunity to speak directly to Him, which is exactly what I do.

When the Mass ended, Eileen and I led the procession one more time down the aisle toward the glass doors. My dad got another picture, my mother smiled and waved. Everyone looked so happy.

Chapter Three

THE FIRST STEP

I t was an unusually hot and muggy Saturday afternoon in September of 1967 when I walked into St. Bede the Venerable Church for my orientation as an altar boy. My mother had this fifth-grader dress nicely in navy blue slacks, white collared shirt, and shined black wingtip shoes—typical attire for Sunday Mass. I had arrived fifteen minutes early with the intention of going to Confession first. Confession is what Reconciliation used to be called in the 1960s. It's a simpler, more direct term that is easier to understand.

Unfortunately as I walked through the double-glass door of the church, I noticed there were about ten sinners lined up next to each of the four confessionals, each a wooden three-door booth recessed into one of the two longest walls of the church. I wouldn't have enough time to go to Confession, so I walked up to the first pew with hands pointed reverently toward Heaven, pulled down the brown padded kneeler, and began to pray.

By this time, St. Bede's had grown to become one of the largest parishes in the Catholic Archdiocese of Chicago. I was just an eleven-year-old kid so I had no perspective on this magnificent church or the history behind its inception. For me, St. Bede's was the only church I knew, conveniently located one block from my house. Nice of them to build it so close to home, I often thought.

But the founding and growth of the parish was a result of baby boomers making their grand entrance onto the Southwest Side of Chicago as well as white flight west from the far South Side. St. Bede's was located on the very tip of the southwest corner of Chicago and, because city employees were required to live in the city, this neighborhood was a prime location for Chicago cops, firemen, garbage men, and water department workers like my dad.

Keeping pace with the demand and growth was no small task. It all began on July 7, 1953, when Samuel Cardinal Stritch officially founded St. Bede the Venerable Parish and named a former United States Marine chaplain, Rev. John P. Griffin, pastor. When the military is faced with a tough challenge, they call on the Marines. Why shouldn't Cardinal Stritch?

Over the next few years, it was obvious neither Father Griffin nor Cardinal Stritch could have projected the enormous growth of the parish. Over the next nine years, they built three churches, each structure significantly larger than its predecessor.

Father Griffin said St. Bede's first Mass on July 12, 1953, in a warehouse at the corner of 83rd Street and Cicero Avenue. After only three months, the pastor broke ground for a real church and a parish hall a few blocks east at 83rd and Scottsdale Avenue. The first Mass was celebrated at the new site on Christmas Eve of 1953, but it didn't take long for Father Griffin to realize that this facility wouldn't be large enough to keep pace with the growth of the parish. Within two years, and with the support of the Archdiocese, Father Griffin sold his church property to the city of Chicago after purchasing seven acres along 83rd Street west of Kostner Avenue.

Griffin built a larger church at 83rd Street and Kenneth Avenue, celebrating the first Mass there on June 22, 1955. At the same time, a one-story orange-bricked school and two-story rectory were built to accommodate the Sisters of St. Joseph of Carondelet and the 300 students who would launch the grammar school on September 11, 1955. Father Griffin also got some much-needed assistance as Rev. William Barry was assigned to the parish in 1956, followed by Rev. John Curran in 1958 and Rev. Francis Ciesielski in 1959. But even with the help of additional priests and more Masses on the schedule, St. Bede's was a baby boomer's haven and Father Griffin had to work hard to keep pace.

By 1961, the number of families in the parish grew to 2,300, with 1,900 students enrolled at the grammar school (grades two through eight), so new classrooms were built to accommodate the expanding student body. At this point, Father Griffin realized it was time to take a giant step.

The pastor contracted Andrew Stroeker to design his vision of a new church, and ground was broken for the $700,000 facility on November 27, 1961, at the corner of 83rd and Kostner. This new St. Bede the Venerable Church was cathedral-size, with a capacity of 1,500 plus a basement prepared to accommodate up to 1,200. At the packed dedication Mass on June 23, 1963, Father Griffin knew this was the last church to be built for the parish.

Now his challenge was paying for it—and over the next decade many parishioners felt that objective became his obsession, placed ahead of his role as the spiritual leader of his Catholic community. But there was no denying this new church was a magnificent testament to God in the tradition started by Roman Emperor Constantine in the fourth century.

Now, with my prayers finished and another ten minutes before the start of altar boy training, I sat back on the hard wooden pew and tried to shift my attention away from the anxiety I was feeling about my upcoming training.

The sinners' line along the walls had grown longer outside the confessionals, with about ten people ridden with Catholic guilt waiting to enter each of them. Some people were leaning against the course light brown brick wall, while others nervously shuffled their feet as they prepared to spill their souls to the priest-confessor seated behind each of the middle doors. Those who had already received their penance knelt in pews praying for forgiveness.

That was always the focus with the kids. Even if we received a large number of Our Fathers and Hail Marys as our penance, we said them fast so no one would know how many sins we had confessed. If we knelt there for ten minutes, kids would come up to us asking what bank we robbed or who we murdered.

Regardless of the many sinners standing outside the confessionals, the church was quiet, with the exception of an occasional loud cough or sneeze echoing off the walls. I gazed up at the imposing altar where I would either succeed or fail as an altar boy: a daunting thought for an eleven-year-old. I knew once I stepped through the opening in the middle of that white marble altar rail, I basically would be onstage; up three steps to that impressive religious platform. The red marble altar table looked elegant with its wavy white highlights. My place would be on the left side, on one of the three wooden kneelers.

I looked at the podium near the front of the altar and knew I would have to stand next to it as the priest read the Gospel. I wondered how that would feel, standing there looking out at everyone as they looked back at me. Would I get stage fright?

Another cough echoed off the wall. That didn't sound good. I looked at my watch. Another few minutes and I would have to walk up to that altar and back to the altar boys' room next to the sacristy, all hidden behind the back wall of the altar. Then I saw my best friend, Marty Durks, walk past me on the side aisle and disappear into the altar boys' room. He was wearing blue jeans, short-sleeved blue collared shirt, and black Converse All-Stars. Was I overdressed? A few minutes later another good friend, Eddie Crandell, walked past and through the same doors Marty did. Eddie was wearing black dress pants and a blue Oxford shirt with shined black shoes. Maybe I was dressed okay. I wasn't sure, but at least Eddie was dressed like me. It was nearly time to go.

I could do this, I knew I could. But just in case, I thought it a good idea to say one more Our Father. After kneeling back down and making the Sign of the Cross, I looked up at the statue of the crucified Jesus presenting a lifelike depiction of the Crucifixion. The cross was high above the altar, along the back green marble wall. It was the focus of the church, and the cross-shaped ceiling lights illuminated it beautifully.

That cross is an image that got my attention from the first day I entered the church as a first-grader, and it lives in my memory to this day. This was the Jesus I knew and loved; the deceased Son of God to whom I prayed throughout my childhood.

Without knowing it, the church and that cross are embedded in my heart, soul, and mind, keeping me on the path of Christianity throughout my life.

It was time to go. I made the Sign of the Cross again, rose, and stepped into the center aisle with hands together in prayer, just as the nuns had taught me. I walked toward the altar rail opening and stopped just in front of the red carpet. I had never been at the altar before. Just as I lifted my right foot to step onto the hallowed rug, a voice filled my ears.

"Hey, what are you doing?"

I turned to see an older, taller, blond-haired boy in blue jeans, T-shirt, and white Converse sneakers, standing in the side aisle looking at me.

"Are you here for the altar boy training?" he asked, not looking very happy.

"Yes, I am," I mumbled, wondering who was this kid barking at me from across the church.

"Well then, follow me," he ordered, and he stepped through the wooden doors.

My first step up to the altar would have to come later. I had to believe this older boy was in charge, so I walked around the altar rail, following him through the door and into the altar boys' room.

On that day in 1967, how many other boys across the United States were entering their parish church feeling anxious about becoming an altar boy? No doubt thousands, maybe a million.

The next four years would be a very important time in my life as a Catholic. I would become an altar boy.

Chapter Four

A LONG WAY FROM GALWAY

My father, Bernard Joseph Ruane, was born on April 26, 1926, on a farm in County Galway, Ireland, outside of the town of Balinasloe in a parish called Ballymacward. Making his entrance after his two older sisters, Delia and Mary, he was the first son of John and Mary and named for his paternal grandfather. Dad's parents were good Catholics who delivered five more children into the world, three boys and two girls.

The final child, Margaret, was born in 1937 when Dad was eleven years old. This was a very sad day, though, because his mother died in childbirth. He told us later how a silence filled their farmhouse for several weeks after the passing. His grandmother, who lived with them and was called Nana, along with his eldest sister, Delia, took on the responsibilities of their mother, running the household while my father and the other boys, Johnny, Peter, and Patrick, all helped their father on the farm.

Growing up on a farm, Dad worked closely with his father in cultivating their fifty acres. They planted potatoes, wheat, barley, oats, beets, and turnips and also raised typical farm livestock. He learned at an early age the facts of life on a farm, with a bird's-eye view of the cattle placed in the pen alongside the house so they could conduct their mating ritual without disturbance from the other bulls. And my dad would stand next to his father in the shed behind the farmhouse watching the local veterinarian deliver calves—a bloody, messy sight, to be sure.

His education covered the animals' entire life cycle. He laughed about it later when he described it to us, but it must have been shocking the first time he watched his dad break the neck of a chicken, then chop it off as it would become the family meal. That was the reality of growing up on a farm.

At the age of four, Dad began attending primary school in a two-room schoolhouse that was located on his family's land, about 100 yards away from the house. His sister Mary, who was his best friend growing up, led him to school each day and made certain he was looked after properly. He recalled later how wonderful it was to have a sister who cared about him so much.

One of Dad's younger brothers, John, joked that the schoolhouse was so close to home it ruined all chances of skipping school because it was literally right in their backyard. John, who went on to become the head of the Patrician Brothers religious order in Ireland, described my dad as a very happy child who was proficient at reading and mathematics in school.

There were fifty-five children in school at the time, and Dad was in one of the classrooms with thirty other young children, all taught by Miss O'Loughlin. At fourteen, he completed seventh grade, which was the requirement in those days. Secondary education, or high school, was available only at fee-paying boarding schools, which was not an option his father could afford.

In school, Miss O'Loughlin was required to teach half an hour of the school day from a chart that had religious doctrines and spent the remainder of the day on secular subjects. On occasion, the school inspector from the Department of Education would make unannounced visits to the school to be sure the teacher was meeting requirements. My dad, like the others in his class, viewed this man as a continuance of British rule and disliked him very much. They were told to bow to him, which resulted in clenched teeth thirty years later when Dad told the story.

A quick mile walk down the dirt road in the morning to Rafferty's Store was required to purchase the newspapers for keeping up with the news of the day. The local newspaper, the *Connacht Tribune,* as well as the two national newspapers, the *Irish Press* and *Irish Independent,* kept the Ruane clan up to date on all the important happenings in Ireland and around the world. Outside of a rare visit to the local pub with their father to catch up on gossip, the newspapers were their only connection to events around the world. While my mother and her family were dealing with the Great Depression in Oak Park, Illinois, my father would only have known about it through the newspapers. Two youngsters growing up in the same time period, but under completely different circumstances that would one day converge.

As it was for most kids growing up on farms in Ireland in the 1930s, life was simple. The family never needed much money because it raised its own food, and anything else could be acquired through barter. When the kids needed clothes, their father would take them to Cullen's Store in Balinasloe for their wardrobe, which was small but satisfactory for their needs. It may have cost two head of cattle and a sheep to clothe all eight kids, but they were always dressed well.

As for the other conveniences of life, hot and cold running water was only a rumor to them in Ireland then. Showers were a fantasy, and a washing machine—well, what's that? A deep well close to the house was the source of water, which was boiled to wash the clothes on a washboard in a large round metal tub. The same system was used to wash the body, boiling water and pouring it into the bathtub located on the second floor between the three bedrooms. And the toilet was located outside, in what is commonly referred to as an outhouse.

"That's all we knew," Dad said. "So in our minds, we had everything we needed."

When my father reached fifteen, his beloved Nana died, and once again another few weeks of silence filled the Ruane home. The full burden of running the household was placed squarely on Delia's shoulders. The eldest Ruane girl was nearly eighteen and fully capable and willing to take over the duties. She pretty much had taken the reins since she was fifteen anyway, so things fell in place naturally, although everyone missed their Nana greatly.

Working to lift everyone's spirits, Delia organized "singsongs" each night off the song sheets with the great Irish tunes of the day. There was always singing at the Ruane farmhouse. This was their form of entertainment. Television hadn't been invented, and there was only one radio in the village, which was run on occasion off a car battery. So their home entertainment system was left up to their own talents, which were plentiful.

One of the big events for the Ruanes, as well as for their neighbors in Ballymacward, came on a spring day in 1937 when relatives in Boston sent them a gramophone and stack of 78 rpm records. The gramophone was a record player that had to be cranked up to rotate the turntable. The day Delia first cranked it up, the house buzzed with excitement as the entire family listened to Bing Crosby, Glenn Miller, and Tommy Dorsey. All of a sudden, they felt like they were living in Hollywood and singing all the great songs. For my father, those three talents influenced his taste in music the rest of his life. Before long, the Ruanes were singing all the hits of the day.

At one point in his teen years, my father began playing the drums, a musical instrument he really enjoyed. One of his good friends, Bill Kilkenny, played the accordion and they began playing together, performing the popular Irish tunes of the day to the delight of his father, brothers, and sisters.

"You are a regular Glenn O'Miller," his father quipped to him about his musical ambitions, referring to him as the leader of the Irish Glenn Miller band.

During this same time period, Dad watched some of his buddies start to smoke and drink. He was determined to keep his life on the straight and narrow and enlisted in the parish Pioneers, an organization of teetotalers and nonsmokers.

As he grew older, Dad's responsibilities on the farm increased. He had become a very strong young man, capable of helping his father in the preparation, planting, and reaping of the crops, digging the peat and attending the markets. Peat was dug up from the bogs behind their farmhouse and used to heat their home and provide the fire for cooking the meals. It is still used today and the rows of dug peat are visible from the family farm, looking much like the World War I trenches in France.

At eighteen, with his brothers growing old enough to take over most of his responsibilities helping his father on the farm, he took a job with a peat supply company during the summer months and quickly earned a reputation as the hardest worker in the village. He was muscular and could dig up the turf in the peat fields for hours on end. This was during World War II, when wages were low but products were inexpensive and food readily available for those on farms where most of the unrationed food was produced. During the winter months, Dad became an apprentice to a building contractor, Mr. T. Mitchell, and helped cut stone to renovate the church at Ballymacward. The church had been built in 1847 during the famine years and still stands today.

The boys he worked with on the building site as well as in the peat fields became his close friends. He made more friends when he began playing Gaelic football for the Kilconnell Parish team. Turns out Dad was quite good. Because he was strong and very competitive, he was recruited at an early age, fourteen. Over the next four years, he excelled on the football field and was regarded as a prospect for the Galway County football team. In Ireland, playing for your county team is a great honor and distinct privilege.

When he reached his twenty-first birthday, the family gathered around the dining-room table awaiting a strong wind from his lips toward the white candles on his birthday cake. It was then apparent he must set a course for his future. There wouldn't be enough work on the farm for him to stay at home. His options seemed limited to farming, building, or emigrating to America to begin a new life. This was the same situation so many Irish boys had confronted over the decades. On the farms, livestock and crops were raised, but plenty of children were raised as well.

Only one in each family would be needed to keep the farm going, while the others would have to move on to something new.

As luck would have it, his late mother had relatives in Chicago, including her brother, Jack Naughton. When Jack visited the family homestead to see his mother, he stopped by the Ruane farm and was impressed by my dad and invited him to come to Chicago. Jack promised to set him up and open his eyes to the opportunities there. Mick Naughton, Jack's younger brother, also was interested in going to America.

After a great deal of consideration and consternation, Dad made the decision to sail to the United States and begin a new life. This was the most difficult decision of his life. He loved his family, his friends, and his life in Ireland, but he reached the point where he realized leaving Ireland for America was his only choice. He was not fond of the British and would never live in England, as some of his contemporaries had elected to do.

On May 22, 1948, his neighbor Mick Lally parked his blue Ford on the road in front of the Ruane farmhouse, prepared to drive Dad and Mick Naughton to Cobh in County Cork, where they would board a ship to America. One of Dad's younger brothers, Pete, went along for the ride and a final farewell. It was a tearful sendoff, and Dad had second thoughts just before entering the backseat of the car as he looked at his crying family and friends waving goodbye to him. As the tears poured down his cheeks, he found the courage to turn his head away, ready to begin his new life.

"It's going to be tough for both of us for a while," Mick Naughton told him as they drove away from the family farmhouse. Dad couldn't talk. He just wanted to get through the day.

As Mick Lally drove south down the dirt roads of the farmlands of Ireland, Dad looked out at the beautiful green pastoral scenes wondering if he ever would return. He looked over at his young teenage brother Pete, with whom he had enjoyed so many an afternoon playing Gaelic football. Would he ever see him again? He hadn't even left, but he missed Ireland already.

Two hours later, Mick Lally dropped them off alongside a small boat that would take them out to the massive three-story black-hulled passenger ship, which seemed to fill the entire harbor. The four young men stepped out of the car to take a good look at this behemoth vessel. My dad knew once he stepped on to it, his life would change forever. He didn't want to think about it as he purchased his one-way passage for the six-day voyage to America. Dad took his heavy double-strapped black leather suitcase from his younger brother and shook hands with Pete for maybe the last time. Both were brokenhearted as their eyes welled up with tears. Then, after a quick "thank you" and handshake with his considerate neighbor Mick Lally, Dad stepped on to the gangway leading to the boat.

The trip across the Atlantic was rough, and Dad remembered he became extremely seasick during the first few days and regretted getting on the ship. At one point, he said the sea had become so rough, he thought for certain they were going to sink.

"People were panicking," he said, recounting the night they sailed through a bad storm. "We were getting tossed around so badly. So many people were crying, screaming, throwing up. I was certain we were all going to die out there."

But they didn't. They survived the storm, and early on the morning of May 28, the captain announced they would soon be arriving at Ellis Island in New York Harbor. Dad and Mick Naughton ran up two flights of metal steps to the second deck, where they found a place along the rail on the port side of the ship. The two young Irishmen stared out into the distance, straining to get their first glimpse of America, the New World that Uncle Jack promised would provide a wonderful new life for them. Off in the distance through the morning haze, it appeared. First it was very small, but as they continued through the haze, the skyline became clearer and Dad saw his future homeland, America.

"It was so foggy, and we could hear the tugboats but couldn't see them," he said, remembering the excitement he felt that Friday morning they sailed into New York Harbor. "And as we broke through the fog, there it was—the Statue of Liberty, just as we had seen it in all of the pictures. Except it looked so much bigger. So much more wonderful!"

He made the Sign of the Cross and looked up to Heaven and prayed the Our Father to thank God for getting him to this new land safely. "God, You have brought me to America. Thank You!" He prayed with hands together as he gazed through the clouds toward Heaven.

"We had never seen anything so remarkable," Dad recalled. "The tallest building we had in Ireland was maybe four stories. I saw the Empire State Building and the Chrysler Building touching the clouds and could not believe my eyes."

With the view of America in front of them, all of a sudden the pain of the voyage seemed to dissipate and Dad was very excited to begin his new life. They walked off the boat at Ellis Island feeling somewhat tired and weak, but simultaneously elated and energized by the opportunity in front of them.

It took half the day before Dad and Mick were passed through the customs agents. Some people were directed to stay on the island until the doctors were certain they were not carrying disease. No problem for Dad and Mick: A two-minute exam for these two healthy specimens and they were on their way to the ferry boat that would take them across to Manhattan.

"There were buses waiting for us the second we stepped off of the boat, ready to take us to the train station or airport," Dad said, impressed with the efficiency of the system that had obviously been in place for several decades. "Mick wasn't about to let us get on one of those buses before we saw New York. We found a fairly cheap hotel near the Chrysler Building and spent Friday and Saturday walking around New York. Everything was so expensive, we knew we couldn't stay very long."

They did pay five cents each to go to the top of the Empire State Building, which Dad said was worth every one of the five pennies for the most amazing view he had ever seen. The trip up the world's most famous skyscraper satisfied Mick's tourist curiosity, and they took a bus to LaGuardia Airport and a plane to Chicago. Neither had ever been on an airplane, but they decided if they could make it over the rough Atlantic Ocean, they could fly to Chicago.

Like most from the Old Country, the only thing these two Irishmen knew about Chicago, other than that Jack Naughton was going to give them a chance to begin a new life, was that Al Capone and his gangsters ruled the city in the 1920s. They half expected to see gangsters carrying Tommy guns riding around on the running boards of cars shooting at Irishmen who might be in Bugs Moran's gang.

The two-hour plane ride on the propeller plane was thrilling, Dad remembered. "Mick and I kept looking out the window trying to see as much of America as possible from the sky," he said. "We could see the farms and houses. When we saw what looked like an ocean, we thought the captain had made a wrong turn. But the pilot announced that we soon would be landing. That ocean was our first look at Lake Michigan."

Dad and Mick gazed out the airplane window at the city that would become their new home. It was nothing like what they had just seen in New York, with its miles of tall buildings and tall skyscrapers, but it was not small by any means. They flew right over the downtown area, and Dad and Mick were relieved Chicago wasn't as big as New York, which was far too overwhelming for these two fellows used to digging up peat and walking down dirt roads.

At two o'clock Sunday afternoon, May 30, the plane landed at Municipal Airport, which later would become Midway Airport. Jack, whom they knew well by this point, was standing behind the rope in a crowd of smiling and waving strangers.

When Dad walked off the plane, a pretty young brunette girl ran up to him and threw her arms around him, giving him a kiss on the cheek.

"That is how I first met my cousin JoAnne Naughton, my uncle Jack's eldest daughter," said Dad, who became like a big brother to JoAnne over the next few years. "It was so nice to receive that greeting. It made me feel like I was with my family. She will never know how much that helped me get over the emptiness I had been feeling up until that point."

Uncle Jack introduced the new Americans to his wife, Ellen, and daughters JoAnne and Patricia in the family Chrysler during a forty-five-minute ride to the Austin neighborhood on the western end of Chicago and the Naughton home at 1504 N. Massasoit. Dad had been a devout member of the Pioneers until his trip to America, but after getting settled in the basement and coming up the stairs, he found his uncle Jack standing in front of him holding out half a glass of whiskey. This is a tradition of the Irish when greeting newcomers to their home. My father was well aware of it and realized he did not have his Pioneers' pin on. He certainly didn't want to offend the man and family that was generous enough to claim him and give him a new life in the United States. So Dad took the glass of whiskey and drank it right down, just as he had seen done by so many others in Ireland. He gulped hard and felt the warm rush of the alcohol fill his body. He watched Mick do the same. His life was changing quickly.

Dad and Mick were given jobs as bartenders at Uncle Tommy Naughton's tavern. One night, he and Mick together decided they could not continue their alcohol abstinence in America while working as bartenders. So one night after closing their uncle's establishment, they each raised a glass of whiskey and toasted their new way of life in America.

They stayed with Uncle Jack's family for about a month, until they were able to get settled in their own flat, which is what they called an apartment back then. Over the next year, Dad became an American, learning all about baseball and American football from his uncle Bill Naughton. During the summer of 1948, Uncle Bill took him to his first baseball game at Comiskey Park to see the White Sox play the Yankees and Joe DiMaggio. He quickly fell in love with the sport. His uncle Tommy loved football, though, and he took him to Soldier Field to see the Chicago Cardinals play the Chicago Bears. There was a competitive rivalry between the fans of the Cardinals and Bears, as there was between fans of the Cubs and White Sox. Dad was a White Sox and Cardinals fan.

Mick wasn't impressed with either sport and found a local Irish Gaelic football club, the Harry Boland Hurling Club, which my dad also joined. He became one of the stars, given his experience in Ireland.

One day, he overheard one of his bar patrons talking about an Irish bandleader named Tom Tracey, who was looking for a drummer.

"I play the drums," Dad said, hoping to bring music back into his life.

An audition followed two days later, and Dad became the drummer for Tom Tracey's Irish Band.

Dad was fitting right in as an American. He would send letters home to his family letting them know about this big new world with skyscrapers, paved roads, big houses, and not a peat bog in sight. His brother Johnny, the writer of the family, would keep Dad updated about life on the farm and his own intentions to take the vows as a Patrician Brother.

His cousin Patricia knew it would take a while for Mick and Dad to make a complete transition to American life because instead of using the sidewalks when traveling by foot, they walked down the middle of the streets just as they had in Ireland.

Just as Dad was feeling comfortable in his new land, a letter arrived from the U.S. Army on November 1, 1949. He had been drafted and had to report to Fort Benning, Georgia, for basic training on December 1. This letter came from the country he was quickly learning to love, so off he went willingly and later described this time as two of the best years of his life.

"The army was one of the best experiences," he said often.

He had been placed in a tank unit where he learned how to operate M-24 Chaffe Light tanks. He spent six weeks training at Fort Benning before being transferred to a base in Berlin, Germany. He was stationed there for nearly a year; his unit was part of the large American force protecting U.S. interests west of the Brandenburg Gate. Mostly, he told us, they conducted routine training operations, guard duty, and maintenance of their equipment and vehicles.

After a few months in Germany, Dad was given a two-week furlough and he traveled to his homestead in Galway. He had been away from the farm for three years when he arrived in Mick Lally's car for the visit.

"Everything looked the same, but different," Dad said. "By that time, I had seen so much that it all felt so different."

Dad looked quite impressive in his U.S. Army uniform, which became the talk of the parish. His brother Johnny said it may have only been three years away, but he had become thoroughly American, accustomed to hot showers, real washrooms, and a more comfortable lifestyle than the one on the farm. Dad spent twelve wonderful days with his father, brothers, sisters, friends, and neighbors. And since he had broken his commitment against liquor, he joined his father, primarily a teetotaler, down at the local pub, where he drank his first pint of Guinness in Ireland.

"It was evident he would return to Chicago after his time in Germany," recalled my uncle Johnny, who was studying to become a Patrician Brother at the time. "Ireland was in the past for him. I was glad he was making a new life for himself, but I felt a bit sad that I lost my big brother. But that's how it is in Ireland. Only a few can stay while the others must move on. It has been said many times that our greatest export is our people. It's so true."

Dad returned to Berlin, but on June 25, 1950, the North Koreans crossed the 38th parallel dividing the north and south of Korea. President Harry S Truman initially announced support of the South Koreans with equipment and training. But within four days, the United States shot down North Korean planes and President Truman ordered General Douglas MacArthur to bring in the troops stationed in the Pacific region. America was at war again.

As the war heated up in 1951 and 500,000 Communist Chinese troops pushed the United Nations forces behind the 38th parallel, taking Seoul, Dad's unit was ordered to South Korea. Dad said most of the guys in his unit were excited about it. They had worked so long and hard in training that they were ready for action.

But three days before they were scheduled to fly to Korea, my father and his unit were returning to base after a training exercise when an army truck came speeding around a corner near his barracks. Dad tried to dive out of the way, but the driver had spotted him too late, and could only slam on the brakes.

The front fender of the truck hit my father's left leg as he dove away, sending him hurtling in pain along the side of the road. The driver, a private who had a reputation for being irresponsible, jumped out of the truck to help Dad, who was quickly surrounded by the other men in his unit. As a few of the men attended to Dad, three others started punching the private, who ended up in the same hospital ward as my father.

Dad's leg had been broken and he spent the next two weeks in the army hospital. He felt horrible, watching his unit ship out without him. When he had healed, he was kept in Germany where he finished off his tour of duty. Sgt. Bernard Ruane returned to the United States on December 1, 1951, with an honorable discharge.

Half of the men he had trained with were killed in Korea when the Chinese attacked with 250,000 men in April of 1951. Dad knew full well he could have been killed if fate hadn't intervened. If it had been up to Dad, he would have been with his unit and the five American army divisions fighting back twenty-seven Chinese divisions.

Dad received a hero's welcome from the entire Naughton clan when he landed at Municipal Airport. Dad had written often to keep everyone updated about his time in the military, but they all wanted to hear it firsthand and spent the next week listening to all the stories about Germany, training, his return to Ireland, and what he planned to do next.

"Once you experience the army, everything else seems easy," Dad once said.

"Coming back, I knew how to run a bar and I had saved enough money to open one."

And that's exactly what he did when he opened "Bernie's Place," a fairly good-sized Irish tavern at 51st Street and Halsted Avenue on Chicago's South Side, where he offered good food, plenty of drink, and Irish music. This area was inhabited by a large population of Irish and was known as the Back of the Yards, referring to the stockyards where so many of those Irishmen worked each day. After work, Bernie's was just the place for them to go meet friends for some chitchat and a drink.

The weekends were the time Dad devoted to his music, which had become the great love of his life, playing with Tom Tracey's Irish Band. They played at all of the biggest Irish music venues in Chicago and were invited quite often to perform on the Saturday morning radio show, *The Irish Hour.*

Over the next two years, Dad did very well financially as a bar owner and musician and was really enjoying life. In only a few short years, he had gone from a fellow digging up peat in the bogs of Ireland, to an army tank sergeant, to an entrepreneur and musician with plenty of money to show for it. By December of 1953, he knew he had built a good life. But at twenty-seven, the time had come to start thinking about settling down and starting a family. He was scheduled to perform at Flynn's Dance Hall on New Year's Eve and wrote on his calendar under the engagement: *New Year's Resolution—Find a wonderful Irish girl and marry her.*

One of his regulars at the bar was a fellow named Jim Conoboy, an Irishman from Wisconsin who had become a good friend. Jim was an engineer for the railroad and would stop by Bernie's Place about three times a week. On Christmas Eve of 1953, Jim stopped by the bar to tell Dad about the new girl he was dating, a redhead named Ann McInerney from Oak Park.

Listening to Jim talk about Ann as a beautiful Irish redhead who was smart, funny, and had a great personality, Dad chuckled at Jim's proud description and quipped, "Does she have a sister?"

Turns out she did, and her name was Therese.

Chapter Five

FIRST
MASS

My first day as a real altar boy left a bitter taste in my mouth, literally.

    I entered the sacristy with my white Converse gym shoes slung over my left shoulder and newly purchased altar boy vestments draped over my right shoulder. This was a big day for me. It all felt so important.

I would be participating in my first Mass with the eighth-grade altar boy who trained me, Tim Rink, whose family was well known for their devotion and participation in the parish. They were holy people and somehow everyone seemed to know it.

Aside from the fact that Tim lived only a block away from me, I really knew little of him and his family before that day. He wasn't an athlete, and everyone with whom I hung around or was familiar with was involved in sports. He was a fairly tall, slightly heavyset boy with blond hair, combed moptop style to the side like most kids at that time.

He had obviously forgotten that I was one of those he had just trained a few days before, because I had to reintroduce myself to him. Then it was time to get ready. I pulled the plastic off my vestments and quickly put on the black cassock that ran down to my ankles. I snapped the buttons and then placed the white surplice over my head, pulling it down and straightening it so it hung neatly past my waist. All of a sudden, I felt holy—like a mini-priest.

In the next few minutes, I learned that being friendly or understanding was not a priority for Rink. His focus seemed to be on making sure I knew what I was doing, so one of the priests wouldn't yell at him. Regardless, with his holy reputation, I was certain I was in good hands.

"Did you study the Latin prayers?" he barked, referring to the prayers altar boys had to recite with the priests at the foot of the altar at the beginning of each Mass.

"Yes, I studied them, but I'm really having trouble," I explained, hoping he would understand that I had never read or spoken Latin before.

"Well, you had better know them, or else you're going to make me look bad. And I don't like looking bad. I'm working hard for that altar boy scholarship Father Griffin gives out each year so I can go to Quigley. Am I clear?"

"You're clear. I'll go over it again before Mass."

"You don't have time. Let's go, we have to set the altar."

The one-hour altar boy training from Saturday seemed like a blur to me. I remembered some of what Rink tried to teach us, but he had a similar attitude on that day as well. It was apparent his focus was receiving credit for doing additional work so he would get that scholarship.

Rink looked like a veteran in his cassock and surplice, like he had worn the vestments his entire life. He stood in front of the sink in the altar boys' room with the freshly washed cruets and a large green bottle.

"You pour the wine into the cruet," he instructed, then demonstrated for me. "But it's vitally important that you check to make sure the wine is not stale. You don't want to give the priests old wine. They may get sick. So you test it."

Tim picked up the bottle of wine and took a swig right from the bottle. He stood a moment.

"Not sure."

Then he took another drink.

"Yes, I think this is fine. Yes, we can use it.

"Now, if I am here, or one of the other older altar boys, you always should have us test the wine. We are experienced. We know the difference between good fresh wine and old bad wine. If not, then you may proceed, but you have to learn what is fresh wine and stale wine. Take a small drink of this."

Never quite realizing that wine-tasting was part of the altar boy experience, I was a bit skeptical about this procedure.

"Isn't this alcohol?" I asked, wondering if this was all some kind of demented joke he was trying to play on me.

"Technically, it is," Tim said, quite sure of himself. "But this is holy alcohol, so it is okay for you to test it."

I took a small sip of the wine from the bottle and grimaced.

"Ah, that's terrible!" I blurted.

"Perfect! That means it's good and fresh," veteran Tim said, watching me fill a cup with water and quickly drink it down. "Very good! You are getting the hang of it. With a few months of practice under your belt, you will be a great altar boy."

The next ten minutes were a complete frenzy. We were really running late.

"Let's go, Ruane, I'm not here to do this alone," Rink snipped. "Get your ass in gear."

Get my what in gear? This kid came from a holy family? I was beginning to have my doubts.

"Bring the water and wine cruets out and place them on the altar boys' table."

"Where's that?"

"Right there on the left side of the altar next to our kneelers, dumbbell."

"I knew that."

I quickly ran the cruets out and nearly tripped. Some of the wine spilled on my hand. It really smelled bad. How does anyone drink that stuff? I wondered. We finished setting up the altar and I had only a few minutes to go over the Latin prayers before Mass started. I could see a priest had arrived in the sacristy. I took a closer look, only to see it was Father Griffin. Why me? Why on my first Mass? There was no way I would be able to remember the Latin. Pig Latin maybe, but not the real stuff.

"Ruane, let's go," Rink barked again, pointing toward the entrance to the church, where we were supposed to line up for the start of the Mass. I hustled through the sacristy and could feel Father Griffin's displeasure staring at me for running through his sacred preparation room. Rink was standing next to the entrance doors and had a perturbed look on his face.

"Don't run through the priests' room like that," he reprimanded me.

"Sorry."

We stood in the hallway waiting for Father Griffin and heard the organ begin to play the entrance hymn. Father Griffin walked down the steps exactly the same way he walked up the steps at my First Communion: right hand over his midsection, little lean to the right, just like Father John Wayne in priest vestments.

"You may proceed, boys," he instructed us in a low monotone.

Veteran Tim and I, at the front of the procession, made our way around that beautiful white marble altar rail toward the foot of the altar. I walked with my hands together pointing toward Heaven in perfect form, praying that I would remember my part of the opening prayers,

"*Dominoes Nabisco.* No, that's not it. That's an Oreo cookie. Oh God, what am I going to do?"

I could see there weren't many people at the Mass, maybe thirty, which made me feel a little better because the entire parish wouldn't see the worst altar boy performance in the history of the church.

With Tim on the left and me on the right walking in front of Father Griffin, we turned up the center of the altar at the opening of the altar rail, making our way up the three steps. Father Griffin stopped at the final step, and Tim and I knelt down on each side of him.

The priest bowed his head and made the Sign of the Cross, saying, "*In nomine Patris, et Filii, et Spiritus Sancti. Amen.*"

I glanced up to see if it was my turn yet. He kept going; guess not.

"*Introibo ad altare Dei,*" he said, then stopped and glanced down at me. My turn!

I leaned in toward him, just like I had been taught, and said, "*Ad Deum qui laetificat juventutem meam.*"

Oh man, where did that come from? I wondered. How did I remember that? No time for bows, here comes the next one.

"*Judica me, Deus, et discerne causam meam de gente non sancta: ab homine iniquo et doloso erue me,*" recited the priest, then stopped.

I felt my teeth clenching as I tried to remember what I was supposed to say.

"*Quia tu es, Deus, fortitudo mea: quare me repulisti, et quare tristis incedo, dum affligit me inimicus?*"

I wasn't sure if that was right, but Father Griffin kept going, so I must have gotten it right. I knew the hardest part was ahead, the real long one.

"*Confiteor Deo omnipotenti, beatae Mariae . . .*" I said, having no idea how I remembered this language. I made it all the way to the end, the part of the prayer some of the altar boys made jokes about, saying it sounded like the priest was saying "*Dominoes Nabisco*" and we replied "*Two two oh.*" As I thought of that, I lost my focus for a few seconds.

"*Dominus vobiscum,*" Father Griffin said, then paused to let me reply.

I completely blanked. The silence began filling my ears. I could feel Father Griffin above me, staring down. Nothing popped in my head. Not a thing. I looked over at veteran Tim. He glanced at me quickly, then looked straight ahead. He wasn't going to bail me out. Time to think quick.

I leaned in and in a very low, muffled voice said, "*Dominoes Nabisco two two oh.*"

There was no way Father Griffin could understand it. He would either have to say "What?" and ask me to repeat it or move forward. The priest bought it and continued on.

"Oremus," he said, which meant "Let us pray." I knew that was the cue for Tim and I to stand and follow the priest up onto the altar, where I could hide behind my kneeler.

As I stood at the corner kneeler, I could feel a huge sense of relief fall over me. I had certainly dodged the bullet from Father John Wayne today, but what about the next time? The second I got home I was going to study my Latin prayers. I came so close, missing only one line. If I had only stayed focused, I know I would have recited all of it correctly, but I had to think of that stupid joke. Then the line popped in my head: *"Et cum spiritu tuo."* Too late. I was just glad I made it through.

My next duty was to bring the large red Bible up to the priest, so he could read the blessing. This seemed simple enough. I knew the specific cue, but veteran Tim thought it necessary to throw a left elbow into my ribs as a subtle reminder.

"Move your ass," he whispered to me.

I turned left, grimacing from the subtle reminder, took the large red Bible off the altar boys' table, and walked up those three red rugged steps behind the altar table, where Father Griffin was finishing his greeting to the gathering. I held the binding of the book against my chest with my hands on the bottom of the Bible, acting much like a human podium. Father Griffin grabbed the red string and pulled it back, opening the Bible to the passage from which he would read. He raised his hands, holding two fingers straight up together, and stared straight into the holy book and read the prayer. When he finished, he closed the book for me and held it so I couldn't turn. He leaned in and whispered in a very firm tone, *"Dominoes Nabisco!"* He just stared at me with a very angry look in his eyes. I looked down at the Bible, hoping he would let go. I was in trouble.

When he did let go of the book, I quickly turned and returned the Bible to its rightful place. As I returned to my place behind the kneeler, I felt sick. My stomach felt horrible, my head was buzzing, my heart was racing.

I must have looked sick too, because veteran Tim leaned over toward me. "What's wrong with you?"

"Nothing. I'm all right."

"Well, you don't look all right."

"I'm fine!"

I was determined to get through the Mass without making any more blunders. After the two readings, Father Griffin walked toward the large wooden lectern at the front of the altar on the right side as the organist played "Hallelujah." This was our signal to walk up by his side and stand with him next to the podium as he read the Gospel.

It was so strange to be standing next to Father Griffin and looking down at the people in the pews. I realized this was what I must have looked like down there all those years. And here I was next to the man to whom I had listened from those pews.

I don't think I heard a word of the Gospel that day. I was looking at the faces of the people. Some watched and listened intently. Others seemed bored. One man actually yawned. On this day the Gospel was about living up to one's responsibility. How appropriate! When the reading was finished, the people sat down, and Tim and I walked back to our chairs behind the kneelers. I couldn't wait to see the parishioners' reaction to Father Griffin's homily.

Father Griffin chose to talk about the importance of trying to identify and understand one's own responsibilities and living up to them.

"Parents have a responsibility to raise their children properly, sending them to school, feeding and clothing them," he said, adjusting his thick black-rimmed glasses. "Children have a responsibility to honor and respect their parents and work hard in school. And we all have a responsibility to try to live as good Catholics, followers of Jesus and the lessons He taught us.

"We all have a job to do and the responsibility to do our best work. The bricklayer has an obligation to lay his bricks in perfect formation to build a sound structure. The plumber has an obligation to fit the correct pipes together so the water will pass through without leaking. The altar boy has a responsibility to know his Latin prayers, so the Mass can be presented in the holy fashion worthy of the tradition of the Catholic Church."

I felt my jaw drop

I couldn't believe he said that. I guess this wasn't going away. Out of the corner of my eye, I could see veteran Tim leaning forward to look at me. I just looked straight ahead past the altar at the people in the side pews. They had no idea what the priest was referring to with that analogy. Bricklayer, plumber, altar boy—made sense to them. Regardless, I started feeling sick again.

The rest of the Mass was a blur. All I could think of was how badly I wanted to get home and study my Latin prayers. When the Mass was over and we led the procession back through the wooden doors, I walked right up the stairs into the sacristy. I didn't look back at Father Griffin, and he didn't say a word. Once in the altar boys' room, I pulled off my white surplice, unsnapped my cassock, and placed them on a hanger and into the closet filled with white and black altar boy vestments. Then I headed for the door before Father Griffin could get to me.

"Hey, where are you going?" Rink yelled, trying to stop me. "You have to help me clean up and get the altar ready for the next Mass."

I never even looked at him. I ran down the stairs and went right out the side doors into a sunlit courtyard next to the convent. I sprinted the one block to our home at 8355 S. Kostner and ran in the front door, right into my bedroom at the end of the hallway next to the kitchen.

I dove into my twin bed. I wasn't going to cry. I was embarrassed and mad. Jerk priest has to say something to me during Mass and then in the homily. The homily! Was there no reverence for that one very important section of the Mass where the priest can provide some guidance for the parishioners, so they can lead their lives more like Jesus. Not for Father John Wayne. No, asking for more money and embarrassing altar boys was the extent of his homily topics.

"Johnny, what are you doing home?" my mother said, walking into the bedroom only to find me lying down with my face buried in my pillow.

"I don't feel well," I said with authority.

"You don't sound sick."

"Oh, I'm sick all right. Sick of being an altar boy. I'm quitting."

"Johnny, you are not quitting the altar boys. What happened?"

"I couldn't remember my Latin prayers and Father Griffin scolded me during Mass and embarrassed me during the homily."

"What?"

"Yeah, right at the beginning when I brought the Bible up, he mocked me. Jerk!"

"Johnny, you can't call Father Griffin a jerk. After all, he is the pastor of this parish and a very holy man."

My mother called the front office at St. Bede's Grammar School to let them know I didn't feel well, which was true, and wouldn't be going to school. She spent the next four hours working with me on the Latin prayers. By lunchtime, I was like a professional reeling off the Latin. There would be no more *"Dominoes Nabiscos"* coming out of my mouth again.

Two days later I was back in church, and luckily Father Thomas Henry was saying the Mass. Veteran Tim was not my partner on this assignment either, so I knew I was really catching a break. Instead, I was paired with Kevin Harlin, another eighth-grader. When we got to the foot of the altar and Father Henry began the prayers, I leaned toward him and knelt perfectly upright so he could hear every word.

"Et cum spiritu tuo," I said perfectly, to finish up my participation in the prayers.

As embarrassed as I had felt during my first Mass was as proud as I felt during my second. At the homily, Father Henry never mentioned a bricklayer, plumber, or altar boy. After this Mass, I helped clean up and set up the altar for the next

Mass. There was no wine testing in my altar preparation. I would leave that up to the expertise of the Rinks of the world. When finished, I walked across the sunlit courtyard to the entrance of the grammar school.

My introduction to the service of an altar boy taught me a tough lesson about living up to my responsibilities in life. As painful as it felt, I think it was a good lesson. The next Mass I served with Father Griffin was a packed 10:00 A.M. Sunday Mass. My mother was in attendance and seemed proud to see her son up on the altar with the priest she respected. Father Griffin never said another word to me about my blunder during my first Mass. And when we arrived at the foot of the altar for the Latin prayers, I recited them perfectly—loud enough so the people in the first few pews could hear me. I would leave no doubt in Father Griffin's mind on this day. He would know this altar boy knew his Latin, and he would not embarrass me during the homily again.

Chapter Six

A BLESSED SINGING
STAR

M aking the decision to become an altar boy was an easy one. My mother, Therese McInerney Ruane, was like a number of devout Irish-American Catholic mothers and wanted one of her sons to become a priest. I was her oldest boy, so her priestly wish was placed on my shoulders. Because of my love for her and the desire to make her proud of me, I set out on the path to ordination that began with becoming an altar boy.

My mother set a holy example in our home. Every morning she sat on her bed, looking out her bedroom window toward Heaven as she prayed novenas. Often I would poke my head around the corner to peek into her room and see her praying. I never thought, not for one moment, that God wasn't listening to her with praying hands, eyes focused up toward the sky as she recited her prayers. I can't count the times I looked at that sky to see if God or Jesus or Mary would appear on a cloud. I never saw Them, but I knew They were there.

When my mother was growing up in Resurrection Parish and attending Resurrection Grammar School at the corner of Jackson and Leamington boulevards on the far West Side of Chicago, she was destined to become a nun. Her older sister, Ann, said she was the holiest girl in the parish, and her two best friends eventually joined a convent. But Terry, as she was called, developed a liking for Irish dances and boys. She obviously felt a very strong connection to God, but at some point she believed her calling was more toward her ability to sing.

By the time Mom was eighteen, she was tall at 5 feet 7 inches, and slender. She had dark brunette hair and a bright smile that lit her kind face. Her sister, Ann, said her good looks and personality introduced a presence to any room she entered.

"She really did resemble Ann Miller," her sister said later, comparing Mom's appearance to one of the major musical stars of their day. Like Ann Miller, Mom was inspired musically and began singing as early as four years old. As she grew older and her singing became a daily staple in the McInerney family home on Oak Park Avenue, both her brother and sister would roll their eyes and poke fun at her. My auntie Ann recounted the day that all changed.

"All three of us—Terry, Jack, and I—went to a party one Saturday night at a friend's house just a few blocks away. This was 1947, and my sister had just turned nineteen. The party was down in the basement and they were playing all of the big hit records of the day: Glenn Miller, Tommy Dorsey, Frank Sinatra, Bing Crosby were all really big at the time. But because we were mainly an Irish crowd, we played a lot of the great Irish tunes on a new phonograph machine. At one point, one of the girls—Carolyn, who was a professionally trained singer—was asked to sing 'Galway Bay.' Well, the three of us McInerneys sat there and listened to her in absolute awe. She was really good, hitting all the notes cleanly while moving up and down the musical scale with ease. When she finished, everyone in the room gave her a nice applause. That's when the host of the party, Mary, stood up and asked if anyone else could sing a song. Three of the girls knew my sister loved to sing and prompted her to perform 'Danny Boy,' which our family had heard her sing many times. Jack and I just looked at each other and rolled our eyes. I thought, This is going to be embarrassing. She had never sang publicly before. Oh sure, anyone within a hundred yards of our home could hear her whenever she was singing at our house, but I didn't count that as a public performance.

"Jack and I cringed as we watched our sister step to the middle of the room. She didn't seem fearful at all, which I found surprising. She started singing low and quietly, 'Oh Danny boy, the pipes, the pipes are calling. From glen to glen, and down the mountain side.'

"I looked around and everyone's eyes were glued to my sister. I looked at Jack, wondering what was wrong with them. And when she hit the high notes, ''Tis I'll be here in sunshine or in shadow,' she filled the room completely with her voice. I looked around again only to find the boys and girls wide-eyed, mesmerized by Terry's performance. I didn't know what to think. A few minutes later, faces started appearing in the basement windows. People outside could hear my sister and wanted to see who was projecting this magnificent voice. At the end of the song, her voice dropped back down nearly to a whisper as she presented the lyrics slowly with a sad look in her eyes: 'I'll simply sleep in peace until you come to me.'

"Mary, who was sitting at the other end of the room, reached for a tissue and wiped her eyes. Terry finished the song and dropped her head and arms, as if she had performed it millions of times. Jack and I didn't have to wait for the verdict. Everyone jumped to their feet and began applauding. 'Wonderful, Terry!' 'Beautiful, Terry!' Mary came up to her and gave her a hug. They kept clapping and whistling. My sister stood there smiling from ear to ear, not really knowing how to react. After years of listening to Jack and me put her down, she was now being appreciated for her talent.

"Carolyn, the trained singer, raised her hands up in the air and put a halt to all of it. 'Stop, stop! Wait a minute,' she demanded. 'As many of you know, I have been singing for years, have been trained by the best teachers and sang with some of the best in Chicago. Terry, you are the most naturally gifted singer I have ever had the pleasure of listening to in person. That was incredible!' Everyone began cheering again.

"My brother and I just looked at each other in amazement. Our sister was a great singer and we never gave her any credit. Well, from that day on, she began receiving requests to sing at weddings, funerals, and parties. She became a very popular singer in our area."

It was obvious that any thoughts my mother still may have harbored about becoming a nun dissipated that evening in that small basement on the West Side of Chicago. Now the idea of becoming a professional singer was something that seemed real to her. But how would she ever do it? Her mother had just passed away and she was taking care of her father and their home. At seventeen, she began working part-time at the Leo Burnett Advertising Agency downtown as a receptionist, managing the phone switchboard and taking dictation. But when a talent scout for *Major Bowes Amateur Hour* came to Chicago to audition talent in 1945, my mother took a crack at the big time.

This day was quite memorable for her, and she and her sister, Ann, relived it many times for us. When she arrived at the famous Chicago Theater on State Street, she was directed to the green room below the stage, which was filled with aspiring singers. Some were sitting staring intently at the theater door, awaiting their turn. Some stood in the corners doing vocal exercises, while others rehearsed in whispers so they wouldn't forget the lyrics.

She walked in and examined a scene of nervousness and ambition, finding the sign-up sheet at a small table along the side wall next to a pot of coffee that smelled like it had been burning for days.

Mom sat patiently for more than two hours. She didn't have to rehearse her song or tune up her voice. She had sung Irving Berlin's "Easter Parade" nearly every day for five years. Al Jolson had made it famous, and Judy Garland was making it even more famous in the film of the same name. Mom knew that when called, she would just walk in there and belt it out as if she were singing at home. Each time the door opened, a Carole Lombard look-alike appeared with clipboard in hand prepared to announce the next casualty.

"Therese McInerney!" she said finally.

Mom rose quickly and followed her out the door, up the steps, and onto the theater's massive stage, where she saw a young woman behind a grand piano.

"Just go right out there next to the piano," the woman instructed my mother. "The man in the first row will direct you."

"Thank you," my mother said confidently.

She walked out onto the semi-lit stage where Kate Smith, Sinatra, Garland, and Al Jolson had all performed. At this point, she said her nerves started to get the best of her and she actually had thoughts of running out the door. But she took a deep breath and regained her composure. The musical director was sitting in the front row of the large empty auditorium. He was dressed in black and looked like a jazz musician with long, dark, slicked-back hair, a goatee, dark-rimmed glasses. He sat with legs crossed, puffing on a Camel cigarette like it was his only source of oxygen.

"What's your name?" he asked.

"Therese McInerney," Mom mumbled after clearing her throat.

"Great, Therese! What are you going to sing for me today?"

" 'Easter Parade,' " she said in an upbeat fashion, hoping to get herself in a positive state of mind.

"Now I want you to relax, enjoy yourself, and sing us your song."

That helped her, but she still felt uneasy performing on a cold dark stage with a strange-looking Camel-puffing man staring at her. To relax, she visualized standing on the podium at church. That helped a little. But now she would have to sing out into the empty theater. Thank goodness there was a piano to support her.

After giving the pianist her key, she listened to the song's intro, then started singing softly to her one-man audience: "In your Easter bonnet, with all the frills upon it . . ."

Throughout the song, she never once made eye contact with the director. She looked over his head, to one side, then the other. She didn't like the look of this weird, cigarette-smoking beatnik with the slicked-back hair. When finished, she looked straight at him. He was holding his smoldering Camel and just looking at her.

"Therese, that was beautiful," he said. "Absolutely outstanding."

My mother was shocked. How could this man like her singing?

"Thank you," my mother said, thinking this was a good sign.

"Have you ever sung professionally before?"

"No sir."

"Well, I think you have a good chance of doing very well. The only thing I can tell you is I'd like you to work on your presentation. Use your hands more, make eye contact with your audience, get into it, sell your song. I'm not going to send you to New York to be on the show this year, but when I come back next year, I would like to see you again. And I'd like you to sing the same song and really sell it to me. Will you do that for me?"

"Yes sir, I will," she said, feeling relieved she wouldn't have to deal with him any longer.

My mother obviously knew that she could have done a better job delivering the song, but somehow the inside of that dark theater was an uncomfortable environment for her.

She walked down the steps on the side of the stage, up the long inclined red-rugged aisle, and pushed hard on the heavy doors taking her into the lobby and out of the front entrance into the bright sunlight of a beautiful Saturday afternoon. She stood in front of the theater looking up at the grand marquee, thinking about all those singers, so eager to get on that stage and show the world their talent, or lack of it. And here she was, a young lady with tremendous talent, but now she was a bit ambivalent about pursuing it.

When the talent scout returned, he called my mother to invite her back, but she never returned to the theater. Something didn't feel right to her. She didn't have the heart to pursue it. She loved to sing, but something had changed for her. Instead, Mom returned to churches, Irish dances, and parties—the kind of singing she enjoyed. She had made up her mind that the glitz and glamour of Hollywood was not for her. No, she wanted a normal life, a stable life, to marry a good Irish man and raise a churchgoing family in an active Catholic community. That idea felt right to her. Now all she had to do was find a good Irish man.

On Christmas Eve of 1953, her sister Ann's new boyfriend, Jim Conoboy, came to their family's apartment for dinner. Ann was still getting over a divorce, and Jim was just what she needed to right her life: a good solid Irishman, who worked hard and had his heart in the right place.

That night after dinner, Jim invited Ann to a New Year's Eve dance at Flynn's Hall, a popular Irish dance hall on the Southwest Side of Chicago at 63rd Street and Kedzie Avenue. He told her how Tom Tracey's Irish Band would be performing and his good friend Bernie Ruane was the drummer. Ann loved Irish dances and beamed her approval, with her father and younger sister looking on. Then Jim turned to my mother and asked her if she would like to join them.

"I can introduce you to Bernie, if you're interested," he offered.

Dad said that our mother looked like a movie star when he was introduced to her that New Year's Eve in 1953. She was wearing a light green dress that ran to her knees, the style of the day, and her brunette hair was done in the style of Dorothy Lamour, a famous movie star. Mom fell in love at first sight with Dad, who she said was quite handsome, with strong broad shoulders, a wonderful smile, and a great sense of humor.

The smoke-filled hall was packed that night, the large dance floor affording each Fred Astaire and Ginger Rogers's wannabe only a few inches to exhibit their skill. Mom and Dad talked a great deal that evening, getting to know each other during each musical break. As midnight was about to strike and bandleader Tom Tracey counted down the seconds, Mom was standing to the right of the bandstand closest to my father when Tracey yelled, "Happy New Year!" As the horns blew, confetti filled the air and kisses were traded, and my mother gazed at my father while he provided the baseline as the crowd sang "Auld Lang Syne." The song concluded and the New Year's revelers cheered loudly as Dad stepped away from the drums and toward my mother, whom he kissed for the first time under the bright lights of the bandstand. Her sister, Ann, and boyfriend Jim turned and looked at each other, knowing they had made a good match.

Over the course of the next six months, the courtship proved to each that they had found exactly the type of person they both were seeking. They were both good, honest, hard-working people, and that understanding cemented their bond. And they were both musical. Tom Tracey's band was becoming quite well known among the Irish in Chicago, and I think my mother enjoyed all of the excitement of singing in front of a band that featured the man she loved on the drums. This was fun! Maybe it wasn't a spot on national radio or television, but she loved every single minute of it.

Dad proposed to Mom on April 3, 1954, and they were married on September 18 in front of family and friends at Resurrection Church. They look so happy in their wedding photos, filled with the hope that their lives together would be blessed with children and good fortune. A flight to Miami Beach for their honeymoon followed, and Dad found out the hard way that a fair-skinned Irish man sunbathing on the Florida beach is not a great idea. He suffered a second-degree sunburn, which didn't ruin their trip, but it did cut back severely on their time outdoors.

The newlyweds bought a house at 1057 Monitor Avenue in Oak Park, close to Mom's family and Dad's relatives, the Naughtons. Mom resigned from the Leo Burnett Advertising Agency to stay home and prepare for their own family. Dad was the breadwinner, managing his bar each day from noon until midnight; Mom often joined him to spend time together. During this time, they spent many an afternoon on State Street shopping at Marshall Field's, Goldblatt's, or Sears. This was a new and different life for Mom, having a husband who took care of her, not having to work and shopping in the afternoon. She and her sister, Ann, would often meet at lunchtime at a coffee shop on Michigan Avenue to catch up with each other's lives, which didn't take much because they talked on the phone each day. Ann and Jim Conoboy got married as well, so the two sisters had new husbands and lives to discuss. And in February of 1955, Mom told her sister the biggest news: She was pregnant. Life was good.

Maureen Therese Ruane was delivered at 6:00 A.M. in October at Loretto Hospital on the far West Side of Chicago, only ten minutes from their home. One year later, they were back at Loretto to deliver their first son, John Bernard Ruane. Over the course of the next year, the realities of caring for young babies with a husband who wasn't home most of the day became all too apparent for Mom. I wasn't much of a help. Mom said I nearly burned the house down one day when, at the age of one, I decided to repair the electric alarm clock in her bedroom. Luckily, she spotted the small fire before it spread and quickly doused it with salt.

About this same time, the fall of 1957, Mom was pregnant again and decided it was time for a change. While spending the past two years at home with two young babies while her husband was at work most of the time, it became very clear that the lifestyle of a bar owner didn't mesh with that of a family man. It was a lot of fun while it lasted, but the honeymoon was over. After much discussion, Dad agreed to sell the bar and take a job as a civil servant. He could swallow giving up the bar to become a policeman or fireman; those were both highly respected professions. But my mother vetoed that idea, saying that line of work was too dangerous.

Dad took a job with the city of Chicago's Water Department, a safe job that would provide a stable lifestyle for this new family man. It was a lot to ask of him, but he did it for her. Only a man in love would give up so much to spend five days a week digging ditches and laying pipes for Chicago's Water Department.

It was also time for a move. Mom's brother, Jack, had just moved into a new parish called St. Bede the Venerable on the far Southwest Side of Chicago. Uncle Jack's red-bricked home was one of the new houses being built on an open prairie that ran between 79th and 87th streets and between Kostner and Pulaski avenues. When Mom and Dad had visited her brother's new home on the 7900 block of South Kolin, she fell in love with the thought of building a new home in this new parish and having her kids grow up with all of the other new families. It would be a fresh start.

Mom and Dad delivered their third child, Kathleen Ann Ruane, at St. Ann's Hospital. A few months later, Mom visited the newly built Catholic church and school at 83rd Street and Kenneth Avenue. That was the day she met the pastor, Rev. John Griffin, who greatly impressed her, sharing his hopes for this new parish.

"We just finished building this church, but we may have to build another larger one if we continue to grow," he told her.

Well, if he was going to build a larger church someday, Mom was going to build a house right down the block. And that's exactly what she did, signing a contract for one of the new homes being built. Mom took the second one from the corner at 8355 S. Kostner Avenue. It would be completed in August, and Mom and Dad said goodbye to Oak Park forever.

Over the next five years, the Ruane family settled into their new home and delivered two more children, this time at Little Company of Mary Hospital in Evergreen Park: Daniel Michael—followed by Margaret Mary to complete the clan.

With five children it was a struggle to make ends meet on Water Department wages. The carefree world of singing with a band was a distant memory for Mom, but Dad was determined to continue playing the drums. He gave up the bar but wouldn't part with the music. Plus he was paid for performing, so it made sense financially for him to continue with Tom Tracey's orchestra. Perhaps it was his last link to his homestead in Ireland and the singsongs his sister Delia used to organize, but he kept drumming with the Irish band for the rest of his life.

We all remember the Saturday night in July of 1968 when we watched Dad perform with Tom Tracey's Irish Band on WGN television's presentation of *The Irish Hour*. This was quite an exciting event for us. We cheered every time the camera panned across the bandstand or showed a close-up of Dad keeping the beat and smiling happily. Wow! Our dad was on TV, playing the drums. All my friends watched it and thought we were rich, because everyone knows when you are on TV or in the movies or write for the newspaper, you are rich.

I know my mother was thrilled to see him on television as well, but I think she watched the show that night and suddenly was confronted with some questions about her own life. What if she had called back the talent scout from *Major Bowes* and gone downtown for that second audition? Would she have been on television singing for Ted Mack, who took over the show after Bowes died? Would she have received a contract from a recording company? Her singing was often compared to the styles of Garland and Ethel Merman, both world-class belters. Might that have been her future? But did she have what it takes, whatever that is, to survive in that business? Would she have been happy? Would she have gotten married and had five kids? What would her life have been like?

Certainly these were questions that must have haunted her on the days that followed as she sat alone in our yellow-linoleum–floored kitchen smoking her Kent cigarettes and drinking coffee. Was she happy as a housewife? Would she have been happy if she had made it big? She never would know. But she watched her husband on television for one night and somehow the appeal of being a star that was lost on her after the audition, all of a sudden seemed exciting and attractive. Is that what's important in life, getting your face on television? It sure seemed to be the case that evening.

After a few weeks of talking at the dinner table about the big night on WGN, the subject just sort of faded away, almost as quickly as it arose. Fame is fleeting. Maybe that was the lesson. But when it was happening, it certainly was exciting.

The fact is, if Mom had become a professional singer, she would never have met our father and had her five children. One little turn in a person's life can affect so many others' lives and destinies. As it was, we were her destiny.

Mom was somewhat content singing at home, but we knew she enjoyed singing in front of an audience as well. This was apparent because each Sunday at 8:30 A.M. Mass, Mom found it necessary to lead the entire church in song, despite the fact that there was a ten-person church choir prepared to do the same.

Just as the choir began to sing from the loft at the back of the church, it only took Mom four notes to drown them out. Each Sunday, the organ and choir performed five songs. Each Sunday, my mother took the lead. And each Sunday, the five Ruane kids hung their heads, embarrassed. All of us were very aware that our mother loved to sing. She sang all day and night. She sang songs from every hit musical. She sang them so often, I even knew the words, which was something I wasn't about to share with any of my grammar-school buddies.

At this time, none of us were aware our mother had once sung in churches and with bands. It never was talked about. We knew our dad was a drummer, but we just thought our mother loved to sing and tried out for *Major Bowes* once.

We all felt very lucky the day our neighbor Mrs. Roman, who could hear Mom's daily home concerts from her kitchen window, suggested she offer her services to the church. Mom probably had thought about it too, but she was too busy with her family duties to make the commitment. Mrs. Roman's suggestion came at the right time. In the spring of 1970, Mom decided to make the commitment, taking her from the third-row pew with her five embarrassed kids to the choir loft in the back of that massive church where she was placed in the starring role. To our great amazement, the parishioners loved her singing voice. Mom was most proud of introducing "Let There Be Peace on Earth," her favorite song, to St. Bede's. After each Mass, she was approached by a number of people, wishing to make known their appreciation for her performance. All of a sudden, it seemed everyone in the parish knew her—even some of my teachers.

"John, your mother has a wonderful singing voice," Sister Linda, one of my seventh-grade teachers, informed me nearly every other week.

"Thank you, Sister." I blushed.

Sister Linda was one of the new, hip nuns at St. Bede's, so her compliment carried a great deal more significance for me than a rave review from one of the older, more traditional nuns.

All five of us were hearing the same compliments. So now, all of a sudden, the mother who used to embarrass us was a singing star in our parish. This was a weird change and a perspective we had to learn to understand and appreciate.

After that point, it seemed half the time I answered the phone, it was someone from the church rectory calling to try to schedule my mother for a Mass, funeral, or wedding. The word was out: St. Bede's had a singing star and everyone wanted her singing at their special occasion. We couldn't go anywhere without someone approaching us. I vividly remember an older man, still in his blue suit from Mass, approaching my mom at the McDonald's about a half mile from our home.

"I was at the eight-thirty Mass today and heard you singing," he said, reaching out to shake my mother's hand. "What a wonderful voice you have. It really made the Mass special!"

A big smile crossed Mom's face as she shook the man's hand. She was happy. Her life was complete. She had her family and her stage.

Chapter Seven

THE BELLS ARE RINGING

During my service time as an altar boy in the late 1960s, we had so much more to do than the altar servers of today. One of the key duties was the ringing of the bells during the consecration of the bread and wine into the Body and Blood of Christ. In some churches, this ritual is still performed and comes during the most sacred part of the Mass, the re-creation of the Last Supper, when the priest blesses the bread and wine transforming them into the Body and Blood of Jesus Christ.

In the blessing ritual, the priest uses a very large round host, about six times bigger than the hosts distributed at Communion so all the parishioners in the church can see it. During this sacred section of the Mass, all the parishioners kneel and watch the priest begin the ceremony, reciting the prayers aloud for all to hear. When he reaches the blessing of the bread and wine, he holds the host with both hands in front of him, reciting a prayer, then raises it up high toward Heaven. It is at the very moment when he begins to raise the host up high that the altar boy is required to ring the bells.

Tim Rink and I were scheduled to serve the 7:00 A.M. Mass one Friday in October. Tim told me to arrive ten minutes earlier than normal so he could teach me about the protocol for bell ringing. He said it wouldn't be difficult, but I needed to know the requirements of each priest. I was nine Masses into my altar boy experience and had never been required to ring the bells.

"It seems like such a simple thing," he had told me a few days earlier after finishing the Tuesday service. "But each priest does it differently. Some hold the host up longer. Others just show it for a few seconds, then bring it down. But you have to know their tendencies or it could be a disaster."

Those words dominated my thoughts as I waited for Rink to arrive that morning. I watched the clock tick ahead: 6:30 A.M. soon became 6:40. Having already set up the altar and altar table, I began pacing the altar boys' room, peeking out the folding door every few minutes, looking for Rink. It was 6:55 A.M. and no sign of him.

I heard a rattling in the priests' room. Did Rink come in the other door? I wondered. I quickly scooted to the doorway and saw Father Griffin putting on his vestments to prepare for Mass.

I leaned against the wall realizing that I may have to serve solo for the holy Father Griffin with no bell training. I walked back to the folding door, peering toward the back of the church, looking for Rink to emerge through those large metal doors. Still no sign of him, and the pews were filled with about sixty older people, the usual crowd for this Mass. I glanced up at the clock. Seven o'clock!

"Where is the other altar boy?" Father Griffin asked, now standing in the altar boys' room.

"He didn't show up," I replied, watching a look of concern cross the priest's face.

"Are you able to serve this Mass on your own?" he asked, looking toward the stairs, probably hoping Rink would appear.

"Yes, Father Griffin, I think so," I replied, and I walked past him through the priests' room toward the two wooden doors we would enter. "I don't think I have much choice."

"Yes, I guess you don't," he said, following me down the steps.

I was on my own. I led the priest around the marble Communion rail to the steps of the altar. I went through my Latin prayers like a pro and then walked up to my altar boy kneeler on the left side of the altar. Everything seemed to be going just fine, but I did notice Father Griffin would glance up toward the church entrance every few minutes, probably looking for Rink or any other experienced altar boy to save the day.

As we got closer to the consecration, it occurred to me that I wasn't quite certain about one aspect of the bell ringing: When do I stop? Do I wait until the priest brings the large host down and then stop? Or do I stop and then he brings the large host down? And this was Father Griffin! He doesn't like mistakes. I decided I would try to read his expression as he held the host up to make my decision.

When I brought the water and wine cruets up for the blessing, I thought—for just a brief moment—about asking Father Griffin very quickly when I should stop ringing the bells. But as I poured the water and wine into his chalice and looked at his grim face, I thought it better to just take my chances.

So there I was, bent on my kneeler, with no veteran server to guide me. The three bells were attached at the top to a long golden handle. I was right-handed, and the bells rested on the rug just to my left. I wouldn't have any trouble ringing them with my left. The question was, for how long?

Father Griffin took the large host and started reciting, "Take this, all of you, and eat it. This is My Body, which will be given up for you." I reached down to grab the handle of the bells and craned my neck up to watch for him to raise the host. He did, and I began shaking the bells. I watched his face to see if he would bring the host down. He didn't. I kept ringing. He still didn't bring it down. Should I take a chance and stop ringing? What if I'm wrong? He'll be holding the holy host up with no ringing. That would be embarrassing. The whole church would look at me and wonder, why did that altar boy stop ringing the bells, leaving the holy Father Griffin standing there holding the holy host up with no ringing? This was getting embarrassing.

As the ringing went on, I noticed Father Griffin's head turn toward me just slightly. That was it. That was the signal. I stopped ringing. He brought the host down. He never looked over at me. I had it. I knew how to do it. I ring the bells and decide when to stop. Easy! My worries were over.

I wondered how the church could give a fifth-grader all of that power. I was the only altar boy at the 7:00 A.M. Mass, serving for the holy Father Griffin, and I get to determine when he lowers the Body and Blood of Christ. What if I was a rogue altar boy, looking to ridicule the holy Father Griffin with his stern face and John Wayne walk? He could raise that host and I could keep ringing that bell. His arms would ache as his blood drained from them. But I wouldn't stop the ringing and the pain would fill his arms. I know he would not only glance at me. He would stare at me. Maybe he would even say, "Hey, rogue altar boy, would you stop ringing that damn bell? My arms are killing me!"

But no, I wasn't a rogue altar boy. Father Griffin then took the chalice of wine with both hands in front of him and recited, "When supper was ended, He took the cup . . ." I reached down once more, craned my neck to spot the right moment. " . . . Take this, all of you, and drink from it. This is the cup of My Blood, the Blood of the new and everlasting covenant. It will be shed for you and for all so that sins may be forgiven. Do this in memory of Me." Then he raised the chalice toward Heaven, and I began ringing the bells. After about three seconds, I thought that was enough. I'll let him bring the chalice down now. Oh wait, I'll give him one more second. The power had gone to my head!

I stopped ringing and set the bells back on the ground. But Father Griffin didn't bring the chalice down right away. No, he kept it up there toward Heaven. Should I go back to ringing? All the heads in the church turned toward me, wondering why I had stopped ringing the bells. I went back to the bells and began ringing. It was most definitely a double-ringing during the wine blessing. I thought it was better to deliver a double ring than let Father Griffin stand there with the chalice in the air and no bells while all of the people in the church looked at me. I'm certain they thought I was a rogue altar boy. I didn't recall ever hearing of a double-ringing during the consecration. No, I had set an altar boy precedent in letting the power of the bells go to my head.

I watched his head again to see when I should stop. Obviously, Father Griffin really liked his chalice of wine blessed with a good, long bell-ringing. After all, he had to drink it all, and who wants to drink half-blessed wine at seven o'clock in the morning?

Father Griffin turned his head just a bit and I stopped ringing the bells. He brought the chalice down. I looked at the elderly people in the pews. They seemed to all nod their approval, as if to say, "That's better."

Throughout the remainder of the Mass, I tried to read Father Griffin to see if he was upset with me for the double bell-ring. No, he was as stone-faced as usual. I'm sure he would fare well in any game of poker. After Mass was over, I was cleaning the altar to prepare it for the next Mass when he called me into the priests' room.

"Mr. Ruane," he said in a very stern voice as he looked down at me from his six-foot perch. "Who trained you on the bells?"

He was angry! I really blew it on the bells.

"I was never trained on the bells, Father. Tim Rink was supposed to train me this morning, but he never showed."

"I noticed," he replied sarcastically. "Don't stop ringing the bells until I am ready. You need to watch me, and when I bring the host or wine down, that's when you stop. It's that simple. Do you understand?"

"I am sorry, Father. It won't happen again," I chirped, fighting back tears.

"It better not!"

I felt horrible as I walked through the exit door and across the courtyard toward school. First I get the Latin prayers wrong and now the bell-ringing. Two huge mistakes in a three-week period was not acceptable; everyone knew that, especially the wide-eyed neck-craners and finger-pointers in the parish. They probably would be contacting Pope Paul VI in Rome to let him know about the incompetent altar boy at St. Bede's Church and ask him to have me excommunicated. I wouldn't blame them. I could just imagine that conversation.

"Yes, Your Holiness, we have a young man here who stopped ringing the bells when he felt like it during the blessing of the wine at Mass today," Father Griffin would tell Pope Paul on the overseas call.

"Oh really!" Pope Paul would respond, sounding surprised over the static-filled phone connection. "Is he a rogue altar boy? You know, we have had reports of rogue altar boys letting the power of the bells go to their heads."

"No, we don't think he's a rogue altar boy, although many of the elderly parishioners who attend the seven o'clock Mass seem to think so," Father Griffin would explain. "We just think he's just unprepared."

"Ah yes, not ready for the duties of the altar. By chance, did this same altar boy forget his Latin prayers at the foot of the altar?"

"He did."

"And did he try the '*Dominoes Nabisco*' line to get off the hook?"

"Exactly!"

"Well, we will have to bring him to Rome and have him walk out on the papal balcony with me, so all of the wide-eyed neck-craners and finger-pointers can humiliate him."

"Good idea, Your Holiness. If you need any additional neck-craners and finger-pointers, I have quite a few in my parish."

"No, we have plenty here in Rome as well."

My imagination ran wild that morning on my walk across the courtyard. I wondered how something as simple as ringing a bell could cause so much trouble. I was pretty upset with Tim Rink for not showing up, but knew I had learned a lesson about the authority and power of the Church, especially when it came to the bell-ringing protocol.

Chapter Eight

THE IKES

My parents were good Catholics who were blessed with five healthy children, three girls and two boys. Five kids in a family, or sometimes more, wasn't unusual for that time.

My three sisters each had their own unique qualities. Maureen, a fairly tall brunette, was one year older than me and was blessed with brains. She earned straight A's each year at St. Bede's Grammar School, and they seemed to come easily to her. She loved to read, and I think her literary interest helped her excel in the classroom. During the 1960s, my sister was like a lot of girls who read the Nancy Drew mysteries. I always felt a bit guilty not having her interest in books, and once I even went so far as to visit the local library to check out one of the Hardy Boys mysteries. I read about five pages before I realized I would rather be outside playing baseball.

A year younger than me, Kathy was a cute, freckle-faced Irish-looking kid with a bright smile. More like me, she had to work to earn her B average. She loved playing outside with her friends. Kathy would join us whenever we got some kids together on the block to play sixteen-inch softball or touch football. Both of these games were often played with both boys and girls on the block, and Kathy turned out to be quite good. She had a very good throwing arm and could hit as well as anyone. This was before organized sports were offered to girls, which is too bad for Kathy because she would have been a star player.

Margaret was always the lovable baby sister. She was thin, with long brown hair, the spitting image of our mother. We all looked out for Margaret, almost like surrogate parents.

Once when Margaret was nine years old, Kathy and I were with her at the Marenos' house across the street, climbing the small tree in their front yard. When it was Margaret's turn, she grabbed the lowest branch and tried to lift her leg to pull herself up, but she slipped and fell. She hit the ground hard and cried out in pain. Kathy and I ran to her side and could see her left arm looked horrible, crooked. The middle of her forearm dipped down almost into a U-shape. It was most definitely broken, and we tried to keep her from looking at it. Kathy and I got her home as quickly as possible. Mom took over and quickly led Margaret to the backseat of the family Chevy to rush her to the emergency room at Little Company of Mary Hospital. The attending doctor soon had a gas mask over her mouth to knock her out, and that was the end of her pain for a while.

When Margaret woke up, she found her arm straight and in a white plaster cast, which started at her knuckles and ran all the way up to her elbow. Every kid in the area seemed to stop by our house over the next few days to sign it. Although the cast itched terribly, she was a local celebrity for about a month. When Dad took all of us to a White Sox game, Margaret wasn't able to clap with both hands. Dad helped her out by letting her clap her right hand against his left—a nice and memorable moment for my little sister.

One of the best family bonding experiences each summer were our trips to the Isaak Walton Club in Dolton, Illinois. Of course, we never could afford to join this club, or any club for that matter, but my mother's sister, Ann, was nice enough to invite us as guests. Several times each summer, Mom would organize her five children for the trip to the "Ikes," as it was called. Getting ready to go was always pure chaos, but somehow we managed to get packed and out the door.

"Okay, now I will pack lunches in the cooler. Maureen, you gather up all the towels. Johnny, you make the Kool-Aid. Kathy, you help Margaret get ready. Danny, get a few rubber balls from the garage to play catch. And everyone, PLEASE DON'T FORGET YOUR BATHING SUITS!" my mother would instruct us on the summer mornings she wanted to take us to swim. "We should have everything together and be ready to go in a half hour, so let's get going."

This was our call to action. Immediately, each one of us did our jobs, then loaded up the light-blue 1967 Chevy and off we went. These trips were really special for us, because we never could afford to go on vacations. So the mention of a day at the Ikes was quite a treat, and the car rides there were quite memorable. Our poor mother!

First of all, she was never that comfortable driving. To drive on the Calumet Expressway was really pushing it, especially with five screaming kids for the duration of the one-hour drive. Mom would take the southbound entrance ramp to the Dan Ryan Expressway at 87th Street and then try to work her way over to the third lane, so she would be able to merge onto the Calumet. The Ryan was always busy with fast, bright-colored, white-walled Cadillacs, so this was no easy task for even the best of drivers. For Mom, that one and a half miles proved the most anxious of times, with five young children yelling and fighting while she tried to drive on this very busy expressway.

Once on the Calumet, she could sigh in relief and stay in the right lane, moving along at about 45 mph with angry drivers lining up behind her.

"Mom, Danny called me an idiot," Kathy would complain as my five-year-old brother would push her, trying to get more space in the cramped backseat.

"Danny, don't call your sister an idiot," Mom would holler back, trying to keep her eyes on the road while the car behind us would honk the horn and Danny would whisper to Kathy, "Idiot."

"Mom, he called me an idiot again."

"I did not."

"Did too."

"Kids, if you don't stop arguing, I am going to turn around and go home."

Because we wanted to go swimming, that would shut everyone up—for about two minutes. But the evil youth in us would quickly rise again and the arguing would continue every time we made the trip to the 147th Street exit and on to Dolton. How my mom ever survived those drives is beyond me. Obviously she really wanted to go to the Ikes because she endured those trips down the expressway about once a week each summer during the late 1960s.

The Ikes was a private club hidden in a neighborhood at 144th Street off Chicago Road. If someone didn't provide exact directions, one would never know it was there. But Mom did have directions, and she parked in the white gravel parking lot next to the brown wooden clubhouse that featured a smoke-filled bar at the front and game room and dance area off to the side. The bar was pretty much off limits to us kids, but my cousin Sheila, Auntie Ann's daughter, often sneaked in there to beg her dad for a bag of Vitners potato chips or pretzels, both of which she loved.

The best part of the club was the lake. It wasn't big, but it had a floating pier about thirty yards from shore that Maureen, Kathy, and I swam to the second we jumped in the water. On the green metal square floating pier was a diving board where the three eldest Ruane kids would perform dives, backflips, cannon balls, and even an occasional belly-flop for guffaws. The water was fairly deep near the pier, about twenty-five feet, and I knew fish surrounded me after each dive, which made me somewhat anxious. I chose never to dive with a pair of goggles, preferring not to see the fish.

Because Danny and Margaret were younger, they weren't allowed past the safety rope set up to separate the deeper water from the shallow swimming area.

"C'mon, Johnny!" my freckle-faced brother would yell, waving one of the rubber balls at me. "Let's play catch."

Once I had my fill of diving, I would swim to one side of the shallow section while Danny stood on the other side and began tossing the ball to me. Back and forth we threw it, diving to catch it, skipping it across the water, throwing high fly balls to see if we could catch it—a real blast for any kid. Kathy also joined us in this game many a day. As we played catch, Maureen would buddy up with our cousin Sheila to eat the potato chips she had finagled from the bar, while chitchatting about nothing in general: probably Nancy Drew books, for all I knew.

Mom would sit with Auntie Ann and gab away while watching little Margaret, who was only two years old. Margaret would often take naps in her blue-covered buggy, which gave our mother a break. Mom enjoyed this time greatly because she was outside in the fresh air, away from the burdens of our home and talking with her sister. She also would take little Margaret along the shore to watch her build sandcastles with her big sisters.

After a few hours of swimming and playing catch, Mom would call us all in for our peanut butter and jelly sandwiches along with the Kool-Aid I had prepared. Kool-Aid was perfect for our family because it was a cheap, flavored drink that we loved because of all the sugar I added. It was nothing compared to an ice-cold Pepsi, a delicacy in our household.

We all wolfed down our sandwiches and Kool-Aid as quickly as possible so we could go right back in the lake. "You have to wait thirty minutes after eating before going in the water again," Mom would say each and every time we finished snarfing down our lunch. This was always met with a Ruane children's chorus of "But, MOM!!!!" It didn't matter how much we whined and complained, and we were world-class whiners and complainers. As a matter of fact, if there were a children's whiners and complainers Olympics, I believe my brother and I would have won a gold medal or two. No matter, we never saw that lake water until thirty minutes had passed.

As a kid I never understood the thirty-minute rule because all we wanted to do was go back into the shallow water to play catch. My mother knew better, realizing if she gave us permission to go in the shallow water, it was only a matter of time before one of us justified a reason to swim out to the pier. Sure, I could imagine it now. A couple of preteens with full bellies ready to go off the diving board again. "Hey, Kathy, that was about thirty minutes, wasn't it?" I'm sure I would bellow out to my younger sister, back on the beach working on a sandcastle with Margaret. "Sure, thirty minutes," Kathy would reply, not really paying attention to the question.

In my mind, Kathy said it was thirty minutes, so I could go to the pier. Sure, thirty minutes—sounded right to me. And as I would begin swimming out there, I would hear my mother bellow, "Johnny! Get back in here!"

And on my return, she would interrogate me: "What is the big idea going into the deep water? You just ate."

"Well, Kathy said it was thirty minutes."

"Kathy!"

Besides swimming in the lake, the other big event at the Ikes was the shrimp fry, an annual tradition the first weekend of August. Now remember, we were five kids from the Southwest Side of Chicago—kids accustomed to hamburgers, hot dogs, and P&J sandwiches. None of us knew what a shrimp looked like, let alone had the ability to comprehend the concept of actually eating one.

Our first shrimp fry experience took place on a hot Saturday in 1967. I walked up to the large oblong silver metal tub that was filled with the little orange and white things. A man who looked to be a dad-type in his forties, with a prominent belly displayed in his blue-checked collared shirt, walked up to the shrimp tub, took the metal tongs, and pinched a serving of about ten creatures onto his white paper plate. He followed with a scoop of the red sauce from the metal bowl sitting on a table off to the side. Then I watched as he dipped one of those things into the sauce and lifted it high. He admired it for a moment before plunging it down into his mouth while holding the fanned tail, which was all that was left after he took his bite. Oh, this was disgusting!

As I watched the man lift the next shrimp to repeat this dreadful act, I spotted my five-year-old brother out of the corner of my eye, walking right toward me. I jumped between Danny's sightline and the man devouring the shrimp. I never let my brother near the television set when the *Wizard of Oz* was on, so I certainly wasn't going to let him see this horrifying sight.

"Stop, Danny!" I yelled, holding up both hands like a traffic cop. "Don't take another step." I ran up to him, took his right hand, and led my little brother back to the wooden picnic table where Mom and Auntie Ann were gabbing away like two schoolgirls.

"Mom, they're eating these orange and white things over there, and Danny almost saw it," I huffed and puffed, completely out of breath after having rescued my brother from the madness surrounding the oblong metal tub.

"It's okay, Johnny, it's a shrimp fry," she explained. "We are going to have some as well."

I stood there wide-eyed. What was this about? Was she trying to punish us for being so bad during the car rides? Was this some form of brutal discipline? That's when I saw it. Kathy was walking toward us with a white paper plate filled with the white and orange things.

"Kathy, what are you doing?" I barked. "For the love of God, put the shrimp down before you do something silly, like eat them."

Kathy smiled wide, seeing the opportunity to have a little fun. She lifted up one of the foreign creatures, then slowly dipped it into the red sauce as Danny and I watched in disbelief. Then she lifted it, held it over her open mouth, took one more glance at me to make sure I was watching, and plopped the sauce-covered shrimp into her mouth.

"Mom, do you see what Kathy just did?" I asked, but Mom and Auntie Ann just laughed and went back to their schoolgirl chatter.

"Idiot!" Danny said to Kathy, knowing how to push her button.

"Mom, Danny called me an idiot," Kathy complained. Mom didn't care. She was deep in conversation.

That's when I saw Maureen and Sheila walking toward us holding plates of shrimp. The world had gone mad. I took my brother away from this lunacy and wandered back over toward the shrimp area. A long line of people now stood in front of the tub, each holding their plate and looking anxious to dip into the smelly seafood.

"Danny, you wait right here, I'll be right back," I said, placing Danny on a wooden picnic table bench where I could watch him while I went on my reconnaissance mission. I quickly ran up to the table with the plates, grabbed one, ran around the side of the tub, grabbed one of these slippery little smelly things by the tail, threw some sauce on the plate, and walked back toward Danny as I heard "Hey, kid, get in line!"

I didn't look to see who was yelling at me but sat down on the wooden bench next to Danny. We both examined this white and orange thing that smelled, well . . . not good.

"Can I try it?" asked my naïve little brother.

"Danny, are you crazy? You are only five. Don't you want to live to see six?"

I had to be brave and taste this thing for my brother. I dipped the shrimp into the red sauce and took a small nibble of it. Huh, that wasn't too bad, but it felt kind of rubbery. I think the sauce was making it okay, but I wasn't sure. I nibbled again. That's actually pretty good. I bit the entire shrimp and chewed it. Feeling much like the Cat in the Hat discovering the benefits of green eggs and ham, I realized I really did like shrimp.

"Danny, this is really good!"

"I want some," he pleaded.

"Okay, you wait here, I'll get some for you."

Once again I slipped over to the table, grabbed another paper plate, shot over to the other side of the shrimp tub—where no one in line could really see me too well—and loaded up both plates, then stepped to the other side for sauce.

"Hey, there's that kid again," one irate man said. "Hey, kid, get in line."

"Okay," I said, not looking to see who was yelling, then walked back toward Danny with the shrimp. We sat at the picnic table eating these mystical delicious creatures of the sea. Danny seemed to be enjoying them as much as me.

Later we walked back by the table where Kathy, Mom, and Auntie Ann were finishing their shrimp dinners.

"Johnny, you are going to have to eat something before it gets too late," Mom said, believing we still had not eaten.

"Yes, Mom, but I could never eat those shrimp!" I said, trying to set up my younger sister, who had two more shrimp on her plate. Kathy was determined to extend her maniacal shrimp-eating torture on us one more time, just for fun. Not today, Kathy. As I walked behind her, she lifted up her shrimp in a teasing manner. I snatched it from her hand and placed it in front of my brother, who quickly bit it, leaving only the tail. He chewed it with great delight.

"I thought you didn't like shrimp!" Kathy said.

"You thought wrong." I laughed at our small act of revenge.

"Idiot!" Danny whispered to her.

"Mom!"

Chapter Nine

AN EARLY HAPPY HOUR

I t was November of 1968 and I was in my second year as an altar boy. Serving Mass had become quite easy. By sixth grade, all of the altar boys could perform our altar duties in our sleep. Unfortunately, it seemed some of the boys were serving the Mass in their sleep because sometimes we were assigned to the 7:00 A.M. Mass, which required being at the church no later than 6:45.

On this rainy fall Friday, I was serving the 7:00 A.M. Mass and standing on the side of the altar holding a glass cruet in each hand, waiting for Father Carl McInerney. The other altar boy, Mike Wendell, had not shown up, so I was once again serving solo. The priest was standing behind the altar table after consecrating the hosts. Now it was time for him to receive the wine, and my job was to pour the water and wine into his chalice when he was ready.

Father McInerney arrived at St. Bede's during the summer of 1967, the first year I became an altar boy, so I was fairly familiar with the red-faced, middle-aged priest who had developed a grouchy reputation. He finally turned toward me, indicating it was time to approach the altar table. As I walked up the three steps to Father McInerney, I noticed through his glasses that his eyes were incredibly bloodshot. He looked old and in bad health. He was balding in the back, although his thinning light brown hair was slicked back to cover his dome. Even with the long, loose green vestments covering him, it was obvious he had a serious pot belly. The middle of the gold cross on the front of his vestment jutted out notice-ably farther than the other priests for whom I served Mass.

As I approached, he held out his chalice and recited a prayer. I lifted the cruet of wine to pour, and he lifted the chalice, meeting me halfway. I poured about a third of the glass vessel into his chalice, the standard portion I was trained to issue during this ceremony. When I stopped and began pulling the cruet back, the priest tapped his chalice against it. I looked up to see one unhappy priest. He quickly nod-ded, which I interpreted as a call for more wine. I poured about half of what was left into the gold cup and began pulling the cruet back once more. Father McIner-ney moved the chalice up again, demanding more wine from this young bartender. As I emptied the entire contents into his chalice, I could see him glaring down at me. I shook the cruet over his chalice to make sure every drop was dispensed. The priest smiled, while I stood dumbfounded.

Then I lifted the water vessel to pour into the chalice. Just as I began pouring, no more than a few drops, the priest quickly lifted his shiny cup away as some of the water spilled onto the red rug below. Unfazed, he grunted at the mishap and swished the chalice around to mix the one cruet of wine with the two drops of water. He returned to the middle of the altar table, raised his chalice with both hands, and recited a prayer. A few minutes later, after consuming the Eucharist, the priest took the chalice and said, "May the Blood of Christ bring me to ever-lasting life."

He lifted the chalice to his lips and emptied it promptly. I wondered why this priest would want to drink that much wine so early in the morning. None of the other three priests I served acted like him. Was this his Holy Happy Hour, or did I just meet my first alcoholic priest?

I never really noticed this about him before that Mass. I had always found him to be a completely boring priest who seemed uninterested in the reverence of the service, always rushing through the Mass, putting no sincere effort into any portion of it. His homilies basically retold the same Gospel story he just read, adding no perspective for his parishioners. If he ever spent more than three minutes on one of his sermons, it would have been a record for him. Some altar boys looked forward to serving for him because they knew it would always be a quick Mass.

After that day, it became more apparent that he probably did have a problem. A few weeks later, while walking down Kostner Avenue past the rectory, I couldn't help but notice the metal garbage can filled with empty cans of Old Style beer and glass bottles of gin. I wondered if he was responsible.

Every Mass after that, whether I was serving or not, I watched the new altar boys relive the same scene I had experienced with the wine. Each would pour the correct portion from the cruet into the chalice and stop, just as we had been taught. Father McInerney would then bang his chalice against the glass container, demanding all of it, just as he had done with me. Then two drops of water, a quick swish, and down the hatch.

It seemed some of the altar boys knew better. One morning I served Mass with my friend Kevin Fox, who didn't skip a beat with the priest. Kevin quickly walked up the steps with the cruets and just as quickly dumped all of the wine into Father McInerney's chalice as if it were water for a dying, dehydrated member of the Foreign Legion stranded in the Sahara Desert. When the priest chugged the wine, I was waiting for him to say "Hit me again, altar boy!" But no, one full cruet of wine was enough to quench his morning thirst.

About a month later I was serving another early-morning Mass with the wine-loving priest. It was an 8:00 A.M. weekday Mass, and only a few elderly people were in attendance. When I approached the altar table to pour the water and wine, his bloodshot eyes once again grabbed my attention. Did this man sleep? He finished the prayer, then turned toward me and accidentally yawned. His breath nearly knocked me off the steps. Wow! What was that? I thought. I turned my head slightly to avoid his stale breath. As I stood there holding the water in my left hand and wine in my right, he became impatient and cleared his throat. Much like the feeling the day I was hit in the mouth with a fastball during a Little League game, the force of his breath slammed against my face, sending me two steps backward. I almost fell but staggered to maintain my balance. The priest glared at me. I looked up at him. What was I going to do? Could I venture back up those steps to face that breath, that air pollution, that stench? I had to. It was my duty as an altar boy. I would face that breath head-on, literally.

Determined to do my job, I took a deep breath and held it so the putrid smell could no longer penetrate my nostrils. Up the two steps I went. Father McInerney was agitated and breathing heavily. Holy Mother of God, please help me, I prayed.

Each blast of warm air bounced off my nose, eyes, and cheeks. Squinting, I could see the priest hold out his chalice. I could barely hold my breath anymore. I had to move quickly. I poured a full cruet of wine into his chalice just as I had watched Kevin Fox do a few weeks before. Then, just as quickly, I poured two drops of water, pulling the water up high and back, so there could be no dispute. There would be no clanking of the chalice against my wine vessel on this day. I had made sure to give it all to him. I stood there content, watching the priest swishing the chalice around. After the cleansing of his hands, I returned to my kneeler and watched him begin the blessing ritual. I was glad to be far away from him and knew he was eager to gulp his morning drink. He lifted the chalice to his lips, slugging it straight down.

Just then, his eyes shot wide open. He brought the chalice down and looked inside of it. Then he looked over at me. What was wrong? Why was he acting like this? I had given him all the wine I had in the glass. I looked over at the two cruets on the altar boys' table and saw one still filled with a light yellow liquid. That's the moment I realized I had mistakenly poured the full container of water into his chalice and only two drops of the wine.

This priest had no intention of jumping off the wine wagon that morning. I quickly rose, grabbed the cruet of wine, and proceeded up the three steps toward the altar table where the priest was awaiting me. Bang! He clanked his chalice against the wine cruet. "Sorry," I said softly, and I dumped it in as fast as it would pour out. And before the last drop hit, Father McInerney was raising the chalice toward his lips, and he downed it in an instant without blessing it.

Once again he looked content, happy. It was like closing time at the local saloon where last call had been sounded, and he was there to claim his final drink. As I returned to my kneeler, I wondered why this man had become a priest. Free wine? The wine is supposed to be transformed into the Blood of Christ, not cocktail hour for Father McInerney.

I hoped the priest wasn't too angry with me for my unintentional mistake. I wondered if he was going to scold me after Mass. It turns out he couldn't wait that long to retaliate. During Communion, as I stood next to him moving along the altar rail, placing my golden paten under each parishioner's chin, he made a point of breathing hard right on me every time he said "Body of Christ." Every twenty seconds, I turned my head, grabbed as much air as my lungs could hold, and held my breath as we continued along the rail. I was like a swimmer grabbing a breath and making my way toward the finish line, which was the twenty-seventh person along the white marble rail. Although it seemed much longer, the onslaught of his breath only lasted a few minutes. I was so happy it was over. There would be no other opportunity for him to breathe on me again. And I would make sure I never served another Mass with him. His putrid respiratory abuse was over. He couldn't hurt me anymore. Or so I thought.

As I followed him up the steps of the altar, walking right behind him where it was safe, a loud sound erupted from the back of his vestments. A barnyardlike stench engulfed me and I staggered. I couldn't believe it. Father McInerney had just ripped a nuclear stink bomb that smelled worse than a pile of manure on a hot August day. I turned my head quickly. It didn't help. Turned the other way. No luck. I walked as fast as I could past the flatulent priest to the altar table, where I returned the paten. I was out of the smelly danger zone, but it had taken its toll. I was not feeling well. I looked up at the priest, who had a big smirk on his face as he cleaned his chalice. I hope he didn't think I made that wine mistake on purpose.

At the conclusion of Mass, I gingerly walked to the front of the altar, making sure to stay to the far right of the priest. We knelt in unison, making the Sign of the Cross, and I led the two-person procession back around the marble altar rail through the brown wooden doors. I was angry, and retaliatory thoughts filled my head. As I went through the doors, Father McInerney's voice echoed through the hallway.

"Thought you were pretty clever out there today, didn't you, altar boy?" he bellowed, obviously not familiar with my name. "Didn't they teach you how to pour the water and wine? It's not that difficult. The wine has a very different color than the water, which is clear. Or hadn't you noticed?"

"I'm sorry, Father, I made a mistake. I apologize," I said, feeling like I was about to cry.

I ran up the steps through the priests' room and into the altar boys' room.

After arriving home from school that day, I informed my mother about the incident, and she could barely wait for my dad to come home from work.

"Bernie, you go up to the rectory right now and meet with Father Griffin," she said in a rage, as my father sat on the top step of the back stairs, taking off his work boots. "Let him know that he has a priest working with him that drinks too much and farts on the altar. What kind of a priest does that? I'll never go to another Mass he presides over."

My father, filthy from a full day's work for the city of Chicago's Water Department, had no idea what my irate mother was talking about. But he did know she was asking him to go up to church to have it out with a priest. This was like Christmas for Dad, who was not particularly fond of Father Griffin or Father McInerney.

So there he sat, given approval by my saintly mother to confront a priest. He didn't have to be asked twice. Right back out the door he went, still covered in dirt and sweat, walking quickly in his mud-stained brown work boots toward the rectory. Maybe he figured the priests would be intimidated by his appearance, which would be easy to understand. My muscular father stood 5 feet 10 inches and weighed about 200 pounds. We knew he was tough, although he never really had to prove it to anyone. When we visited Ireland many years later, we heard all of the stories of how he was the strongest young man in the county. His work in the bogs digging peat for hours on end, as well as his athletic abilities on the Gaelic football field, were well known throughout the town of Balinasloe in County Galway. To us, he was our father. But later, we could understand how his physical presence could be intimidating.

When he returned from church about an hour later, he told us that Father Griffin was extremely apologetic. We had heard many things about Father Griffin, but making apologies was never in his repertoire. The pastor said he was well aware of Father McInerney's problems—the drinking and bad breath. But he was completely shocked by the flatulence. My dad said when he informed the pastor of McInerney's behavior, the priest just sat straight up in his large black leather chair in total disbelief.

"He farted on the altar?" he asked, with jaw dropped.

"Right on the altar," replied my dad.

"On the altar?" he repeated for a confirmation.

"That's right. Right in my son's face. Is he around? I want to see him."

Father Griffin claimed the ill-mannered priest was not in the rectory that evening. He informed Dad that he had already discussed Father McInerney with John Cardinal Cody, and disciplinary measures were under consideration.

"He will have to answer to the cardinal about this now," the pastor said.

"You tell that priest if he ever goes anywhere near my son again, he'll have to answer to me. And I can promise you, I'll be a lot tougher on him than Cardinal Cody."

When Dad arrived home, I sat in my bedroom and overhead him relate the entire encounter to my mother. She was relieved to hear that Cardinal Cody would be reprimanding Father McInerney, and it quickly restored her full faith in her beloved Catholic institution. However, she wasn't so happy to hear that Dad had upset the holy Father Griffin.

"Griffin was so shaken that he began to stammer," Dad said, chuckling about the change in demeanor of the always stone-faced priest.

After dinner that evening, my mother had me come into the living room to talk with me privately.

"The Catholic Church is a good institution, Johnny," my mother explained. "But like all organizations, sometimes bad people find their way into it and do things that aren't right. They abuse their privilege and the authority they have been given. You did the right thing by speaking up about it. If you had let it go, he may have been allowed to continue his disgusting actions, which would have been very unfortunate.

"So always remember that. When you see a wrong, speak up. Because if you don't, there's a chance no one else will either."

I was pulled out of Mrs. Lemonnier's sixth-grade class the next day and sent over to the rectory to meet with Father Griffin. The secretary directed me to his office and instructed me to sit in front of his desk. Father Griffin entered and closed the door behind him, walking behind his desk, but not sitting down.

"John, I know you are a sixth-grader and a fairly new altar boy, but I don't want you to think that Father McInerney's actions are acceptable or reflect on the other priests here at St. Bede's," he said, looking down on me in his typical John Wayne monotone style. "I do not want you to share this incident with the other altar boys or other children in the school. It may be taken the wrong way and reflect poorly on our parish. Do you understand?"

I nodded my head, a bit perplexed at the request.

"You need to understand that sometimes—not very often, but sometimes—priests make mistakes. Father McInerney made a mistake, and we will work to correct it with him. Do you understand?"

I nodded again, but the only thought running through my head was how badly I wish my dad were sitting there with me. He wouldn't like this.

I left his office that day wondering why it took this incident to deal with Father McInerney's problems. The pastor obviously knew about it. And like my mother said, what if I didn't speak up? Would they have ever dealt with it? That uncertainty about Father Griffin's true intentions bothered me. That evening, I told my father about the impromptu meeting with the priest and he told me he would take care of it and to let him know if Father Griffin or McInerney ever spoke to me about it again. They never did.

Father McInerney wasn't reassigned, but I believe that incident may have helped him to mend his ways. Over the next few years, he gained a reputation as the priest who would visit the sick at home or in the hospital, as well as working closely with the senior citizens of the parish. He became a popular figure among some of the altar boys as well as the older adults of St. Bede's.

However, I never spoke to him or served a Mass he presided over again. He was reassigned to St. Gabriel's Parish in 1975.

Chapter Ten

SUNDAY MASS

Before I became an altar boy, Sunday Mass was the most dreaded event of the week. All of the Ruane kids hated getting up early on a weekend to go to church and sit there while the priest bored us to tears. Granted, the Mass was being said in Latin at the time, and the ceremony was very different than Pope Paul's New Mass instituted in 1969. Nonetheless, we were kids who had no perspective. The bottom line for us was having to get up early to go sit in church and be bored for an entire hour.

This was just one of the many challenges for my parents, raising a family of five in the 1960s. But my mother knew that if she stayed true to her convictions, her children would one day appreciate her efforts to get us to Mass each Sunday. Whenever Mom faced a challenge, she leaned heavily on her faith in God and prayed for help. This religious devotion set the standard for commitment to the Catholic Church for each of us. She was most certainly our role model.

The best example of that conviction was her insistence that all five of us attend St. Bede's Grammar School. My parents really couldn't afford it on one income, but it was a priority for Mom, so there was no discussion about it. It was that decision plus her requirement that we attend Sunday Mass each week that shaped us into the people we are today.

So each Sunday morning in the mid-1960s, whether we liked it or not, she woke up her four eldest children early to attend 8:30 A.M. Mass. Margaret, the fifth and youngest child, was only a baby and allowed to stay home, with Dad watching her.

Somehow, however, my young mind reasoned that going to early Mass was somewhat optional. After all, the church offered six Masses, so why get up so early? No such luck. Mom held steadfast to this early weekend wakeup tradition and hauled each of us out of bed, quickly turning our home into a scene of great chaos.

"I don't want to go!" my four-year-old brother, Danny, would yell. "Can't I just sleep, Mom?"

"Johnny, get your brother up and dressed right now or we'll be late for Mass," Mom demanded. "Maureen and Kathy, I expect you to be ready in five minutes."

I pulled my little brother's clothes out of the closet, and now it was my turn to yell, "Danny, get your butt out of bed."

"Make me!"

Ah yes, "Make me!" These were the fighting words of the 1960s. Anytime anyone, anywhere, said "Make me!" that was like a hockey player dropping his gloves. It was fight or be labeled a coward. Even though I was five years older than Danny, I couldn't allow the challenge to go unanswered, and before he knew what hit him, my brother was on the wooden floor of our bedroom. "Get dressed, Danny, now!" I said, throwing his clothes on him. I walked out of the bedroom, down the hallway through the living room, and out the front door, to sit on the top of the three-stepped cement porch until the craziness was over.

A few minutes later, my brother, with his white dress shirttail hanging out over his navy blue dress slacks, came out of the aluminum-framed front door and walked down the steps past me to sit on the bottom step. "Jerk!" he proclaimed, never turning around to look at me.

"Well, next time get up when you're told, JERK!" I said, staring straight at the back of his dark brown crew cut.

He turned angrily and looked up at me on the top step. As he stood up to challenge me, my mother and two sisters arrived, ready for Mass. The walk down Kostner Avenue always seemed long, but it was only one block. My brother and I bumped and shoved each other as we passed each of the sixteen houses on our street, while our mother appealed to our better senses.

"Stop it!" she said. "Do you understand me?"

More pushing and shoving.

"Stop it or you will sit in your rooms the rest of the day."

He pushed me. I shoved him.

"Jerk!" shot Danny.

"Jerk!" I returned.

"Okay, when we get home, I am going to have your father punish you both."

The pushing and shoving stopped abruptly. We moved away from each other for the remainder of the walk to church. We always knew when Mom drew the line, and the line usually involved the words "Father" and "punish."

The nearer we got to church, the greater the crowd grew around us. By the time we reached the cyclone fence that lined the east side of the parking lot, we were walking in a large crowd of churchgoers streaming across 83rd Street and through the tall silver doors of the new church. As we entered, the bells from the church tower rang loudly, signaling that Mass was about to begin.

My mother led us through the two glass doors down the middle aisle, looking for a pew as close to the altar as possible that would accommodate all of us. She wanted to be close to the action. If they had a pew for parishioners on the altar, I can promise you my mother would have had us sitting in it.

Usually three rows from the altar on the right side of the aisle, we found enough room for the Ruane clan. Mom pulled down the padded kneeler and in unison, it seemed, we all knelt on the brown foam-padded support and made the Sign of the Cross to begin our silent prayers, just as we had been taught at St. Bede's School. I always had the same ritual. I prayed the Our Father, a Hail Mary, and then asked God to bless my mother, father, sisters Maureen, Kathy, and Margaret and, oh yes, my brother, Danny. We may have given each other a hard time, fought, wrestled, and generally ticked each other off half the time, but my brother and I loved each other—well, like brothers should.

Finishing up my prayers, I could hear the organ begin to play. I looked up, then glanced over at my older sister, Maureen. We knew what was coming next and unfortunately had no appreciation for it, only dread. As Mom's head rose to belt out the opening hymn, our four respective heads sank, hoping our friends wouldn't notice us. It wasn't cool for us to be around our mother singing in church so loudly and drawing so much attention. We preferred the anonymity that surrounds the kids next to the parents who basically whisper-sing in church, looking like they are singing in case anyone looks at them, but not loud enough to draw any attention to themselves. Ah, those kids really had it made.

Mom's singing was the least of my problems. No, I had a much bigger obstacle to overcome each Sunday. How do I stay awake so I don't get in trouble? It was a challenge, no question about it. But at nine years old, I thought the priests were the most boring people on earth, saying the Mass in Latin with their backs to us. How rude! And what was the point? I could go watch my friend Lenny Michaels's relatives speak Lithuanian to each other and be far more interested than sitting at Sunday Mass. I didn't understand either language, but at least Lenny's relatives looked like they were yelling at each other half the time, which was definitely more interesting. Plus his grandmother had gold teeth, which scared the living daylights out of me. An argument in Lithuanian by grandmothers with gold teeth—that's what they needed up on that altar.

One Sunday morning, as I sat watching Father Henry give his homily, I felt my eyes start to close. I fought to keep them open and pretend I was listening. They kept closing. I couldn't stop them. I was in trouble. They would find me asleep and take me to Father Griffin, who would sit me down, place a hot light over my face, and conduct the inquisition.

"Did you fall asleep in church, young man?" he would ask sharply.

"I couldn't help myself, Father," I would plead. "I tried to keep them open, but Father Henry bored the crap out of me with his homily."

"That's no excuse," the priest would snap. "Father Henry bores the crap out of me too when he speaks, but I still pay attention. I don't fall asleep."

"But, Father, could you just give me one more chance?" I would beg.

"No more chances," he would direct. "You must be punished."

"Could I suggest that you put Lenny's relatives up on the altar? They argue in Lithuanian and have gold teeth—"

All of a sudden I felt a sharp poke in my ribs. I jumped forward quickly in my seat. "Ah!" I looked around and realized I actually had fallen asleep. My brother, Danny, was laughing to himself. He had reached behind my sister Kathy, who was sitting between us, to punch me. I reached back behind Kathy and poked him back. He returned it and I retaliated again, just as Mom turned toward both of us. In unison, we both pointed at Kathy, to whom Mom gave a disapproving look. Danny and I both nodded our heads to support our mother's punishing look.

"Jerks," Kathy mouthed to us.

After Mass ended and we worked our way up the aisle toward the exit, Mom ran into a neighbor, whom she just *had* to talk to about nothing important. This happened every week. Here we go through the misery of a Mass and now she is going to make it even longer by talking to someone while we are left to stand there with our hands in our pockets, kicking walls until she was done gabbing. I was convinced Sundays were created to see how many kids actually could be bored to death.

Once we all arrived home, we could count on finding Dad sitting in his brown easy chair watching the Sunday news shows, which were always followed by the Bears games in the fall and White Sox games during the spring and summer. Dad was always the one staying home to watch us when we were too young to go to Mass. He would attempt to bring us to Mass on special occasions—Christmas and Easter, to be sure—but never on Sunday. I don't recall Mom or Dad ever talking about it, but it was something all of the kids noticed.

One Sunday when Danny was seven, he became bold enough to request more sleep instead of going to Mass.

"It's a sin not to go to Mass on Sunday," our mother scolded him.

That's when it came flying out of my brother's mouth. I don't think he planned it. It just happened.

"Dad doesn't go to Mass!" he argued.

Mom stood straight up and looked very angry, folding her arms. She turned her head toward the front room, where she knew our father was watching television. She looked angry as her bottom lip stiffened and began to quiver.

"He has to watch Margaret!" she snapped, and she pulled Danny out of bed, saving me the trouble.

One Sunday after an extremely boring Mass followed by an unending wait in the hallway kicking walls while I waited for Mom to finish talking to our neighbor, Mrs. Vogner, I made up my mind that I would have to skip Mass the next Sunday. There was always one failsafe excuse that I would normally use for not going to school.

"Mom, I really want to go to church, but I am afraid I will throw up and make everyone else sick," I whined that day, knowing this threat never could be overruled. But it also required some pretty fancy faking once Mom returned home from church to find me in bed.

"Johnny, are you feeling any better," she asked with great concern.

"Well, I threw up about twenty times while you were at church and I think I'll be better in a little while," I informed her, while my brother, Danny, stood behind her, making faces at me trying to make me laugh.

"Twenty times!" she exclaimed, her voice rising with panic. "I had better take you into the hospital."

I realized, then, I may have overdone it with the claim of twenty trips to the bathroom. I should have said "a few times."

"Mom, when I said twenty, I may have counted wrong," I backpedaled, trying to correct my estimate. "It may only have been a few times, like once or twice. And I think I am feeling much better now."

She just looked at me, realizing that I probably wasn't sick. Her mouth dropped. She didn't have to say it, but I could see she was disappointed in me.

As she turned to leave the room, I confessed. "Mom, I am sorry! I'm really not that sick. I promise I won't miss Mass again. I don't care how badly I feel."

She turned and looked at me, the hurt look on her face evaporated upward into a smile.

"I know, Johnny. You're a good boy."

I never pulled that stunt again. My stomach actually did start to ache. I had hurt my mother's feelings, let her down. I knew then I would rather attend two boring Sunday Masses each week and kick the walls for a couple of hours afterward waiting for her to finish talking before I ever let her down again. And I never did let her down after that Sunday.

Once I became an altar boy and the Mass changed to English, my perspective changed with it. I actually became very interested in the Mass and looked back on my youthful behavior in embarrassment. I wonder how many kids did the same thing. I'm just glad they changed the Mass.

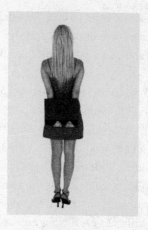

Chapter Eleven

MISS PASCO

When I entered my fifth-grade class, Room 104, for the first time in September of 1967, little did I know the impact the upcoming school year would have on my life. I walked in to find my best friend, Marty Durks, sitting in the first row next to the windows. That was great! I was so happy he was in my class.

I had known Marty since the second grade and we quickly became best friends. His father, like mine, came over from Galway in the late 1940s. He was about average height, on the thinner side, with strawberry-blond hair combed to the side and a pale face filled with freckles. The thing I liked about Marty was his upbeat personality and great sense of humor. He was a funny kid, and over the course of my seven years at St. Bede's he provided me with more laughs than anyone.

I looked around to see if I knew anyone else. The Morton twins, Gale and Dale, were sitting next to each other in the front row, perusing the room to see if they had friends in the class. Gale and Dale were identical twins with short, pixie-cut blond hair. These two girls were as tall as most of the boys in our class and looked to be in good shape, like runners, and were probably as good as most of the boys at sports.

Rita Fitz, the most talented artist in our grade, was sitting next to them. Rita was a fairly pretty girl with light brown hair down to her shoulders, decorated with two light pink bows. Unlike Gale and Dale, Rita didn't look like she would ever consider running. Her passion was drawing, and she was an incredibly good artist. She could draw anything and make it look lifelike. We would all just stare at her artwork in amazement.

Three boys walked into the room whom I recognized but didn't really know very well. Kevin Fox, a tall thin kid with blond stringy hair hanging over his forehead, loped in first with his long stride. He was followed by Eddie Crandell, a muscular boy with short light brown hair, who was about my height and wore black-framed glasses. Mike Hannon, a taller, athletic-looking kid with dark black hair presented in the popular crew-cut style of the day, was the last one in the room. The three of them sat in empty desks next to Marty and I. We all exchanged the quick lift of the chin to indicate our recognition of each other and greeting.

As we waited for our teacher, the room began filling with chatter. No one knew who had been assigned to our class, which inspired talk about all the possibilities so we could mentally prepare ourselves. Waiting for this unknown teacher was like waiting for our sentence over the next nine months. Would it be a mean old nun? God help us. Or maybe it would be a nice nun like Sister Mary in second grade. I was just coming off fourth grade and Miss Darlene Lausus, who was a very good teacher but strict. I was hoping for a kinder, gentler teacher.

It was 7:58 A.M., two minutes before school was scheduled to begin, when she walked into the room. It was a moment I will remember forever. I watched the most beautiful woman I had ever seen enter our classroom, carrying a large shiny black purse in her right hand and stack of schoolbooks in her left. She had straight, shimmering blond hair, cut just above her neckline, and a beautiful face with a soft pale complexion and high cheekbones. Her eyes were stunningly beautiful—big, deep-blue teardrop eyes that seemed to sparkle.

Once she passed my row of desks, I could see she was wearing a light pretty yellow summer dress that was cut conservatively at the neck and arms, exposing her long neck and toned shoulders and arms. The dress extended down to only about an inch above her knee, revealing a very nicely shaped pair of legs. There seemed to be something else that had drawn my attention to her. I couldn't quite put my finger on it. Oh yes, I remember. She had an outstanding figure. That was it. I didn't know what an outstanding figure was at that time, but I knew I couldn't take my eyes off of it.

Before then, I never quite understood why those 1960s movies, like *How to Succeed in Business,* would take close-up shots of a woman's behind as it moved from side to side with each step. But all of a sudden the appeal made a great deal of sense to me. From the reaction I witnessed around me, this was a shared experience among a good number of the boys, who were suddenly quiet and staring at our new teacher.

"Hello, I'm Miss Pasco," she said in a wonderfully sweet and gentle voice.

Well, that did it. Not only was she gorgeous, but she had a voice that melted us down to nothing more than droopy-eyed schoolboys who had fallen in love with our teacher.

"I will be your teacher this year, and I would like to welcome all of you to my class."

Hey, it's great to be here, was my first thought. What happened, did they run out of cranky old nuns to throw at us? Was Father Griffin raising the tuition so much that he wanted the kids to go home and trumpet how wonderful school is and how they would never leave St. Bede's? Or was this sort of prepubescent education for the fifth-grade boys to teach them what happens when they see an attractive woman? Heck, I didn't care why they brought her into the school. She was more than welcome to teach me all four of my final years at St. Bede's. She could come with me to high school and college as far as I was concerned.

Although the boys in the class had a strong reaction to Miss Pasco, the girls seemed to have an equal acknowledgment of our new teacher, because they were looking at each other in dismay. They knew immediately that they couldn't compete with this woman for the attention of the boys. The game was over. They would have to wait until sixth grade to tease the guys and have us chase them around, while they coyly pretended not to care.

For the next six months, each day I came to school with a new exuberance for the education system and the wonderful opportunity to sit among my classmates and study mathematics, science, and English. This was my chance to expand my mind and prepare myself for high school. Oh, who am I kidding? I couldn't wait to see Miss Pasco and what she was wearing.

And she wore all types of different dresses and looked great in every one of them. But on one particular day during that first month of school, she walked through the door in a dress that will live in the minds of every fifth-grade boy who sat in her class: a tight yellow miniskirt that revealed her physical attributes. Until that day, legs were just legs. But all of a sudden, Miss Pasco's legs caused a reaction that I wasn't prepared for. All of a sudden I was the captain of a submarine who had lost control of his vessel, which began to surface on its own while the sound of alert horns blared in my ears. I couldn't stop it. From the look on the faces of my buddies—Eddie, Mike, Kevin, and Marty—I wasn't the only captain who had lost control. It looked like alert horns were blaring in their ears as well.

Miniskirts were the fashion of the day, so I'm sure Miss Pasco had no idea what she was doing to us as she began wearing them fairly often. It didn't matter what color they were—light blue, pink, red, white—she looked great in all of them. On the days she wore them, there weren't many boys raising their hands during math. None of us were too eager to stand and walk to the blackboard to solve the problem. On miniskirt days, every boy in the class knew it would be a parade of girls answering the questions at the blackboard.

We were attending a Catholic school, and each of us had just become an altar boy. I wondered if we were supposed to be having these kinds of thoughts, these kinds of reactions. Were we all sinners or just normal little boys?

"Mr. Durks, would you like to come up to the blackboard to answer this question?" she asked my best friend on one occasion, when she was dressed in a very short red mini.

Marty hemmed and hawed. "Uh, I'm not feeling very well."

"Oh, I'm sorry," she replied. "Maybe you should go down to the nurse's office."

Panic crossed Marty's face. "No, that's okay. I think if I just sit here, I'll be fine."

"Okay, well let me know if you change your mind," the kindhearted teacher replied.

"I will. Thank you, Miss Pasco," said my relieved friend.

"Mr. Ruane, would you come up to answer the question?" she asked with a soft but seductive tone in her voice.

"Uh, I, uh . . ." I fumbled, looking over at Marty, who was trying to hold back a laugh, realizing I was now in trouble. "I don't feel very well also, Miss Pasco. I think I caught what Marty has. I'll be all right in a little while if I can just sit here."

And sit there we did as a group on miniskirt days. None of us dared venture away from the security of our desks until one day when Mike Hannon must not have been thinking clearly and raised his hand to answer a math question on the board.

"Okay, Michael, why don't you take this one," Miss Pasco said, sitting behind her desk with most of the mini danger zones hidden away.

Mike was up and walking toward the blackboard before Marty and I could remind him about our teacher's outfit. Hopefully she would not get up. Either way, this was a risky situation Mike had placed himself in. He was out in the deep all by himself, with no desk to protect him from a submarine attack. Eddie, Marty, Kevin, and I all looked at each other, realizing the danger.

Mike was one of the best math students in the class and perhaps he thought this division problem was so easy, he could compute it quickly on the board and sit down. He would have been successful, if one of the Morton twins had not raised her hand.

"Miss Pasco, when we do long division, shouldn't we always show our work on the side?" Gale asked, perhaps aware of what she was instigating. Mike had not shown his math work on the side of the problem, but as Miss Pasco stood revealing her very short and tight pink miniskirt to help him, he soon would be showing more than his work.

Seeing her stand, I'm sure the submarine alert horns were blaring in his ears as he quickly turned away from her and looked toward his four friends, his eyes growing wide, hoping we somehow would bail him out.

"We have to do something," I said to Eddie behind me.

"A diversion," he suggested with clenched teeth, intent on helping his friend. "We need a diversion!"

Kevin overheard the suggestion and jumped on it.

"Miss Pasco," he blurted out, raising his hand. "I don't feel well, can you take me down to the nurse's office please? I think I'm going to be sick."

Our teacher looked very concerned as Kevin rose, diverting his eyes from her, and bent over to hide any surprise submarine attacks.

"Of course, Kevin," she said, moving toward him. "Michael, you go ahead and sit down. Class, I'll be right back."

Gale Morton quickly stood up.

"Miss Pasco, I can take Kevin down to the nurse's office," she offered.

My four friends and I looked at her, completely bewildered. Did she know exactly what she was doing? Or was she really just trying to help? Either way, Kevin was too quick for her as he began making heaving noises and the beautiful blonde rushed him out the door before another word could be said.

Mike scampered quickly to his desk to sit down and we all realized what a close call that had been for him. We also knew we couldn't trust the Morton twins anymore. That would have been very embarrassing for Mike.

I don't remember how we found out where Miss Pasco lived, but somehow we did find out. It was October and the weather was getting colder, when Marty, Eddie, Mike, Kevin, and I rode our bikes to the two-story yellow and orange–bricked apartment building at 8655 S. Tripp, where our beautiful teacher and her mother lived. This short ten-minute bike ride became almost a twice-a-week ritual. Upon arrival, the five of us stared up at the second-floor apartment to the right of the doorway, hoping she would come out. Most days after about five minutes of looking up at the white shear drapes that never moved, we gave up and rode our bikes the two blocks back to Durkin Park where we could talk about her.

"Do you think she has a boyfriend?" Kevin asked.

"Yes, I happen to know that she does," Mike replied. "And you're looking at him."

"In your dreams," Eddie said. "She told me she thought you were ugly."

"Yeah right, when did she say that?" Mike smirked, laughing at Eddie's attempt to one-up him.

"Last night on our date," Eddie said. "Right after I kissed her good night."

Everyone burst out laughing. Hey, if we couldn't actually be with a beautiful, sophisticated woman like Miss Pasco, we at least could pretend it was possible.

I do remember the one time someone came up with the idea to actually walk into her building, ring the buzzer to her apartment, and let her know we were there to see her.

"Sure, she'd love to see us," Kevin said, smiling wide at his big idea. "Especially me. Goes without saying."

Somehow this idea didn't seem so ridiculous to me, so I volunteered to be the point man. Or "guinea pig," as Marty described me. When I walked into the doorway of the apartment building, I looked to my left to see four narrow silver mailboxes lined up next to each other on the wall. Each mailbox had a paper strip across the bottom with the name of the tenant typed on it. I scanned each name until I came to "Pasco." The apartment number was 201.

By this time I really wanted to see her, even though we had just left her classroom an hour earlier. I pushed the small yellow button under the mailbox but did not hear a sound. I hoped that the doorbell rang on the second floor. All of a sudden, an older woman's voice came over the intercom, "Yes!" It didn't sound like Miss Pasco. I wondered if I had made a mistake.

"Hello," I responded. "Is this the Pasco residence?"

"Who is it?" the unfamiliar voice said.

"I am a student of Miss Pasco. Is she home today?" I asked.

"No, she hasn't come home from school yet. Who is this?"

I wondered if I should let this lady know who we were. Would we get in trouble for showing up at her front door?

"Oh, I see. Would you let her know that Marty Durks . . . No. Would you let her know that John Ruane and some of his classmates stopped by to see her."

"Certainly. I'll let her know. John Wayne stopped by."

"No, it's RU-ANE."

"Oh, I'm sorry. Okay, RU-ANE. Got it."

"Thank you."

And with that, I walked back out the heavy wooden door with the golden door-knob to my group of friends.

"Hey, what happened?" Kevin asked, barely able to contain his excitement.

"She's not home. Some other lady answered the doorbell."

"Who was it?" Mike piped in.

"I don't know. She spoke to me over the intercom. Probably her mother, since that's who she lives with, right?"

"Yeah, probably her mother. What did she say?" Eddie asked, getting back on his twenty-six-inch blue-black Schwinn.

"She said that Miss Pasco hadn't come home from school yet."

Just then, we saw a familiar green Volkswagen Beetle turn into the alleyway on the north side of the apartment building, where the parking lot was located.

"Oh my God, that's her!" Marty shouted.

"That's her?" Eddie asked. "Are you sure?"

"That's definitely her," said Marty.

"Let's get out of here," Mike said, and before I could get a word out, they each were standing high on their pedals, pushing down hard to race south toward 87th Street and away from the apartment building.

I couldn't understand why they were taking off. Since I had come this far, I was going to finish it. I rode my bike around to the parking lot and there she was, getting out of her car. Out of the backseat, I watched her retrieve her big black purse, a large stack of books, and a folder full of papers. As she straightened up, she spotted me on the sidewalk.

"Hello, Miss Pasco," I said, feeling a very big smile cross my face as a very warm feeling crossed my entire body and a ringing filled my ears.

"Hello, John," she said. "What brings you by? Did you forget something at school?"

"No, we all came by to see you today," I said, then realized that I was the only one standing there. "I mean, a few of us wanted to come by and say hello, but they thought you weren't home, so they just rode off on their bikes."

"Oh, I see," she said, with that very familiar sweet voice. "Well, that's very nice of all of you. Who else was with you?"

Who else was with me? Would they be angry if I told her? Or would they be more disappointed if I didn't?

"Well, you know Marty Durks, Mike Hannon, Eddie Crandell, and Kevin Fox. We are all in your class."

"Yes, that's right," she said, trying to close the car door with her elbow because her hands were full of books and papers.

"Here, let me help you with that," I said, jumping off my twenty-six-inch green

Schwinn, kicking down the kickstand and hustling over to close the driver's side door.

"Thanks, I appreciate that," she said, smiling, and I realized I was standing only a few feet away from her, close enough to smell her very appealing perfume. "Well, I'm sorry they left. I think it's very nice that you would all come by to see me. Would you let them know that for me?"

"Yes, I will, Miss Pasco," I said, staring into her beautiful blue eyes. Then it occurred to me. I was an eleven-year-old fifth-grader; an altar boy. She was at least twenty-two. What in God's name was I doing?

"Miss Pasco, we all think you are a wonderful teacher and we wanted to let you know that if there is anything you ever need, please let us know. We'll be here to help."

"Thank you, John. That's very nice of you," she said, walking toward the white wooden back door of the apartment building.

"Do you need help carrying those books?" I asked, hoping she would let me assist her.

"Actually, if you don't mind, could you open that door to let me in the apartment?" she requested, handing me her ring of keys with the gold apartment key separated.

"No problem," I said, taking the keys and inserting the gold key into the doorknob, turning it and opening the door quickly.

"Here are your keys, Miss Pasco. Are you sure you don't need help with those books?"

"I'm fine, but thank you, John. And thanks again for stopping by."

"You're welcome. I'll see you tomorrow in school."

"I'll look forward to it."

"And please, I really mean it: If you ever need help with anything, let me know."

"I will," she said, smiling again, then turning and ascending up the back stairwell as I closed the door behind her.

Feeling a tremendous surge of energy fill my body, I ran and jumped on my bike, kicked back the metal kickstand, and pedaled as fast as I could down Tripp toward Durkin Park feeling like I was flying as my heart raced. I was so happy and I didn't really understand why. But that beautiful teacher of ours just talked to me outside of school and said I could help her if she ever needed it. She had accepted me completely.

As I rode closer to the playground, I could see Kevin sitting on one of the six black plastic-seated swings, while Mike, Eddie, and Marty stood in front of him on their bikes. Kevin spotted me first.

"Hey, what happened?" Kevin yelled across the playground as he jumped off the swing and ran toward me. "Did you get in trouble?"

Marty, Mike, and Eddie rode up behind him. I stopped at the bench in front of the large round cement area with the four metal sprinklers that young kids played in every summer. I nonchalantly got off my bike, putting the kickstand down. I could feel all four of them staring a hole through me as they huffed and puffed from their twenty-yard sprint to greet me.

"What happened? C'mon, spill it," Kevin demanded.

I sat on the bench with my four friends looking at me, waiting for the information that would make their lives complete, at least on this day.

"Isn't it a lovely day," I said, knowing it would drive them crazy.

"Okay, that's enough. Get him," Eddie said, and he was joined by Mike, Marty, and Kevin in an attempt to give me a pink belly and make me talk.

"All right, all right!" I said, jumping up and away from them as they tried to grab me. I was laughing so hard that I had to work to catch my breath. This was funny. I had them at my mercy: to toy with them until I decided it was time to fill them in on the details.

"Okay, I told her why we came by and gave all the names," I said, moving away from them toward my bike.

"You told her we were there!" Mike said.

"Yep, told her we wanted to offer our help if she ever needed it."

"Did she ask why we left?" inquired Marty.

"She did," I said, looking a bit grim. "I just told her the truth that you were all a bunch of sissies who didn't have the guts to face her, so you ran off like a bunch of giggling schoolgirls."

That did it.

"Get him!" ordered Eddie, and the others responded quickly, trying to tackle me. I dodged Mike, pushed Marty to the side, and jumped on my bike. The race was on, but I had a good head start and my house was only one block away. By the time they got to their bikes, I was already halfway home. As I entered the alleyway, which ran behind my house, I turned to see how far ahead of them I was by that point: 200 yards easy. I rode through the gate and into my backyard. I put my bike in our yellow wooden garage and ran into the house.

"I'm home, Mom," I shouted, dashing to my room toward the back of the house, next to the kitchen.

"Good, Johnny, dinner is in ten minutes."

"Okay, I'll get my homework organized. Let me know when it's ready."

Just then, a loud knock was heard coming from the back door.

"Hey John, c'mon out! We need to talk to you." It was Kevin's voice.

My mother looked a little angry about the loud banging on our back door, "I'll take care of it, you do your homework," she said, closing my bedroom door. I opened the windows on the second floor, which overlooked the ten-foot-wide gangway running between our house and our neighbor's home. I lifted the bottom screen window up and stuck my head out to see what was going on in the yard. I saw Eddie's back bike wheel but couldn't see them. Then I heard my mother addressing my friends. A few seconds later, I could see them walk their bikes out the front gate of the yard and down the gangway. Just as they passed my room, I shot my head out the window and screamed, "Sissies!!!"

They each jumped about a foot in the air, completely startled. They looked up to see me laughing.

"Oh, you are dead!" Mike said, smiling and appreciating the prank.

"You better stay in that room, John," Eddie said, trying to jump up to grab me through the second-floor window. He could barely touch the windowsill.

Kevin couldn't care less about any of it. "What happened with Miss Pasco?" he pleaded. He had to know. Obviously so did the others, because their attention was right back on me.

"Nothing really," I said, figuring it was time to fill them in. "I told Carol that we came—"

"Carol?" Marty exclaimed.

"Miss Pasco and I are now on a first-name basis," I explained, trying not to burst out laughing.

"Yeah, right," said Mike. "Is that even her first name?"

"I think so," I said. "I thought I heard the principal call her that last week. Anyway, I informed Carol that we came by to offer our help, if she ever needed it. I helped her get into the door of her apartment and that was really about it."

"That was it?" Kevin asked.

"Nothing more," I said. "She kissed me goodbye and I left."

"Hah, hah, you are so funny," said Mike.

"Look, I have to go wash her lipstick off before dinner, but I'll see you four sissies tomorrow in Carol's class."

They left laughing. We had a fun day trying to see Miss Pasco. It would be one of many for us over the next six months.

Chapter Twelve

THOU SHALL NOT FIGHT

The day a boy decides to become an altar boy is not the day he decides to give up his identity and rights of self-defense. This can be confusing, because an altar boy seems to be the first step toward the priesthood. One who serves on God's altar should be a peace-seeking Christian, obeying the Ten Commandments, one of which says "Thou Shall Not Kill." Fighting back is not allowed. If punched on the right cheek, offer the left. If punched on the left cheek, offer the right. Enemies can hurt the body, but not the soul. Faith in God and the belief in a better life after death will help one endure the physical challenges of this world. I received these teachings at church and school.

At ten, you can nod your head in agreement with that philosophy until your neck hurts, but when the bully shows up looking to pummel you, the focus swiftly turns to self-defense. At least it did for me.

It was mid-June of 1967, just after I had completed fourth grade. I had been enjoying the freedom of summer vacation—the one season every kid in America anticipated with joy. Summer meant freedom, sitting around with friends doing nothing. It meant the sprinkler on the lawn as the only means for trying to stay cool, because we had no neighborhood pool and certainly could never afford an above-ground backyard pool. It meant games of hide-and-seek after sunset. Or playing baseball all day long, with only a quick bike ride home from Durkin Park around noon for the two peanut butter and jelly sandwiches and glass of milk. It meant running behind the mosquito repellent truck spraying the clouds of white smoke. Or playing a game of bounce-or-fly baseball right on our block. Boy, was it fun!

When summer came, it wasn't Marty, Mike, Eddie, and Kevin with whom I was playing bounce-or-fly each day. The rules shifted in the summer. It seemed the kids from school stopped hanging around with each other to play with kids on the block, who were obviously closer. On my block, the kids I hung around with were Jimmy Daul, Lenny Michaels, Keith Mareno, and Jerry Volkner.

Jimmy Daul was the leader because he was, without question, the coolest and the toughest of our bunch. I'm not sure how we all came to that conclusion; it just was understood. Jimmy was a fairly tall Irish kid, built solidly, who sported a blond Roger Maris–like crew cut. Jimmy's dad was a Chicago policeman, and we often watched his father scold our young friend. Somehow in our minds, being the son of a tough cop made Jimmy a tough kid.

Lenny Michaels was a tall, thin Lithuanian boy. He was the first kid picked in basketball games because of his height. Lenny had a long, thin face and shiny brown hair that always hung over his forehead like a mop. If he tried to comb it to the side, it would soon revert back to the mop look. Lenny was never considered tough because he was so slender, but his height usually deterred potential bullies. He could have been a very successful athlete, but he struggled with self-confidence.

Keith Mareno was a good-looking Italian boy with a fairly prominent Dean Martin–like nose and thick black hair combed to the side. He was slender and the same height as me, about 4 feet 10. Keith's happy-go-lucky attitude and good sense of humor made him a favorite. He was best known for his lightning-quick running ability—no one could catch him.

Then there was Jerry Volkner. He was an Irish kid like myself, who was the same height, with a slightly lighter build. He had short black hair, a pug nose, and a thin-lipped, round freckled face. He always seemed to have a sarcastic smirk and could be described as a smart-aleck who was constantly taking potshots at other kids, trying to make fun of them. He was not well liked. The only reason Jerry was ever included in the summer group was that he forced his way into our games.

Bounce-or-fly is played with the same rules of baseball, except instead of hitting the ball with a bat, the hitter bounces the ball off the cement front porch steps, then runs the bases. A ball that flies all the way to the street without being caught is a home run. The best way to make the rubber ball go that far is by throwing it off the corner of the step at just the right angle, which is not easy to do. The other way is by throwing it just before the crease in the steps, so it bounces up off the facing of the next step and flies far. This requires a good throwing arm and a good, hard throw. Either method executed properly would usually result in the rubber ball traveling thirty feet in the air and into the street, a home run. And it had to be high enough or the fielder would catch it. The fielder wasn't allowed to go into the street. The curb was like our outfield wall. You couldn't go past it to catch the ball. You could jump straight up and make a catch, but if you landed in the street, it was a home run. Plus you might get hit by a car, which would ruin the day.

Keith had the best cement steps for bounce-or-fly. They were longer than the steps at each of our homes, which meant we had more opportunity to send the balls to different areas of the front yard, resulting in more hits.

No matter where we played it, all of our parents hated it equally for good reason. When one of us tried to hit the corner of the step and missed, a good number of those misses would ricochet up and bang the screen door hard, making a loud noise, especially when it hit the square metal bottom portion of the door. And when it ricocheted up higher and hit the screen, it usually made a huge dent in the thin wire. Before long, all the front screen doors were covered with dents, which greatly upset our parents. Because our mothers were the ones home during the weekdays, our hope was they would be too wrapped up in a telephone conversation, laundry, or house cleaning to attend to the extremely loud banging coming from the front door. But eventually, no matter how busy the mom might be, the sound of the ball smashing against a front door half a dozen times, clanging like the cymbals of a marching band, would usually get their attention and result in a personal appeal to discontinue the game.

"Get the hell out of here before you break my door!" requested Mrs. Mareno, a brunette Irish-Italian beauty in a colorful yellow summer dress.

That appeal alone was embarrassing enough for Keith, but what followed was worse.

"Keith, wait until your father gets home!"

All of us dreaded that line. We could endure screaming mothers in their pretty summer dresses. They loved us. They would get over it. But the ticked-off dad? That usually meant corporal punishment. We knew one of our hind ends was going to be introduced to a ruler, yardstick, or firm hand of discipline. To avoid this ominous threat, we would rotate the game from home to home each day. That usually did the trick.

So every morning during that summer of '67, we slept late, ate a bowl of cereal, then started knocking on doors to see who was coming out to play. The rules for calling someone out were different at each home. At the Marenos' yellow-brick house, I had to go to the back. The white wooden back door was usually open, leaving me looking through the screen door into the kitchen. There was no knocking or ringing doorbells at the Marenos' home.

"Yo Keith!" I would yell.

"Hold on, Johnny," Mrs. Mareno would always answer in a friendly manner. "Let me get him."

After a few minutes of pacing or kicking the wall with my pent-up energy, Keith would appear.

"Hi, Keith. Want to play?" I would ask.

"Sure," he'd reply. "What do you want to do?"

"I don't know, what do you want to do?"

"I don't know. Let's get Lenny," he would say.

And the calling-out ritual would continue to Lenny's and then Jimmy's. At Lenny's house, the front door approach was accepted, because his dad was at work and his mother didn't live with them anymore—a concept I never quite understood at that time. If the door was closed, I would ring the doorbell. If it was open with just the screen door in front of me, there were no rules. I yelled right through that screen.

"Yo Lenny! Hey, Lenny, c'mon, we're out here! Let's go, hurry up!"

No polite stuff at his house. There were no parents there to judge our "call-out" approach.

Jimmy's house was optional. We could go front or back on the "Yo Jimmy." But we usually chose the front door because it was closer and we were lazy kids. Because his dad was a policeman, we were especially well mannered. We didn't want to get arrested for an overzealous "Yo Jimmy!" We might be disturbing the peace or something.

Once Jimmy was out and the four of us were sitting on his porch, we knew it was only a matter of time before Jerry, who lived right across the street, would spot us and walk across Kostner. Besides that stupid smirk he always had on his face, Jerry had a chip on his shoulder to go with an attitude of superiority. Maybe he was that way because his dad was one of the few white-collar workers in the blue-collar neighborhood. He was an agent for State Farm Insurance and drove a Volkswagen Beetle, which we all thought was pretty cool. The Volkners belonged to the Aqua Pool, which also elevated them above the rest of us.

But if white collars and lifestyle perks were reason for a snobby demeanor, Lenny easily could have trumped Jerry. His dad was a bigshot at American Can Company and regularly flew to New York for meetings, jetting back on the same day. That sounded like a fantasy lifestyle to us, but Lenny never tried to pull social rank like Jerry.

There was no doubt the Volkners lived in a different world than my family. His dad came home from work every day at five o'clock and walked up the front steps past the five of us, always greeting us with a chipper "Hello boys." We could see him sit in the upright chair next to the picture window in their living room, waiting for his wife to place a martini with two green olives on the white coaster set on the round table next to his chair. When we found ourselves sitting on Jerry's front porch witnessing this, it all seemed so fancy. Mr. Volkner sipping his martini made it look so good. What a life!

My dad walked through the back door every afternoon about four-thirty covered in dirt and sweat, then sat on the top step in the stairwell to take off his muddy work boots, before going to the bathroom where he would shave and get washed up for dinner. I loved that, though. Visually, it told me that my dad had worked hard, was done for the day and was getting cleaned up to eat a well-deserved dinner and spend time with his family. No fancy martinis, Volkswagen Beetles, or Aqua Club memberships for Dad. We couldn't afford it and, quite frankly, didn't want it. As long as we were together, life was great!

Nonetheless, Jerry Volkner lived on my block, forced his way into our summer games, and we all had to deal with him.

"Okay, so what's the sides?" Jerry obnoxiously blurted out as he walked up Jimmy's sidewalk.

"It's still me and Johnny," Jimmy said, hoping to keep the team with the three-game winning streak together.

"No problem, we can beat you guys," Jerry boasted. "We're up first."

All of us were fairly good, but Lenny and I were the best, because we had the best throwing arms. Keith's speed made him dangerous, and Jimmy was an all-around great athlete. Jerry was clearly the worst player and was always the last pick for every game, which he didn't appreciate.

"Hey, we have to play at Keith's house," Jimmy said. "We played here yesterday."

We all walked across Kostner carrying our baseball gloves and set up the bases in front of Keith's house, while we watched his front door and window in search of his mother. His sister Dawn appeared at the front door. Dawn was a few years younger than us, and she took great pleasure in trying to get her brother in trouble.

"You hit the door and I'll tell Mom," the curly-haired, olive-skinned eight-year-old said through a few missing teeth.

"Shut up, Dawn," Keith replied with great affection. "We're up first."

Jimmy played close to first base. I covered the area near second base, which was right up against the curb, the home run mark. Most of the balls would be coming my way, so it was up to me to either catch them on a fly or field the bounce and throw the runner out before he reached first.

Keith was up first and stood with his left shoulder facing the steps. He stared at the corner of the second stair, then wound up and threw the ball as hard as possible. The rubber ball came off the steps like a rifle shot right at me. I threw my glove up in self-defense and caught it.

"Ahhh!" Keith yelped, jumping up in the air, frustrated he just missed "hitting" a home run. "Lucky. Just lucky. You'll pay for that one."

I tossed the ball to Lenny, who was always Mr. Strategy when it came to bounce-or-fly. He caught it, didn't say a word, but just looked over the top of my head. He turned toward the steps, then glanced back over my head again, indicating he was looking to send that ball into the street. I crept back to make sure I was at the edge of the curb. Lenny wound up and threw the ball—really softly off the face of the third step. Then he sprinted toward first base.

"Bunt!" yelled Jimmy, who ran quickly to his right to field the ball. I ran as fast as I could toward first base. Jimmy slid on one knee across Keith's front lawn, fielded the ball with his bare hand, and threw a perfect strike to me just as I reached first. But it was too late. Lenny had beaten it out easily. And because Jimmy was lying on the ground and my momentum was taking me across first base, Lenny easily jogged into second for a double.

"Nice one, Lenny," said his teammate Keith. "Now c'mon, Jerry, bring him home."

"No problem." Volkner smirked with a swagger as he looked out over my head, just as Lenny had just done. I looked at Jimmy and he nodded at me. We knew what this Einstein was thinking. As Jerry made a big windup, I charged directly toward him. Just as we thought, he threw it softly against the steps. I was three feet behind him when the ball hit the porch. I picked up the bunt, then threw it to Jimmy at first for one out. He threw it back to me as I raced to third base, but Lenny slid in safely.

"Jerry!" Keith yelled. "What are you doing? Do you think they're stupid? Two bunts in a row!"

"Hey, they were lucky!" Jerry snapped.

"You guys can have him next game," said an angry Lenny, who rarely got upset during our games.

With two outs, we knew Keith would be going for the home run. Heck, he always did. It was all or nothing for him.

Once again, Keith stared at the corner of the second step. He turned his left shoulder toward it, wound up, and threw the ball as hard as possible. As fast as he threw it at the step is as fast as it ricocheted the wrong way and boom! It hit the bottom metal portion of the door really hard. We all froze and stared at the front door. Would an irate Mrs. Mareno in her pretty summer dress appear at the front door to yell at us again? The seconds ticked away. No sign of her. No Dawn either. I could see the new dent he had just put in the aluminum bottom section of the door. After about thirty seconds, we figured she didn't hear the noise and we were safe.

"Okay, strike one," said Keith, completely unfazed that he had just put another major dent in his door. He lined up and threw the ball once more. This time he hit the step perfectly, and it shot off the cement corner and sailed ten feet over my head for a home run. The score was 2–0. As I crossed Kostner to retrieve the ball off of Mr. Festerhouse's front lawn, I scanned his picture window to make sure he wasn't watching. Mr. Festerhouse hated anyone going on his lawn. I took two quick steps on his front lawn, bent down, picked up the ball, and out of the corner of my eye, there he was, coming out of his front door to remind me gently about his rule.

"Get the hell off my lawn!" he kindly instructed me.

"Yes, Mr. Festerhouse," I replied. "Sorry!"

"Just stay off the lawn or I'll have to talk with your father."

I walked back across Kostner and there was no sign of Lenny, Jimmy, Keith, or Jerry. I looked in Keith's gangway and there they were, hiding behind the chimney stack running up Mrs. Nesbitt's home. As Mr. Festerhouse disappeared into his house, the three cowards ventured back out.

"Hey, get the hell off of my lawn," Keith mocked me, laughing hysterically because I had been yelled at by our cranky old grass-loving neighbor.

We made it to the third inning before one of Keith's home run attempts hit his front door for the fifth time that morning. That got his mom's attention and the game was postponed due to an angry Italian mother in her pretty summer dress threatening the notification of Keith's father upon arrival home from the firehouse. But Jimmy and I had won our fourth straight game together, 5–4.

We walked next door to Jerry's house and sat on his front porch to recuperate from the game, our white T-shirts soaked in sweat.

"That's four straight for me and Johnny," Jimmy bragged to rub it in on Keith, Lenny, and Jerry. "We only have two guys and we beat your brains out every time. We don't change teams until you beat us."

Lenny and Keith just laughed. Jerry seethed.

"Hey, new sides next time!" Keith said.

"Yeah, me and Jimmy," Lenny blurted.

Keith cut him off.

"No, me, Johnny, and Lenny."

It was obvious Jerry was the kid no one wanted on their side.

"No, you have to beat us to change sides," Jimmy said. "You'll just have to take your lumps."

As Jerry stood there turning redfaced, I could see the anger growing in him. Jerry was the kind of kid who would never take a poke at a kid who was clearly bigger or stronger than him—like Jimmy or Lenny. And he must have had his doubts about Keith as well, because he turned his anger and frustration directly at me, even though I didn't say a word to him. But why not me? I was the perfect target for a bully. I was younger than him and had aspirations of becoming an altar boy: I wouldn't fight back.

As I sat there tossing the rubber ball into my Wilson baseball glove, laughing as the boys bantered in good fun, Jerry got up and stood directly in front of me.

"I can take you," he said loudly, making sure to announce his challenge clearly in front of Jimmy, Lenny, and Keith. I didn't know what to make of this boastful challenge. Lenny, Keith, and Jimmy burst out laughing.

"Look, Jerry, you stink, live with it," Jimmy said, drawing laughs from the others. We all thought Jerry was kidding around, but he had a stern look on his face.

"Stand up, Ruane!" Jerry demanded. I just looked up at him, not knowing what to make of this abrupt challenge.

"Oooooh, *Ruane*! He said his last name," Keith said. "He must be serious."

Everyone except Jerry laughed. Instead, Jerry leaned over toward me and pushed my shoulder hard. The laughing stopped. It was serious.

"Hey, it's just a game, Jerry!" Jimmy said. "Knock it off."

"No, you think you're so tough, Ruane. Stand up."

"Hey, he didn't say anything, I did," Jimmy said, standing up off the porch. "If you want to fight someone, fight me."

That made sense to everyone except Jerry.

"No, he thinks he's better than me, so let's see him prove it," Jerry said.

"He didn't say anything," Jimmy repeated. "I did!"

"Tough!" Jerry said. "Stand up, Ruane. I can take you."

Everything became quiet. I wasn't looking for a fight. I never was looking for a fight.

The only time fights ever broke out usually were the result of an argument about something stupid, and kids would react by fighting. Or when some kid got real angry during a game, sometimes the fists started flying. Other than those flash fights, the only kids I ever saw pick a fight were usually bullies—kids who knew they could beat up another kid and just had to show the world they could do it.

That's what Jerry Volkner was attempting to do to me that day. He lost in a game of bounce-or-fly baseball, so he was going to show everyone he was tougher than me, the prospective altar boy.

"C'mon, are you chicken?" he said, pushing my shoulder again.

I popped up off the porch and moved to the side of him. A surprised look crossed his face as he turned toward me and lifted both his fists up to fight.

"Knock it off, Jerry," Jimmy demanded, stepping between Jerry and me to stop anything before it got started.

"Stay out of this, Jimmy," Jerry snapped and brushed past Jimmy toward me.

"What are you doing, Jerry?" I asked, dumbfounded by his actions.

"C'mon Jerry, stop it," Lenny said.

"Yeah, forget it, Jerry, it's just a game," Keith said.

"I can take you," he reiterated, smiling widely and pushing me with both hands across my chest to knock me backward.

I had never been in a real fight before. I could feel a buzzing in my head as my heart started pounding. I felt like I could hear my heart, it was pounding so hard. I didn't know what to do. I didn't want to fight Jerry. I didn't want to fight anyone.

"Hey, leave him alone," Jimmy said one more time, stepping in between us.

"No!" Jerry snapped back at Jimmy, then stepped around him again. "This won't take long."

Jerry was now face-to-face with me.

"You think you're so good," Jerry said as his right hand clenched into a fist.

The buzzing in my head became so intense, I felt like my head would explode. My heart raced faster. I didn't know what to do as I stood just inches away from a kid who was intent on beating me up to show he was better than me. Jerry reached back and threw his right fist toward my nose. I was so shocked to be confronted that I didn't react, and Jerry connected. As his fist came across my right cheekbone and hit my nose, I could feel and hear the pop of his fist against my face, and my head was knocked back from the force of the punch.

Jerry's face lit up as he quickly shook his hurting right hand.

"C'mon, Ruane!"

His fists came up again.

"Hey, knock it off, Jerry," Jimmy yelled.

"Stay out of it, Jimmy," Jerry yelled back, lining up in front of me with his fists up.

The buzzing got louder. My heart felt like it was going to jump out of my chest. And now my face hurt. I took a few steps back as Jerry came toward me. Jerry reached back to throw another right, but this time I quickly ducked. Without thinking, I bounced into a boxer's stance with my left fist held up in front of my nose and right fist back closer to my chin, just like my dad had showed me a few years earlier. I had watched Cassius Clay do this so many times on TV that it just seemed natural.

"Yeah, nice, Johnny!" Keith yelled.

"Get him, Johnny!" Lenny said.

I now had a cheering section, and it only made Jerry angrier. As he recoiled after the miss, his entire face was left unprotected and I hit him with a hard right uppercut to his jaw. Oh boy, I felt that on my knuckles! I didn't care. I was in a fight now, and there was no turning back.

"Yeah, teach him a lesson, Johnny," Jimmy said, clapping his hands. He was joined by Lenny and Keith, clapping and cheering in unison.

I followed with a hard quick left jab to his nose and another right cross to his eye. Blood started to trickle from his nose. His eyes stared at me in complete shock and then turned to anger. He wasn't done.

Just then Keith's sister Dawn appeared to see the commotion.

"Fight!" she yelled, and ran back into her house bellowing, "Fight! Fight!"

All of a sudden the buzzing left my head and I was filled with rage. I wasn't going to get hit again. Jerry came at me to try to tackle me. I stepped to the side and hit him with a right hand hard to his gut. That stood Jerry straight up.

"Oh yeah! Oh yeah!" Keith yelped, clapping wildly.

"Finish him, Johnny!" said Jimmy.

I followed with a combination of lefts and rights to Jerry's face until he fell back onto his front lawn, crying and hiding his face in shame.

"I don't know what your problem is, Jerry," I said, now feeling the confidence that comes with a victory.

With his right hand covering his bleeding face, he stood up and ran, disappearing into the gangway between his house and Keith's.

As I stood there, I still could feel the sting of his punch across my nose and right cheek. Both of my hands were hurting as well. I was upset, feeling like I was going to cry. Why did Jerry start that fight? I never said anything to him after we won the game. I never said anything to him after any victory. I just wanted to go home.

I didn't say anything to Keith, Lenny, and Jimmy, who were smiling widely and giving each other high fives. I just turned and walked away.

"Hey, where are you going?" Keith asked.

"C'mon, you won, Johnny," Lenny said.

I just kept walking and looked back over my shoulder at them. Their smiles turned to looks of disappointment. Jerry ruined the day. None of us understood why he would start a fight among friends.

"Hey, I'll call you after lunch to play baseball?" Keith yelled to me as I crossed Kostner Avenue, heading toward my house.

I didn't respond. I was confused and just wanted to be left alone.

"Okay, we'll call you after lunch. We don't need Jerry. We can play two on two," Keith said, hoping to salvage the day.

If Jerry Volkner thought I wouldn't fight back because I was a nice kid and planned to be an altar boy, he found out the hard way that summer day that some altar boys do fight back.

But as I entered my front screen door, I walked through the living room, down the hallway, and straight into my bedroom, where I plopped on my bed. As I lay there with my face in the pillow, I felt horrible. I think being raised Catholic and having it drummed into my head at school and church that "Thou Shall Not Fight" had a strong impact on me. I knew the story about turning the other cheek. But when I was faced with a hit-or-be-hit situation, there was no choice for me. I was going to defend myself. It made me realize just how difficult any confrontation is for all of us. To be a true follower of Jesus, I would have to learn how to turn the other cheek. I wasn't sure I could make that transition then, and I never did. How do you just let someone beat you up? More important, why was a kid I considered my friend trying to beat me up?

The next morning, Keith came by my house and called me out to play.

"Yo Johnny!" he hollered through our back screen door.

My mother preferred that kids call us out at the back door. I was sitting in the kitchen reading the sports pages of the previous day's *Chicago Daily News*.

"Hey, Keith, come on in," I said, seeing Keith with his Wilson baseball mitt on his left hand and holding a rubber ball in his right.

For the most part, the emotions of the day before had cleared my head and heart, but I looked at him, wondering exactly what his plans were for a game. And did it involve Jerry Volkner?

"Bounce-or-fly?" I asked.

"Yes," he said, tossing the ball into his mitt, pulling it out, and tossing it in again. "Lenny and Jimmy are waiting at my house."

Keith glanced at my right cheek, which had a slight black and blue mark, but didn't mention it.

I grabbed my glove from my bedroom and went out the back door with Keith. As we walked across Kostner toward his house, I could see Lenny and Jimmy sitting on Keith's front porch, waiting for us. The bases were already in place.

"What's the sides?" asked Lenny, who also seemed to notice the mark on my face.

"Still me and Johnny," Jimmy replied. "And now it's even with just the two of you."

That day, no one talked about the bruise on my face or the fight. It was over, and we all wanted to forget it. We just wanted to play bounce-or-fly and have fun in the summer of '67.

Chapter Thirteen

WRITING ON THE WALL

B esides her obvious beauty, one thing that was apparent to the fifth-grade students in Miss Pasco's class was her talent for teaching. She brought tremendous energy and passion to her classroom, sincerely working to help her students learn and excel. I could see it in her face as she worked to explain a math problem or a historical point or perhaps a writing concept.

That is the subject where her efforts helped provide me with a lifelong direction. It was Tuesday, during the second week of December, when she said, "Okay, I would like each of you to write an essay about Christmas. You can write about anything you want. It can be informative, sad, funny—whatever you want it to be. But I want you to have fun writing it. No rules or restraints, just write whatever comes to mind."

"Have fun writing it?" I wondered what that meant. I can write something funny? Sure, I would love to do that. After thinking about it for a few moments, I decided to write something humorous about Christmas. In the 1960s, the culture in America was changing. We were watching television shows like *The Flip Wilson Show, Laugh-In,* and the *Smothers Brothers' Comedy Hour*. People going to college had long hair and were wearing grungy clothes with peace symbols plastered all over them. There were hippies and yippies seen on Walter Cronkite's

CBS Evening News every night rebelling against America, dropping out. Like most kids growing up in my neighborhood, I thought they were a bunch of freaks and should be kicked out of the country. They looked and dressed weird. The TV shows seemed to be making fun of them, but I was too young to understand the liberal politics of the Smothers Brothers. I just thought they were funny. It all went right over my head.

So as I thought about this writing assignment from Miss Pasco, I came up with a parody about Santa Claus being a hippie delivering the presents to children around the world. He talked and dressed like a hippie, wearing red bell-bottom pants and a red, white, and green psychedelic shirt with a red bandanna tied around the front of his head to hold back his long and straggly white hair. The North Pole was a commune inhabited by his hippie elves. And Santa wasn't married to Mrs. Claus, as was the tradition. No, they were just "living together" at their pad in the North Pole. That was "cool with her baby!"

On Christmas Eve when Santa stood up in his sleigh decorated with yellow peace symbols, he exclaimed, "Oh wow! Like, on Dasher, on Dancer, on Comet, on Cupid. Like, on Blitzen and Rudolph and all you reindeer cats. Let's, like, fly far out, man, make a trip across the world to deliver these crazy-looking presents to all of those cool little kiddies. Go, man, go!"

Rudolph, at the front of the reindeer team, turned to Santa and said, "Groovy, Santa!" And off they flew.

I had a blast writing it. When I finished, I checked with a few kids around me and asked what they had written. Each penned a straight story about their favorite Christmas memory or what they hoped would happen this Christmas. Upon hearing this, I began to get cold feet. I know Miss Pasco said to have fun writing, but would she accept this type of parody? No one else seemed to have taken a risk.

"Okay, everyone, pass your papers to the front, it's time for lunch," she said.

I thought about stuffing it into my desk. But Eddie Crandell's hand came over my right shoulder, handing me the collected papers from our row. I was supposed to add mine to the stack and pass it forward. I stopped thinking about it, slapped my paper on the pile, and passed it to Rita Fitz, sitting in front of me. There, it was done. If she didn't like it, I would live with the consequences.

Over the next ten minutes, we filed up to the entrance of the room to collect our carton of milk, which we had each day with our lunch. In those days, everyone brought their lunch to St. Bede's in a lunch box or brown paper bag, usually purchased at the local Jewel supermarket. Peanut butter and jelly sandwiches were always a popular choice, or cheese sandwiches, ham sandwiches; turkey hadn't made its way into the popular culture at this time. The funny thing is, most kids usually brought the same type of lunch each day. There were always kids who thought they would mix it up a bit and try to work a trade with one of the other students.

"Hey Gale," Kevin Fox said to one of the twins. "Trade you my P&J for your Fluffernutter?" Gale loved her Fluffernutters, and Kevin knew it. No question this was a bold proposition from him, but he went forward with it. He had a real taste for a Fluffernutter.

"No way," Gale shot back. "You bring your own Fluffernutter."

Kevin wasn't to be denied. He spotted her sister, Dale, about to take her first bite from her Fluffernutter.

"Dale!" he said, loud enough to freeze her before she closed the deal with her first bite.

She turned to Kevin and gave him a suspicious look, knowing what he wanted.

"Look Kevin, if you want my Fluffernutter, you are going to have to do better than your peanut butter and jelly sandwich. You know what I mean?"

"I know what you mean," replied Kevin. "No problem. I have Chips Ahoy. I'll throw two of them into the deal."

"Four," Dale fired back.

"Three!" replied Kevin.

"Deal!"

They swapped lunches, and the excitement was over. I looked up at Miss Pasco, which I was prone to do every few seconds for no reason other than to just look at her. She put her head down and was laughing at the lunch barter.

Two days later at the start of our English lesson, our teacher pulled out a pile of looseleaf papers from her file folder and announced, "I have graded the papers you wrote the other day about Christmas. I think it was a good exercise for everyone. I think you all did real well.

"There is one paper, however, that I believe is exceptional. If the author gives me approval, I would like to tack it up on the board so everyone can take a turn reading it. And I would like to request that all of the other fifth-grade teachers have their students read it as well. It shows a tremendous amount of creativity and humor. Honestly, I am truly amazed that a fifth-grader wrote this."

"Who is it?" Dale said, unable to deal with the mystery.

"Yeah, who is it?" mimicked her sister, Gale, thinking it had to be one of the two very bright twins.

"John Ruane," Miss Pasco said, extending a big bright smile in my direction.

Oh my goodness. Everyone started staring at me. I could feel myself become flush.

"John, this is a really great paper. Nice job!"

Everyone in the class started clapping. That was followed by Marty, Mike, Kevin, and Eddie razzing me.

"Great paper, John. You've won her hand in marriage, congratulations!" Marty teased.

"Miss Pasco loves your paper, John. She's all yours," Mike said, while punching my shoulder.

"Kiss me, Johnny, I love your paper," Kevin said, puckering up to toy with me.

I wasn't certain if Miss Pasco could see that I wasn't dealing very well with this newfound classroom fame. She just seemed so thrilled that a student in her class would write something so creative that she was compelled to share it with everyone.

After the English lesson, she placed a big red star on my three-page, blue-lined, looseleaf paper and tacked it to the corkboard at the back of the room, just as she said she would do. During lunch, groups of students went up to the board and read my Christmas story. I could hear them read it out loud, and it resulted in several laughs as the kids got a kick out of the hippie Santa Claus and his far-out lingo. It was nice that they all liked my paper, but it sure felt strange having all of that attention focused on me. I didn't really like it. I preferred being the quiet kid to whom nobody paid much attention.

"Hey, that was a funny story, John," said Kevin after lunch.

"Yeah, I liked it too," Mike said. "You're a good writer."

"Thanks," I said, and glanced at Miss Pasco, who was smiling from ear to ear at me. I felt the hot rush fill my face and my heart started pounding. Then she winked at me, and I was glad to be sitting down behind my desk.

When the final bell rang that day and school was over, I walked into the cloakroom to get my jacket and wool hat. As I followed the other kids toward the door, I felt a hand tap me on the shoulder. When I turned around, there she was again with that big beautiful smile.

"Can I talk to you a minute, John?" she asked, turning and walking back toward her desk.

I followed her but quickly glanced over my shoulder to see Marty standing at the doorway grinning as he witnessed the moment. There would definitely be more harassment later.

"Yes, Miss Pasco?" I said.

"I just wanted to tell you how proud I am of you and the paper you wrote," she said, looking me directly in the eyes.

"Thank you, Miss Pasco. I was so glad you liked it. I wasn't sure when I handed it in if it would be accepted. I felt like I was taking a chance."

"That's right. You did take a chance and you succeeded. And that's the point. If everyone writes along the same lines, very conservatively, it's boring. But when writers go outside the bounds and use their imaginations, that's when wonderful things can happen. I hope you will always remember that."

"I will."

"And you have to know that you have the talent to do it. Some people—teachers and students—will appreciate it. And please remember this: Some won't. Some will criticize your work. That's the risk all writers and artists take when they create. But don't let anyone discourage you from writing the way you want to write. Write what you want to say, not what others want to read. If your heart and instincts tell you that your writing is good, listen to your heart. You are the writer. It's your work. Write from your heart. Write for yourself. If others enjoy reading your work, that's a bonus."

"I will, Miss Pasco. Thank you."

When I walked out into the cold winter weather, Marty was standing outside the door waiting for me.

"So, did she kiss you?" he asked, laughing.

"Twice," I said. "She's a great kisser."

"Yeah, in your dreams."

"She asked me out on a date next Friday. Wants me to pick her up at seven."

"Is that right? On your bike?"

"Yeah, she says she doesn't mind riding on the handle bars."

Marty walked home with me that day and we joked back and forth about the day, my Santa story, and Miss Pasco. It was quite an exciting and important day for me.

After the Christmas break, we were back at school to begin 1968, a turbulent year in America. As fifth-graders on the South Side of Chicago, we were aware of the Vietnam War. How could we miss it? Every evening, my father watched the *CBS Evening News* with Walter Cronkite, who always seemed to be reporting on the war.

During the first week of February, the news really got my attention as Cronkite reported about the sixth straight day of savage fighting in Vietnam. The Viet Cong had attacked half of the forty-four provincial capital cities and killed 983 Americans and wounded 318. The United States reported killing 12,704 enemy over the six days and aggressively counterattacking.

At the same time, word was coming back to the United States from returning troops about massacres. A few years later we would learn about the My Lai massacre and other atrocities in Vietnam. Charles Percy, our Illinois senator, was on TV saying President Lyndon Johnson's administration had purposely misled Americans about the strength of the Viet Cong.

I just sat there next to my dad, stunned at the news. The president was lying to Americans while their boys were getting killed in a country that seemed a million miles away. For what? So President Johnson could "win the war." From that point on, protests against the war intensified in several cities, including Chicago. I was too young to really understand and digest the horrific events in Southeast Asia; nonetheless the war affected our fifth-grade class at St. Bede's.

It was a Monday in March of 1968. We were all sitting at our desks waiting for Miss Pasco to arrive when the principal of the school, Sister Rita, entered our class holding a newspaper. She walked behind Miss Pasco's desk and everyone in the room watched her, wondering what she was doing.

"Children, I have some news for you today," she said in a rather grim and direct manner, laying the newspaper on the desk. "Beginning today, you will have a new teacher."

The word "What?" seemed to echo across the room. "What's going on?" "Where's Miss Pasco? New teacher? What was this all about?"

The nun held her hands up to quiet down the class.

"Miss Pasco is fine. But I think you are old enough to understand this development. Miss Pasco participated in an antiwar rally over the weekend at the University of Chicago and was arrested along with several other protesters. Due to this, we will be replacing her here at St. Bede's. I'm sorry."

I felt numb as I watched the nun lift up the newspaper to show us a picture of the protest, and she pointed to a person in the photo whom the nun said was Miss Pasco. Our teacher's name was listed in the story. Then I thought about Walter Cronkite and the news of the massacres in Vietnam, Senator Percy's statement, and the war protests across the country. This is the teacher who encouraged me to take chances and express myself openly and honestly. All of a sudden it seemed to make a lot of sense.

"Your new teacher, Miss Fleming, will be arriving shortly and will teach you the remainder of the year," Sister Rita informed the classroom of wide-eyed eleven-year-old students. "I would now like you all to sit here quietly until she arrives. Do you understand?"

"Yes, Sister," was said collectively and respectively in unison by a glum group of students, who sat at their desks looking like they had been told the world would be ending.

Sister Rita's description of the events was not enough of an explanation for Eddie Crandell. He really liked Miss Pasco. We all did. Eddie stood up to address the nun.

"Is Miss Pasco okay?" he asked, with a very concerned look on his face. "Is she in jail?"

The nun paused, realizing the news really disturbed the students.

"We received the call this morning from her mother," she explained, again holding up the Sunday newspaper. "As you can see, Miss Pasco's pictured here in the *Tribune* being arrested. Her mother said that her daughter had been arrested on Saturday and was released that evening."

"Then why can't she come back to school?" Eddie asked.

"Yes, why can't she come back?" echoed across the room.

The nun paused, really not prepared for this barrage of support for Miss Pasco.

"The matter was addressed by the pastor, Father Griffin, today and the Archdiocese of Chicago. The decision was made to replace her for the good of the students at St. Bede's."

The class fell silent. I turned and looked around at the other disappointed students. Eddie was angry! We were all angry. We heard the principal, but we still couldn't understand why this wonderful teacher wasn't being allowed back into the school. So she protested the Vietnam War. A lot of people were protesting. It was on the news every night. Give her credit for having the guts to do it. Don't take her job away from her. Was this because the *Tribune* put her name and picture in the paper? Was is too embarrassing for Father Griffin to have a teacher who stood up for her principles? For peace? He had been a U.S. Marine chaplain. Did he view her and all protesters as traitors? It was never addressed again.

About an hour later, a very pretty young lady, about twenty-two, with long brown hair and a purple mid-length dress, entered our classroom in black high heels. We had never seen her before.

"Hello, I am your new teacher, Miss Fleming," she said in a sweet voice. "I just received the notice today that I would be finishing the school year teaching here. I understand there was a problem and they needed me to step in to help. So I will do my best to help you finish fifth grade."

Miss Fleming was a very nice teacher, and she obviously had been thrown into a difficult situation. We spent the rest of the day answering questions for her, as well as asking questions about Miss Pasco's situation. She really didn't know anything about it and was quite surprised to hear the information we had learned from the principal.

That day after school, Mike, Kevin, Eddie, Marty, and I rode our bikes over to Miss Pasco's apartment. When we arrived, the shyness had dissipated from the others. Kevin was the first one off his bike, and he went straight into the familiar wooden door at 8655 South Tripp. We followed behind him, but only Marty and Mike could get inside the doorway while we waited outside the open door. Kevin rang the bell and we all waited for the voice on the intercom. Nothing. He rang it again, waited about twenty seconds, still nothing. I looked up at the window of her apartment, only to see a head duck back behind the white sheer curtains.

"Hey, someone is up there," I said. "I just saw someone in the window."

"Was it her?" Mike asked.

"Didn't look like her. Probably her mother. Miss Pasco must not be home."

We walked back to our bikes, looking up at the window. A shadow appeared and disappeared just as quickly. We got on our bikes and rode up to Durkin Park, where we sat on the swings discussing the events of the day.

"She must be embarrassed and doesn't want to come down to face us," Marty said dejectedly as he sat on the middle swing looking down.

"I wonder if they will give her another chance to come back and teach," Kevin said.

"No way," Eddie said. "You heard the principal. The Archdiocese was called on this one. They aren't going to call them back and ask for permission because a bunch of goofy fifth-graders want their teacher back."

"We should protest," Marty said.

"Yeah, that worked for her," Mike said sarcastically.

That night I watched the local 5:00 P.M. news on channel 7 with Fahey Flynn and Joel Daly to see if they would cover the protest. It was one of the top stories, but I didn't see Miss Pasco in the crowd of people being hauled into the police paddy wagons. I checked the *Daily News,* the newspaper we received at our home each afternoon. Again no photo or mention of Miss Pasco.

At school the next day, Mike Hannon had the *Tribune* and there was her picture, just as Sister Rita told us. She was in a crowd of other protesters, yelling something. She looked really angry. I felt sorry that she had been arrested, but proud that she took a stand. She showed courage and conviction in her beliefs.

With each passing day, the talk about Miss Pasco decreased. But that didn't stop us from riding our bikes over to her apartment for the next week. Every time we rang the bell, there was no answer. We saw the shadow in the window appear and disappear, but no Miss Pasco. By day four, the other guys threw in the towel, even Kevin. But I wouldn't give up. She meant too much to me. The first day I went by her apartment alone, I really hoped she would come down and talk to me. But as I stood in the hallway of her apartment ringing her bell, it became apparent that it wouldn't happen.

I never saw Miss Pasco again, although I have thought of her many times since. She was a beautiful, smart, encouraging, positive, devoted, energetic, sincere, good, and honest teacher. She was a dream teacher! She obviously let her conscience be her guide. That speaks volumes about her integrity, sincerity, and courage. She was a woman and so couldn't be drafted, but she felt strongly enough to join the protest.

I will never forget her. She was the first person in my life to identify and encourage a talent in me that I draw upon nearly every day. And for that I am eternally grateful.

God bless you, Miss Pasco.

Chapter Fourteen

UNBLESSED ACT

The Blessed Eucharist. The host. The Body of Jesus Christ. That consecrated white round Communion wafer distributed to all those who had received their First Communion and were in the state of grace qualifying them to receive Holy Communion.

What makes the Communion wafer holy is not its form or content but what Catholics believe it becomes. The moment the priest stands over the ciborium filled with hosts and consecrates them, they are transformed into the Body of Jesus Christ. At that moment, each host is Heavenly Bread that no one except a Eucharistic minister or priest is allowed to touch. In my youth, only a deacon or priest could touch the consecrated hosts, and prior to becoming an altar boy I believed they were the only ones who could touch them before consecration. That was my understanding until the holy Tim Rink presented me with a different view.

"You know how good they taste," holy Tim said to me one day in the altar boys' room while he sat in the pew set along the wall holding a large plastic bag of un-blessed hosts. "Well, as long as they are not blessed, it's okay to eat them."

Then he plunged his right hand into the bag and pulled out a handful of wafers, shoving them into his mouth as if he was eating potato chips.

In my Catholic education, one of the messages I took away from the Bible teachings was that as children we are too young and innocent to understand our wrongdoing; therefore we are not truly guilty of sin. We are guilty of ignorance, which is exactly what Tim Rink was exhibiting at that very moment.

If Tim had known that early Christians had to hide the Eucharist and celebrate Masses in secret because they feared being persecuted for their beliefs, perhaps he would have understood the importance of the host before it becomes the Eucharist. But he obviously did not have that perspective, nor did any other altar boy I knew at that time.

As I watched him chewing the hosts, I knew it was wrong. Dead wrong! Every instinct in my body told me so. Rink already had taken advantage of my naïveté by introducing me to drinking wine, justifying his actions by saying he was trying to make certain it wasn't stale. It only took me a few days to find out he was taking advantage of my trust in him as an older altar boy who was supposed to be my mentor, my role model. From that point on, I became skeptical of everything he told me. And here he was trying to justify eating unblessed hosts.

"Here, try one."

"I don't think I should," I said, as I stood over the sink full of soapy water, washing the cruets.

"No, it's okay. All the altar boys do it. It's one of the fringe benefits of being an altar boy. Heck, some guys bring a bag into school and share them with the other students."

I never heard about altar boys bringing bags of hosts into the school.

"C'mon, they're not blessed," he insisted. "It's just like eating bread from the store. No big deal. Just try one."

I thought about it a minute, watching him munch away at the sacred manna. I recalled the time in second grade when Sister Mary had given us unblessed hosts to help us practice for our First Communion. She was allowed to touch them and explained to us, "Children, these hosts have not been blessed yet, so Father Griffin has allowed me to touch them and give them to you for practice." That experience stuck in my mind and unfortunately fed Rink's justification and prodded me to join him in his sinful act.

I reached into the bag and took one of the small round wafers, holding it up to take a good look at it. There it was in my hand, a host that no one except a deacon or priest was supposed to touch. Yes, it wasn't blessed, but somehow that didn't seem to make much of a difference to me at the time. I lifted it up toward my mouth, looked at it, and placed it on my tongue. Then I ate it as if I was eating a normal host. It tasted the same as the blessed ones, no difference at all. But I couldn't help feeling as though I had committed an awful sin. The holy Tim Rink had led me down a sinful path.

Over the course of the next several months, I watched other altar boys sneak into the priests' sacristy to the very large gray safe where all of the holy instruments were kept with the unblessed hosts. This was quite a safe. Huge! My friend Eddie Crandell never could understand why Father Griffin felt he needed such a large safe when half of the Chicago police force seemed to be parishioners.

We were not supposed to go into the safe unless we needed candles or extra patens. The sacristy was the domain of the priests. So when an altar boy went into that safe for anything other than the appropriate religious items, he was most definitely crossing the line. If he were caught, he most likely would be dismissed as an altar boy and possibly expelled from school. Yet many of the altar boys sneaked in there to pull out a bag of hosts.

Mike Wendell was the most obnoxious of all. He not only took the small hosts, he took the large hosts the priests used at the moment of consecration. One morning I watched him sitting on the pew in the altar boys' room eating a host sandwich of small wafers smashed inside two large hosts, showing no remorse at all. He looked at me curiously, wondering why I was staring at him.

"What?" he snapped. "I didn't have breakfast!"

This sight had become such a regular occurrence, I almost felt like I was missing one of the great fringe benefits of being an altar boy. Oh yes, I was being corrupted, just as they had been corrupted. But we were all too young and too stupid to understand the significance of our crime and sin.

It was an early-morning weekday Mass when I decided I was going to sneak into that safe and pilfer a bag of hosts. I was wearing only my black cassock and standing at the sink preparing the cruets for the Mass. I looked around the corner through the doorway into the sacristy to see if the priest had arrived.

There was a long corridor that connected the rectory directly to this room. I walked in and opened the door leading to the corridor to see if anyone was coming. No priest. I closed the door and quickly walked toward the safe.

My heart was pounding and I felt out of breath. God was trying to tell me this was a bad idea. I didn't listen and kept going. As I stepped into the safe, I could see all of the holy chalices, ciboriums, candles, extra cruets, patens, and some small collection baskets. It was all in there. And there were the unblessed hosts, bags of them, just like aisle one at Jewel Foods—the bread aisle. I listened to hear if a priest was entering. No sound. I grabbed a bag and ran across the sacristy, my heart pounding like it was going to fly out of my chest.

I made it back to the altar boys' room and stuffed the hosts into an empty paper brown bag from Jewel; just coincidence. My heart was racing. I was sweating. What was wrong with me? Why would I do this? Because all of the other altar boys do it? So what! Well, at twelve years old, I had taken an unblessed bag of hosts. I guess I thought I had to be one of the boys, one of the altar boys.

I had to show the other guys what I had done. I was one of them.

When my friend Kevin Fox, the other altar boy assigned to the Mass, showed up a few minutes later, I showed him my bag of hosts.

"Hey, give me some," he said, not showing an iota of guilt toward his request. I brought out the bag, broke it open, and he took a handful.

"I love these things," he said, popping one in his mouth as if he were eating round Necco candy wafers.

"Yeah, they're good," I said, eating one. "Good thing they're not blessed, huh?"

"It would be a mortal sin," he pointed out.

"Yeah, a mortal sin," I said, not feeling very good and handing Kevin the bag, while I walked out to the altar to finish setting up for Mass. This wasn't the way I normally acted, and I knew it.

To receive Holy Communion then, all good Catholics were experienced at walking up to the white marble Communion rail and kneeling down with hands clasped in prayer until the priest arrived with his golden ciborium filled with hosts. The priest would hold the host in front of the good parishioner at the rail and proclaim "Body of Christ."

The good Catholic in the state of grace—who does not wear an altar boy's uniform or rob large gray safes full of unblessed hosts—would respond "Amen," then present his tongue so the priest could transfer the host without anyone else touching it. Once the blessed host was received and the lips sealed, chewing was not allowed. It just melted in your mouth as you prayed.

This host was so holy that the responsibility placed on my shoulders, as well as on all altar boys, was to hold the golden paten under each recipient's chin in case the host were to drop. It was up to the altar boy to catch any wayward host.

The paten was not only used to catch a falling host. It also proved a good tool for prodding a friend at the altar rail. This became a tradition among most of the altar boys. Any time a friend showed up to receive Communion, that friend knew they would be receiving a small smack in the chin or neck. And they knew it was coming, so they would often try to avoid it by leaning back until the priest said "Body of Christ." Then they would lean in to receive the host. It didn't matter how far they leaned back because it was too easy to make it look like that extra tap to their neck was just part of being a cautious altar boy, making darn sure the paten was under the recipient's chin so the host would not fall to the ground.

This ritual caused many altar boys attending Mass to determine which section of the Communion rail their friend would be serving. Then they would walk to a different portion of the rail being served by the altar boy they didn't know so they could escape a shot in the neck.

During my two years holding the paten, I witnessed several slips and drops but never missed one host. The day I witnessed my first miss was quite a moment.

Rink had briefed me about how to handle such an incident, but until my best friend Marty Durks and I were teamed for a 10:00 A.M. Sunday Mass, the most well-attended Mass of the week, I never actually experienced it. The priest I was assisting during Communion, Father Ralph Mollan, had just run out of hosts. He looked across the rail to see only five people were left to serve. I guess he assumed Father Griffin, whom Marty was assisting, could finish, and he turned and walked up to the altar table to clean his ciborium.

I turned to follow him up the steps of the altar when I heard Father Griffin say, "Don't touch it!" And there it was, a little white host lying on that bright red rug in front of Father Griffin, with a stunned parishioner in front of him and an even more stunned Marty Durks just to his left. The parishioner must have fumbled the host as he received it. And Marty must have missed it with the paten.

The thousand parishioners in attendance seemed to be watching this scene. Father Griffin never flinched. He was like an emergency-room doctor attending to a patient who had fallen from a four-story building. By the look on Marty's face, he was the injured one. The parishioner at the rail didn't look much better. They both felt like they were to blame. The five remaining state-of-gracers waiting along the rail for their Communion just looked on in amazement. What would Father Griffin do? There was no picking this host up and giving it to one of the five holy ones on the rail. First, I wondered if they would even take it. I was sure that host was headed to a nearby garbage can. But could he throw it in the garbage? A blessed host? I soon got my answer.

Father Griffin knew exactly what to do. He called Father Mollan over to take his ciborium and finish distributing the hosts to the holy five still kneeling along the rail. The pastor took the white holy hand cloth, which was always worn over his left wrist, bent down, and lay the cloth over the tainted host. He made a Sign of the Cross and picked it up. Once upright, Father Griffin glanced at Marty as if to say, No Problem, young Durks, I can handle this. Then, to my great amazement, he ate the host. The pastor carried out a holy act in his standing-room-only church that Sunday for all to watch.

Every Catholic knows the consecrated host becomes the Body of Christ and we are all blessed to receive this sacrament. But this demonstrated the tremendous significance of that little round white host. If that host had fallen anywhere—onto the muddy ground of a hut being used to celebrate Mass in a poor Peruvian village; or into the polluted mucky sewers running along the streets of a village in India; or even under the shoe of a violent nonbelieving foreign soldier crushing it with his heal to show his disrespect—I believe Father Griffin and every other priest truly devoted to Jesus would have worked to rescue it, just like one of God's soldiers coming to the aid of their fallen Savior. The cross may represent Jesus' sacrifice for our sins, but the host represents the new life He gives us. As Catholics, nothing can be more sacred.

After that experience, I never touched another unblessed host, and I begged God to forgive me my youthful indiscretion.

Chapter Fifteen

A TRAGIC DAY

It took about a month for our fifth-grade class to accept our new teacher, Miss Fleming. She had been placed in a difficult position, but she was very nice and a pretty good teacher. She wasn't Miss Pasco, but no one could ever meet that idealized standard.

It was a sunny Thursday during the third week of April in 1968 when Miss Fleming called me up to her desk after the final bell rang and class was dismissed. I had no idea why she wanted to speak to me. Slowly she walked around to the front of her desk as I approached wearing my navy blue St. Bede's school sweater and carrying my math and science books for that evening's homework. I could see a look of concern on her face. She didn't look happy, but I couldn't remember doing anything wrong.

"John, I asked you to see me because something has happened," she said.

Something happened? In my mind, I quickly tried to review the day, wondering what I had done. "Yes, Miss Fleming."

"Did you hear the fire engine sirens today around lunchtime?" she asked.

Oh no, I thought. What was this all about?

"Yes, I did," I replied. How could I not have heard them? They were loud and seemed to go on forever.

"There was a fire at your house today," she said.

"What!" I exclaimed.

"Please don't be alarmed, no one was hurt," she said.

"No one was hurt?" I said, starting to back up toward the door, ready to run.

"No one was hurt," she repeated. "Everyone is okay."

"But why wasn't I told earlier?" I asked.

"When your mother called the principal, she thought it better to keep the children in school. There was no point in having you come home with all of the commotion," she explained.

"I have to go," I said, rushing away. Outside, I squinted as I dashed across 83rd Street into the nearly empty St. Bede's Church parking lot. I could feel the adrenaline pumping as I ran faster and faster, despite carrying two heavy books. As soon as I had crossed Kostner, I could see down the block where a number of neighbors were gathered in front of our house. There were no fire trucks, though. They must have put it out, I thought.

Among the throng were about twenty kids from Kathy's fourth-grade class, because their teacher had announced the fire in front of all of them. Real smart!

I saw my brother, Danny, running across 84th Street where he had been talking with one of his friends, waiting for the rest of us to get home. He was a first-grader in public school and must have been home for a while. He seemed to be running as quickly toward me as I was toward him, his shirttail flapping over his blue pants and black hair bouncing off his forehead with each stride.

I reached the front of our house just before Danny, and it looked like a war zone. Our front door was wide open, as the screen door was lying against the brick facing on the blackened cement porch. Orange emergency tape had been placed across the doorway to make sure no one could enter as the place aired out. The cement porch steps were covered with dirt and soot. Our lawn looked like a football team had practiced on it. In the gangway along the side of our house, I could see broken windows, burned closet doors, and a blackened light fixture from the ceiling of one of the bedrooms.

"Hello, Johnny," my next-door neighbor Mrs. Rome said. "I'm really sorry."

"Thanks, Mrs. Rome," I replied courteously, then asked Danny, "Where's Mom and Dad?"

"In the back. Come on, I'll show you what happened," he said, anxious to show me the damage he had already seen. "Everyone's okay."

That was good news, but Danny's face had a look of loss across it like he had just lost the biggest game of his life. I didn't say anything to him. I didn't have to. He knew what I was thinking: What had happened to our house? I followed him as he made his way through the gangway, both of us staying to the side of all the debris. I just looked at the mess, wondering how bad the damage was inside. When we reached the gate to the backyard, there was blackened debris piled on the lawn. There was a mattress almost completely burned, with a large black hole in the middle, revealing bedsprings. Whose bed was that? I wondered. A white dresser and bureau from the girls' room were charred and laying on their sides. The burned drawers were strewn around the yard, and burned clothes were in piles next to the dresser as flies buzzed about them. Once yellow closet doors were now charred along the edges and were butted up against the dressers. What a mess!

"Come on, Johnny, it's okay," my six-year-old brother offered bravely. "I'll show you what happened."

Our back door was open, as were all the windows of the house, in an obvious attempt to air out the brick building. As we entered and ascended the red and gray tiled steps into the kitchen, I was hit with the horrible smell of burned wood. I looked to my left to see the walls of the kitchen covered with black stains, as was the kitchen floor. A stale haze hung in the air, but I was able to see Kathy in the hallway outside her bedroom.

"How bad is it?" I asked her.

"Bad," she said, near tears. "Our room is wrecked."

Her disappointment apparent, my ten-year-old sister turned and walked toward us, her shoes squishing across the wet rug in the hallway.

"I don't know how they are going to fix this!" she said, walking out the back door.

Danny and I continued on through the kitchen, which was a mess but not burned too badly. We looked to our left into our bedroom and were happy to see that the room looked untouched, just as it had before we left for school. I could see my glove and baseball bat in the far corner. I knew the rest of the house wouldn't look like this, especially after seeing Kathy's reaction to her room.

"I guess we lucked out, eh?" I said to my brother as we made our way down the hall.

The second the soles of my school shoes touched the brown and white carpet, they sunk in and squished. The front-room rug was soaked. The sound of the two of us walking across the rug echoed off the walls—not a sound we ever thought we would hear walking through our home. Obviously, the firemen had to use a good deal of water to put out the fire.

As we moved into the hallway, we glanced to our right at the boys' blue bathroom. Looked okay. Then looked to our left into our parents' room. Well, this looked quite a bit worse. The walls were black, just like the hallway walls, covered with soot. One wall of my parents' room, which connected to my sisters' room, was badly damaged by the fire. The red bedspread covering the queen bed was pulled back and the pillows ruffled, as if someone had been sleeping in it. I couldn't help thinking this was the bed I so often had watched my mom sitting on while praying. This day, the sun and blue sky seen through her window couldn't brighten the smoke-filled room. That's when I noticed the burned doorframe to the girls' room next door.

I took another wet step across the rug and looked left into my sisters' room to see the entire back wall, along with half of the two side walls, charred black—completely destroyed, with the wooden studs showing. This must have been where the fire took place. The room had been emptied of the furniture, exposing the burned wooden floor.

I could hear Danny's shoes squishing as he walked up behind me, and we both just stared in disbelief at the damage. We could hear someone coming up the back staircase. It was Mom, looking frazzled. Her jet-black hair was a bit mussed, which was unusual. Her green and white daisy-patterned knee-length dress was wrinkled. That was unusual as well.

"Johnny and Danny, you shouldn't be in there," she said, squishing her way toward us.

"What happened?" I asked my mother.

"Everything is fine, Johnny," said Mom, giving Danny and me a reassuring hug while she gazed into the blackened bedroom. "We are all okay, so no worries."

It was evident on Mom's face that she had been crying. This day would take a toll on her for the rest of her life.

Maureen, dressed in her St. Bede's uniform, came up the back steps having just arrived home from school. Her jaw dropped as she surveyed the scene. She walked directly to where we were standing, totally uninterested in the rest of the house. Kathy already had told her the worst of the damage had been in their room.

"It's okay, Maureen," Mom said, still holding Danny and me against her. She explained that she had been resting around eleven o'clock, the time our four-year-old sister Margaret normally took her daily nap. Inexplicably, the electric outlet on the back wall of the girls' room sparked and started the fire. Margaret later recalled lying there as flames shot up from the outlet and her bed caught fire. She remembers being in a daze, thinking she was dreaming. The mattress burned quickly, and thank goodness Margaret woke up. Once she realized this fire was real, she sprang out of bed and immediately ran through the already smoky hallway to Mom's room next door.

As the smoke billowed into the bedroom, Margaret shook our mother and woke her up. Mom grabbed her house shoes from the closet next to the bed, took Margaret by the hand, and quickly led her out. As she turned into the hallway toward the front room, she saw the blaze in the girls' room, which was spreading across the drapes and walls. It's a good thing Margaret awoke as quickly as she did. They both could have been killed!

Mom led Margaret out the front door to our neighbor's house, where she called the Fire Department. They spent the next ten minutes in front of our home with Mrs. Rome watching the smoke and fire shoot out of Margaret's bedroom window as the blare of the fire engines heard in the distance became louder. A long hook and ladder truck with its powerful engines roared south down Kostner toward our home, which thankfully had no cars parked in front of it. Another smaller fire engine came screaming up behind it.

Two firemen quickly jumped off the back of the hook and ladder and grabbed their axes. The two firemen on the back of a smaller fire engine jumped into the street and pulled the fire hose off the truck, following their comrades up the steps of our home. By this time, a good-sized crowd had gathered in front to hear the chief hollering at them to "Stand back and let the firemen do their job!"

The lead fireman slammed the screen door back, breaking it off the wood at the hinge, and the five men disappeared into our burning home. In 1968, firemen didn't have gas masks. They created their own protection and called them cheater masks, which looked like an asthma mask and helped them avoid breathing smoke.

"I could hear them tearing apart the windows and walls with their axes," Mom said, visibly upset and almost starting to cry as she recalled the scene. "But the important thing is no one got hurt. Thank God, Margaret saw the fire and woke me up."

And that was the point. Yes, the girls' room was destroyed, but it could be rebuilt.

"Where is Margaret?" Maureen asked.

"She is next door at the Romes' house," Mom explained. "She's okay. I don't really want to bring her in here though."

That made sense. At almost four years old, how could my little sister get past the trauma she had endured that day?

We all knew the rest of the house would need major work to get it back in shape. But really, this wasn't so bad. It wasn't like the fire had spread through the entire house. Sure, it was a complete mess, but most of the house just needed a really good cleaning.

"Where's Dad?" I asked.

"He's in the basement with the insurance inspector."

I squished my way back down the hall to the back stairwell and down to the basement, carefully treading on the wet gray wooden steps. The gray cement floor was filthy with black water and ashes across the southwest corner under my sisters' room. Good thing the furnace was not touched. If that had caught fire, who knows how great the damage would have been!

Dad obviously had come straight from his Water Department worksite, still dressed in his green work pants and flannel shirt splattered with the day's grime. His black thinning hair looked damp with sweat and a bit mussed. He stood in a dry area talking with a short slim man in gray dress slacks and white short-sleeved dress shirt. He was asking Dad questions and making notes on a clipboard. A cricketlike sound came from the puddles of water on the floor. I was familiar with this noise that came each time I was ordered to sweep and hose down the basement floor with water from our backyard hose.

The insurance man sounded like he was just finishing up, and I overheard Mr. Allstate tell Dad he thought we would be able to move back into our home in about a week.

Danny came down the stairs, and I saw Mom and Maureen walk out the back door behind us.

"Hello, boys," the gray-haired insurance man said as he climbed the stairs past us. "Don't worry. We'll get your house back in shape."

Danny and I stared at our dad, our family leader, who looked so frustrated seeing his home in such a state. I watched him rub both of his eyes with the palms of his hands. The day was only half over and he was exhausted. On an average day, our mother and father had so much to deal with, given five kids, three in Catholic school, mounting bills, a physically demanding job with the city, and now this— their home nearly destroyed. If living the American dream was buying a home, losing the dream was having it burn down.

My dad had endured worse, though, having grown up on a farm in Ireland with seven siblings. He knew what it was like to live in simple circumstances. And my mother was no stranger to tough times as well, having had to move from one apartment to another in the 1930s and early '40s during the Great Depression. I'm sure they were at an age, though, when they hoped life would start getting easier, not harder. But somehow it never works out that way. Just when you think things are great, something comes along to ruin it. We certainly can plan for the long term, but the truth is, we have to live day by day.

"Don't worry, we'll be okay," Dad assured his two boys peering through the round white stair railings.

"Yeah, but where do we live?" I asked him, having no idea how families survived this sort of thing.

"I don't know," he said. "We will probably have to go to a hotel until they repair our home."

"Can they really fix this, Dad?" Danny asked.

"I think so. Most of the damage is to the girls' room. The rest of the house just has smoke damage and can easily be fixed with sanding and painting."

That made me feel good, but where would we go until then?

One of the things I learned from this experience is that when hard times hit, good people step forward to help. Keith Mareno's dad, who was a fireman and saw this type of tragedy on a daily basis, invited Danny and me to stay at their home that evening. Kathy, Margaret, and Maureen stayed at the Wonaks' home, where Kathy's best friend Gail lived. They were a good Catholic family who lived the values of their faith.

Mom and Dad checked into the two-story Miami Motel at 90th Street and Cicero Avenue, making reservations for the rest of us to join them the next day. Before leaving for the evening, however, Mom and Dad went to St. Bede's Church. Dad knelt next to Mom in the first pew and thanked God for sparing his wife and daughter from the fire. Then he and Mom walked to the statue of the Virgin Mary on the west wall to light a candle, praying for the courage to get past the difficult time.

When I arrived at school the next morning, Miss Fleming asked me to step out into the hall.

"Is everything okay?" she asked, very concerned. "I am really sorry I wasn't able to tell you about the fire earlier, but I had to respect the wishes of your mother."

"It's okay," I said. "Everyone is okay, but the fire damaged one of our rooms pretty badly. My mom said we probably won't be able to go back into the house for about a week."

"Where will you stay?" she inquired. "I can talk with my parents. They may have some room," she added, indicating she lived with her mother and father.

"Thank you, Miss Fleming, I know my parents would appreciate that, but we are fine. We stayed with neighbors last night, but my dad said we will be staying at a motel for the next few days until the house is ready."

This was the really big news for the Ruane kids: staying at a motel. We had stayed at a motel only once before, during the summer of 1967, when we traveled to Wisconsin for a three-day vacation at Lake Geneva. That was the farthest and longest trip we had made away from South Kostner. All of us looked forward to our stay at the Miami Motel, located right across the street from a McDonald's. For five kids who never stayed at motels and loved McDonald's hamburgers, this was a dream scenario.

Over the next six days, we had a great time jumping on the motel beds and swimming in the pool. Plus we didn't even have to make our beds. It turned a bad situation into a good one for us. Plus, with McDonald's right across the street, Danny couldn't get enough of their hamburgers, fries, and chocolate shakes. Neither could the rest of us. This was living!

Mom and Dad had taken all of the clothes that weren't burned out of the house and brought them to a cleaners, the tab paid by Mr. Allstate. But all of the girls' clothes had been ruined in the fire, so Mom took the three of them to Goldblatt's department store at 79th and Cicero to purchase new wardrobes. Buying an entirely new wardrobe was a foreign experience for my three sisters, who normally would receive most of their clothes at their respective birthday parties or at Christmas.

Six days later, we checked out of the Miami Motel and drove back to 8355 South Kostner, just as the insurance inspector from the "good hands people" predicted. On this hot April afternoon, we pulled up in our blue 1967 Chevy to the sounds of pounding hammers and buzzing drills. They were working to turn our house back into the home we loved, maybe even better. On our front lawn sat a large blue metal garbage Dumpster filled with all kinds of burned and water-damaged debris. There was a lot of stuff that looked very familiar sitting on top of the pile of rubble. But all of a sudden it didn't feel like it belonged to us anymore. Now it was just junk, which was kind of sad.

Walking up the cleaned front porch stairs, it was reassuring to see the entrance fixed with a new screen door. Dad entered first with the six of us right behind him. It was amazing to see how much had been done to the house, just a week after the fire. The living room looked very different, with no furniture and the wooden floor exposed. The large mirror and all the pictures had been taken off the walls, which still were covered by smoke stains. The bad smell I had been hit with when I ran in the house the day of the fire lingered, but just barely.

Two Irish painters were applying gray primer to the living-room walls, making the black smears disappear with each stroke. A carpenter was in the girls' room with his apprentice reframing and rebuilding it. The kitchen and two bathrooms had been completed already, which allowed us to move back in. It was hard to believe those were the bathrooms that looked so horrible just a week before. Now they looked beautiful! The pink and white ceramic tiled floor of the girls' bathroom had been replaced and a large mirror had been placed on the wall behind the sink where a medicine cabinet used to be. The blue bathroom had been painted and cleaned, making it look like new. I thought it was too bad we couldn't just close the door and look at this nice clean bathroom from time to time. I knew it never would look that clean again, not with me and Danny trying to pee in that toilet at the same time each night, making a contest out of it to see who could finish first. To put it mildly, great shots we were not.

The kitchen looked incredible, like a commercial, with a cleaned and waxed tile floor and freshly painted walls, cabinets, and woodwork. Despite our love for McDonald's, it was good to see our gray-topped kitchen table and green foam-backed chairs again.

Over the next two weeks while they transformed the upper level of our family nest, we lived in the basement, sleeping on a pullout couch and two mattresses on the freshly cleaned gray cement floor. At least we could live in our home, albeit mostly downstairs, until they finished the work.

That bright sunny April day in 1968 will always be a vivid memory for me. It just shows how quickly and unexpectedly life can change. The fire inspector determined the fire was started by faulty wiring of the electrical outlet in the girls' bedroom. That wiring had been completed in 1957 when the house was built, yet for whatever reason, it sparked and set our home on fire ten years later.

How do you plan for that kind of devastation? How do you defend against it? I think the lesson is that no matter how hard we try to plan for the future and protect ourselves from harmful events, we really don't have total control of our lives. So when bad things happen, we just have to pray to God for the strength and patience to get through those tough times. Conversely, I believe we can't plan or count on good things happening in our lives, so on those good days that we do have I believe we have to pray to God and give thanks. On the day of the fire, I prayed for the strength and patience to get through that trying time, and I thanked God that Mom and Margaret weren't hurt.

In my mind, Margaret and Mom's escape remains a miraculous mystery that has weighed on my mind ever since. What woke up my little sister? Was it just luck? Maybe. Was it the crackling of the fire? Could be. Maybe the pop of the electrical outlet? I don't know. Personally, I believe in angels, and I wonder if one of those heavenly soldiers wasn't sitting there on the end of the bed watching Margaret sleep on the day of that fire. And when the sparks flew from the electrical outlet, setting the bed on fire, did the angel shake Margaret the same way she shook Mom to wake her up? I don't know. But I do know God spared their lives that day.

My sister is now a forty-year-old wife and mother. In 1989 she married Mike Sedlak and together they have two beautiful children. Her son, Brian, ten, and daughter, Marilyn, seven, may never know how important that April day is in their lives. But the truth is, they wouldn't be here if not for Providence.

Thank You again, God, for sparing my sister and mother that day.

Chapter Sixteen

THE SEMINARIANS

I was in sixth grade during the spring of 1969 when St. Bede's offered boys who thought they might be interested in the priesthood an opportunity to spend a weekend at a Catholic seminary in Holland, Michigan. The idea, I guess, was to let young men experience seminary life. This was not a popular camp. None of the boys were forming lines or beating down doors to get into this future priests' school. The three of us who signed up had mothers who wanted their sons to be priests.

Dan Lemmonier, the son of our sixth-grade teacher, and Phillip Barton, who was pretty well known among classmates as one really weird kid, were the only two seminarians I knew. Somehow I never understood Phillip's interest in the priesthood. His reputation in Mrs. Lemmonier's class was gained from two acts of craziness in December of 1968. I never had Phillip in my class before that year, so he may have established his wacky ways earlier.

It all began at lunch. Everything seemed normal, with the students filing up to the front of the room for their always semi-sour milk, then they munched away on peanut butter and jelly sandwiches That's when the fair-haired Phillip took center stage to grab his fifteen minutes of fame. Lunchtime was the only time the class was left unattended by Mrs. Lemmonier, who must have assumed we all would be too busy eating to get into trouble. Plus she needed to eat her lunch, preferably away from us, in the teachers' lounge.

When Phillip was ready to begin his show, he cleared his throat to draw all eyes to him. He slowly reached into his desk to produce a small round container of Elmer's paste. As he brought it out of his desk, he glanced around to make sure everyone still was watching. They were. No matter, he wasn't going to take any chances. He cleared his throat loudly again. All he needed was a spotlight and a drum roll. Slowly, he unscrewed the top of the paste.

"What's he doing?" the whispers spread around the room. "What's he doing?"

No one in the classroom had any idea what this strange kid was about to do, but somehow everyone knew this would be something to watch.

"He's a weird kid, what's he doing?" said the bright and beautiful Eileen McGriff, loud enough for most to hear.

Phillip plunged the orange stick attached to the cap into the paste and scooped up a hunk of thick white goop that would hold together a dozen construction paper art projects.

"Is he going to do an art project?" the whispers continued. "That's a lot of paste. What's he doing?"

But no, this paste was not destined to do its duty in an art class. Phillip held up the stick of paste high, so all could see.

"What's he doing?" blurted out Colleen Bannon, her long brown ponytail flailing back and forth over her shoulder, and she turned her head quickly, hoping not to miss a minute of the show.

"I don't know!" said her best friend, Anita Carick, looking very mature with her dark brown hair set in the Toni-style look of the day. "He's weird!"

Phillip held the stick of paste high, opened his mouth wide, and plunged the stick of goop deep into it. When he pulled it from his sealed lips, the stick was clean and orange. As faces around him cringed and the weak gasped, Phillip knew he had a hit show on his hands. Eileen covered her eyes with her hands, then peaked through her fingers. She knew Phillip wasn't done. He slowly looked around the room, his mouth full of Elmer's gunk. At just the right moment, he began chewing. He knew his audience would appreciate the chewing.

"What's wrong with you, Phillip?" Anita yelled.

"You are weird!" Colleen shouted. Both girls rose quickly from their desks and ran toward the door.

"We're telling Mrs. Lemmonier, you weirdo!"

They stopped. What was this boy going to do next? They were torn between disgust and curiosity as they both stood next to each other at the classroom door with hands over mouths and wide eyes.

Phillip's face froze. He stood up and looked Anita and the ponytailed Colleen in the eyes and slowly raised both hands in the air, forming a fist with each hand.

Then he looked around the room. All eyes were on Phillip. In one swift movement, he brought down his fists like a muscleman flexing and gulped so loudly he could be heard in the next classroom.

Ah, the gulp was quite a touch! It sent Anita and Colleen into a frenzy as they ran out the door screaming. Eileen laid her head on her desk, not looking very well, while nearly every boy stood and cheered, and the girls yelled insults at the paste-eating, fair-haired boy who sat down with a smile of great accomplishment. His place in our collective memory was secure, but in my eyes he later topped that performance.

It was only a few weeks later, and Phillip couldn't let the buzz fade. But what to do next? Paste again? No. They'd seen that piece of theater. And how could he ever top such a great performance?

He had to wait for the right opportunity, the right moment. And it came one day when Mrs. Lemmonier, a round-faced, light-brown-haired, middle-aged woman who exuded kindness and care, lost her patience during history class. Too many kids were talking and not paying attention, even after several high-pitched appeals from her.

"Okay, if you are not going to listen and learn, just go ahead and do what you want for the next hour. I don't care!" she said disgustedly as she took out a stack of papers to grade.

As the entire class sat there stunned, Phillip calmly stood up, grabbed his spiral-bound notepad, and walked to the front of the class, where the wastepaper basket stood.

He looked across the class, then reached into his notepad and ripped out a sheet of paper. He held it up high for all to see. All eyes were once again on Phillip. He loved the spotlight, the attention.

"What's he going to do?" the whispers began.

"Is he going to eat that too?" Colleen asked.

"He can't eat that," said Anita. "And if he does, at least it's not paste."

Phillip crumpled the paper with one hand and tossed it into the wastepaper basket. He tore out another page with his right hand, held it high, crumpled it, and threw it away. And another page, crumpled, tossed. Again and again he tore, crumpled, and tossed. Mrs. Lemmonier, who sat only ten feet away, watching this spectacle of absolute zaniness, stood up from her desk.

"Phillip, what in God's name are you doing?" asked the kindhearted teacher, who was completely baffled by this exhibition of lunacy.

"Well, you said do whatever you want, so I thought I'd just stand up here and throw paper away."

Half the class, mostly boys, burst out in laughter, while the other half (mostly girls) didn't appreciate his humor at all. Mrs. Lemmonier didn't know what to make of this nutcase of a sixth-grader.

"He's weird, Mrs. Lemmonier," Colleen yelled.

"Yeah, just a weirdo," Anita said.

"Phillip, sit down this instant," Mrs. Lemmonier commanded. "I want to see you after school. We are going to the principal's office, and I think your parents need to be made aware of your activities here over the past few weeks."

Phillip sat back in his seat with that smile of great accomplishment once again. The principal's office! He had made it big. The entire school would be talking about him, and he knew it. Obviously, being tagged a lunkhead, weirdo, nutcase, or moron didn't seem to bother him at all. He was on the map, and that's all that mattered.

When spring rolled around and I found out Mrs. Lemmonier's son, Dan, and the infamous Phillip were the only two other boys from the school going to the seminary camp, I knew Dan was the fellow I would be hanging around with over the weekend.

My mother met me in the St. Bede's parking lot outside the gymnasium that Friday after school. She brought clothes for two days, some snacks for the bus ride, and ten dollars in spending money. She was letting me use the same suitcase my dad had used when he came to America, so it had great significance.

"Now you don't have to be afraid while you're there, Johnny," she said, giving me a bear hug of reassurance that I needed. "I want you to call each day. And if you get homesick, just call again. I know this is a big step for you, but I know you can handle it."

"Thanks, Mom," I said, and I felt the tears streaming down my cheeks. "I'll be fine, Mom."

My mom kissed me goodbye and I ducked my head down to wipe my face dry, then walked up the steps of the Greyhound bus. As I reached the top step, I could see the faces of the other boys. I didn't recognize any of them, but some looked like they had just wiped their faces dry as well. As I walked down the middle aisle, I spotted Phillip in the back of the bus—where else?

"John, back here!" he called out to me. Just then I felt a hand on my right arm. I looked over to see Dan Lemmonier leaning over from his window seat to grab my attention. "John, right here," Dan whispered, saving the day for me as I quickly ducked into the seat next to him.

Dan and I were determined to have a great time during the two-hour bus ride to Holland, playing games like hang the butcher and tic-tac-toe. We also were determined not to let Phillip spoil it for us. Neither one of us had ever been to Michigan, so all of the landscape was new to us. Once we got on the Calumet Expressway, it seemed like all we saw for a good hour were big old smelly factories. The air was horrible, and it got worse once we passed what we learned was a garbage dump.

"My eyes are burning!" Dan yelped. "What is that?"

"That smells like my feet when I take my shoes off," a familiar voice in the seat behind us said. We looked back only to see Phillip laughing in appreciation of his own gross sense of humor.

Our heavyset, balding bus driver must have heard him, as he immediately took on the responsibility of becoming our private sightseeing guide.

"As we move down the Calumet Expressway, you will notice to your left a very large hill with several dump trucks on top of it," he announced loudly, so all could hear. "Well, that's not a hill and those aren't dump trucks. That is a very large dirt mound of garbage, and those are garbage trucks dumping their day's collection into the newest hole. At this time some of you may notice a very strong stench."

Phillip jumped up and shouted, "Yeah, that's from my feet!" The boys on the bus burst out laughing. Phillip had found an audience.

The bus driver wasn't about to be upstaged.

"This is coming directly from the garbage dump," he said, not pausing for the reaction from Phillip's audience. "Having once been a garbageman, I can tell you that the odor will not bother you after about two or three years."

He laughed, thinking himself a big crackup.

"That stench is from my feet!" Phillip blurted, hoping to milk his joke for one more laugh. Not this time. Instead fingers were being pointed at him and boys began whispering to each other about the weird kid yelling out about his smelly feet. Phillip crumpled back down into his seat.

As we drove through Gary, Indiana, a city filled with steel mills spewing pollution, we were amazed at how much smoke was being sent into the sky above, which was completely gray. I never had smelled anything so putrid in my life, including all of the times I had to pick up after my dog Sparky. Somehow, the site of Gary made it clear that I wasn't on South Kostner anymore. I was definitely away from home. Dan and I tried to focus on our game of hang the butcher while sharing stories about our favorite episodes of *The Andy Griffith Show*.

"You may notice a very strong smell," our all-too-witty bus driver announced.

"And don't say it's your feet again, you nerd," a rather burly boy in the front of the bus said, looking directly at Phillip behind us. A bully was going to priest camp. That was nice.

The bus driver continued his description of our tour. "What you are experiencing now is the exhaust being strewn into the atmosphere by the many steel mills here. Unlike the garbage, getting accustomed to the smell of the steel mills, I am told, takes many years to accept. It's lucky for you kids, you don't live anywhere around here and probably won't ever have to work in a steel mill—I hope."

Phillip popped up again. He couldn't let this opportunity slip away. He was going to try new material.

"Hey, if you think this smells bad, try coming into our bathroom after my dad has just finished taking a crap!"

He got his laugh. But the fingers were pointing and the whispers followed.

The bully wasn't finished either. "Hey, sit down, freak!" he ordered Phillip.

"I'm sorry," Phillip said. "Did I offend you because your bathroom actually smells worse than my father's? Or just because you are just so full of shit!"

I had never actually seen or heard about a bus screeching to a halt until that moment. It was quite an experience being jolted forward in my seat. But the bus driver, although a lover of fun and comic moments, knew fighting words when he heard them. Dan and I both jumped up to get between the bully and Phillip. I pushed Phillip back in his seat. Four or five of the other boys worked on the bully until the bus driver had parked the vehicle alongside the road and sat the punk down.

"May I remind all of you that this bus is taking you to a seminary, where you are to learn how to become priests," the bus driver said quite angrily. "Last time I checked, priests don't swear, and they are taught to turn the other cheek. Now, any more of this, and I will report both of you when we arrive."

That shut them up for the remainder of the trip. Both boys were embarrassed, and when I peeked back at Phillip, he was crying. This kid sure hit a lot of highs and lows.

We finally made it out of Gary and were back on Interstate 94 over the Michigan border. This state seemed so different, with vineyards along the highway and lots of green trees. It was a much prettier picture of nature than what we had witnessed in Illinois and Indiana. We found ourselves relaxed and we fell asleep, only to be awakened by the bus driver shouting, "Okay, you bunch of sleepyheads, let's go; you are here."

As I walked off the bus, my stomach began feeling queasy. I really wanted to go home. They led us into the dormitory and showed us the beds where we would sleep. It was organized much like an army barracks, with ten beds lined up on each side of a wall. We were directed to take a bed, place our bags in the gray metal footlocker, and get situated.

As slump-shouldered Phillip walked past me, I grabbed him by the arm. "Hey, why don't you grab the bunk next to me?" I asked him. He looked up and smiled as if he had just found his first friend in the world. "Thanks," he said, and he began unpacking his bag.

After we had all unpacked, Phil, Dan, and I went down to the recreation room, which consisted of two Ping-Pong tables and a vending machine packed with an assortment of candy and snacks. This was popular, as each of the kids looked to rid themselves of their homesickness with a Snickers, Milky Way, or Baby Ruth candy bar.

After a few games of table tennis, we were ordered into the auditorium. This was not a large room, but it easily accommodated the sixty or so kids at the camp. A middle-aged priest with graying hair and black-framed glasses entered from the wing and walked to the microphone at center stage. He took a moment to view his audience.

"I want to welcome all of you here today," he said, looking around the room at all of the new faces. "Becoming a priest is a very special commitment for any young man. We hope to show you what life is like in the seminary and try to give you a greater understanding of the religious responsibility you would be blessed with if you felt the calling to become a priest. The calling doesn't come to all of you, but you are here today, so there is a reason you have taken this first step. If your parents have made you come here, then you will have to look into your heart and find out if this is the life for you. If you have decided to come here of your own accord, then perhaps you are destined to become a priest. How many of you have come here today because you personally feel you may have the calling?"

Of the sixty boys in that auditorium, only one raised his hand. That's right, it was Phillip, smiling from ear to ear. I wondered if I had boosted his self-confidence at the wrong time.

"Son, would you stand up and tell us your name?"

As he stood, the smile dropped to a frown, as he realized this was not a good ploy to grab the attention of the class. This wasn't Mrs. Lemmonier's class he was entertaining. He was being addressed by a serious priest running a seminary, looking for real candidates for the priesthood.

"My name is Phillip Barton and I did come here of my own free will. Although my mother did say that if I attended this seminary camp, I no longer would be grounded for standing up and eating a jar of paste during lunch in Mrs. Lemmonier's class."

A huge laugh exploded. Phillip had done it again. His big smile returned. He was the life of the party. But the finger-pointing and whispers followed. Nevertheless, he was going to stay on his roll, or so he thought. "You see, during lunch one day . . ."

"Phillip!" yelled the priest. The boy froze. "Do you think becoming a priest is a joke?"

"No sir."

"Well then, why are you trying to turn this into a comedy club? Sit down!"

He sat down quickly. I watched his face. The tears came pouring down his cheeks. Phillip took a chance and got burned. I was guessing the priesthood was going to be crossed off of his career list that day.

"When Jesus called on His Apostles to join Him, He told them to leave everything behind and follow Him. And they did. They left their families, left behind anything they may have owned to follow Jesus. They depended on the charity of others to survive, while they traveled throughout the area listening and watching Jesus speak, heal the sick, help those who were lost and finally be crucified and die on the cross for all of our sins. Jesus made the ultimate sacrifice for us.

"To make the decision to follow the tradition of the Apostles—leave your families and preach the word of God—is a major decision in any man's life. You cannot enter this vocation thinking, I will give it a few years and if it doesn't work out, I'll try something else.

"To become a priest, you must know in your heart that this is the only life's choice for you. In your mind, there is no option. Unless or until you feel that calling, you won't know if the priesthood is your future. But we are introducing you to the training, so you can see and feel what it is like for those who have felt the calling. Perhaps this will inspire some of you. Perhaps it will dissuade others. Either way, we hope to help you understand the commitment a seminarian makes and why that decision is a serious, lifelong commitment. Do you understand that, Phillip?"

"Yes sir," he whimpered.

Despite the public humiliation Phillip had suffered, Dan and I both felt a loyalty to our parish brethren, and we escorted him to the cafeteria where we snarfed down a dinner of hamburgers, hot dogs, and potato chips. As I sat there eating with Dan and Phillip at my table, I knew bedtime would be the most difficult part of the day. And I was right. I had never cried myself to sleep until that day in the seminary. All I kept thinking was how badly I wanted to be home in my own bed, safe and sound on South Kostner Avenue with my mom and dad there. But then I started to think about what the priest had talked about that night. I wondered how difficult that must have been for those twelve Apostles to leave everything behind and follow Jesus. They really couldn't have known back then just how special Jesus would become in history. Or maybe they did know. Maybe they were certain and that's why they were able to drop everything and follow Him. I wondered if I would ever have that kind of courage, because there was no doubt in my mind that those Apostles had to be very courageous to make that commitment. And maybe that was the point the priest was trying to make that evening. Sure he had made Phillip cry, but he was right. Making that big a decision with a life is nothing to joke about—not even for the paste-eating sixth-graders of the world starving for the attention of their peers.

Over the next two days, we attended Mass and listened to seminarians talk about when they felt the calling and what that experience was like for them.

"I was probably like a lot of you here," said one big and tall seminarian who looked more like a linebacker than a priest. "You go along having fun with your friends, playing sports, not really certain what you will do with your life. But one Sunday during my junior year in high school, I sat at Mass and listened to our pastor, Father O'Malley, talk about how important it is to lead by example. He said not everyone tries to live their lives as good Catholics, good Christians. Many people go the opposite way. And all of you will feel those pressures. We all do. But as my pastor said, the key is to stay strong in your beliefs and stay determined to be good and do good. Some will tease you for this, make fun of you. But remember, they spit on Jesus, put a crown of thorns on His head and laughed at Him as He carried His cross. So let those who will laugh, laugh. Turn the other cheek and give them a second chance. If they slap that cheek as well, do as Jesus said: Kick the dust from your sandals and move on.

"At that moment, I felt my spine tingling all the way up my back to my head. I was filled with the Holy Spirit, and I knew it. That is the moment when I knew I would become a priest. There was no question for me from then on. I had been impressed by some of my football coaches and teachers growing up, but this Father O'Malley had inspired me more than any other person in my life.

"That was my experience. It may happen for you in a completely different way. It may never happen for you. Maybe you will be inspired in a different direction. Perhaps you will be inspired to become a teacher or coach. Maybe you will meet a wonderful girl, get married, and have children. Your life is in front of you today and the path you take in life will come to you at some point. But we are here this weekend to show you the life we have chosen in the event any of you are inspired to follow us."

Phillip jumped up. "I am going to become a priest. I just felt my spine tingling when you were talking."

No one laughed this time. No fingers were being pointed or whispers shared. I think perhaps a few other boys may have felt inspired and believed Phillip was representing their feelings. I looked around at the boys in the auditorium. More than a few sat wide-eyed, their faces flush with the energy of the moment, but they didn't stand to proclaim their career destination.

The next day, the final full day, the priest and seminarians took us down to the beach along Lake Michigan. This was very different from the beaches along the lake in Chicago. The beach was fairly empty, with thick woods behind it. Phil, Dan, and I swam and played catch with a baseball along the beach. This was the most fun I had at the camp since arriving. I had a good arm and could throw the ball fast and far, which always felt so good. That was coming through loud and clear. I loved it, every second of it. As I threw the ball, I knew this is what I loved to do in life. And maybe for me, like the priest said, there is no option. You just know.

That final evening at the camp, we played table tennis, ate more candy bars, and cried ourselves to sleep one more time. I never would complain about my bedroom at home again.

When I awoke, I sat up in my bed and realized that my trip to Holland was a success. I learned that my inspiration in life was toward sports, not the priesthood. I had found a definite direction. As we rode home, I barely noticed the beauty of the Michigan landscape or the stench of the Gary steel mills. I thought about the life ahead of me and how lucky I was to have gone on a trip that helped me grow up a little bit at the age of twelve. I would have to break it to my mother at just the right moment. Her first son definitely was not headed toward the priesthood, so she would have to depend on her second son, Danny.

And Phillip? He stopped acting like a clown after that day. I really think he was inspired to become a priest. Dan? He went on to become an actor, musician, and storyteller—truly a great talent. Perhaps his greatest claim to fame came during the Chicago Bulls championship years, when he was seen on the home basketball court and known as Benny the Bull.

Chapter Seventeen

THE GOOD
PEOPLE

I t seems difficult to understand, but tragedy seems to bring the best out of good people. How often have there been snowstorms, where cars get stuck, and the next thing you know there are two guys at the back bumper pushing, two guys who may never have met that driver before, or maybe even exchanged hellos. Or how about when a tornado hits a town, many of those who haven't been affected step forward to help. Why? Because they can help and it is in their hearts to do so.

In our case, we were five kids and two parents forced from our home for seven days in April of 1968 due to a fire. And the good people noticed our situation and offered to help to buffer the pain of this time.

With no kitchen available to us during our stay at the Miami Motel and McDonald's remaining the strong preference among all five Ruane kids, my parents were eager to take any dinner invitations for their children. Despite how much we were enjoying the fare at the Golden Arches, Mom and Dad would have preferred us eating healthier food. So when the good people called to extend a dinner invitation, Mom and Dad couldn't say "yes" fast enough.

Five days after the fire, the Markey family invited me over to have dinner at their home. I went to school with John Markey, a slim kid with a big Dudley Do-Right smile. I had played with him on the same baseball team, the White Sox, a few years earlier, and his dad was the coach.

Outside of baseball, I really never spent much time with John. Sure, I saw him at school, but he wasn't one of the kids I hung around with regularly, like Marty, Mike, or Eddie. But John was a good kid who came from a good family. When his parents heard about our misfortune, they offered to help by having me over for dinner.

Mrs. Markey was busy in the kitchen making dinner, while John and I sat in the living room trading baseball cards. John's mom looked like June Lockhart of the *Lassie* show; she didn't seem to wear much makeup and dressed in casual slacks and a blouse.

While I sat in the Markeys' living room trading Tiger's first baseman Norm Cash to John for the Cardinals' ace Bob Gibson, Mr. Markey sat in his recliner drinking a can of Hamms beer while watching the Cubs game. He was probably in his early forties, medium build, with a bit of a paunch. He had brown hair combed back to cover his balding top and a fairly narrow face with a prominent nose and ears. Like many dads, he wore casual slacks and a T-shirt around the house. It was funny to see my former coach in his own home environment. Somehow when he was my coach, he was bigger than life—the guy in charge. Now he was John's dad sitting there, drinking beer and yelling at Cubs announcer Jack Brickhouse.

"Ah shutup, Brickhead, you dummy," he shouted at the TV set. It seemed he would stand up every few minutes to adjust the rabbit ears antenna that rested on the top of the set, so he could get a better picture. These were the days when it was necessary to stand up and walk over to a television set to turn the channel or adjust the sound. No clickers back then. And there were only eight channels, not counting PBS, which showed a bunch of stupid educational shows about which no respectable kid I knew cared.

Like every good White Sox fan, I hated the Cubs. In 1968 they had a very good team, with Ernie Banks, Ron Santo, Billy Williams, Glenn Beckert, Don Kessinger, and Randy Hundley. It was enough to make a diehard Sox fan sick.

I couldn't understand why Mr. Markey would turn on the game. I mean, he did live on the South Side of Chicago, where everyone is supposed to be a White Sox fan. I wasn't about to say anything, though, because this was the family that was nice enough to invite me over for dinner. If I had expressed my views, I might not see the kitchen table that evening.

And this was one dinner I wanted to eat, because up until then, I had never eaten lasagna. When I had arrived that afternoon and Mrs. Markey asked me if I liked lasagna, I had no idea what she was talking about. They seemed surprised, thinking everyone must have had lasagna once. Not me.

"Okay, Boog Powell for Carl Yastrzemski," John offered to me, thinking I would give up the second best outfielder in Boston Red Sox history for the overweight Baltimore first baseman, who couldn't run and struck out too much. Not likely.

"Okay, I'll make that trade," I said, watching John's eyes widen. "As soon as you trade me your entire White Sox collection of Pete Ward, Gary Peters, and Tommy John cards for one Fergie Jenkins."

John burst out laughing.

"Fergie Jenkins, he's a good player, John," Mr. Markey said, identifying himself as an even bigger North Side traitor. "I wish he was pitching today, because Ken Holtzman can't throw a strike for his life."

Just then Mrs. Markey's voice was heard from the kitchen, announcing, "Dinner is ready!" John and I immediately stood up and walked into her bright blue kitchen. There was a small square wooden table to the left of the kitchen counter, where Mrs. Markey was busy working. The table was nicely set with silverware, napkins, and eight-ounce green-tinted glasses. John's younger brother, Jimmy, was already seated at the table, drawing red crayon doodles on one of the napkins.

"John, you sit over here next to my John," Mrs. Markey instructed me.

"Go ahead and pour everyone a glass of milk," she directed her son.

With only four in their family, this felt so much smaller than the seven-person dinner environment I was accustomed to at home.

As John was pouring the milk, Mr. Markey entered the kitchen holding his Hamms. "Stinkin' Cubs! They're blowing it again," he informed his wife, who looked like she couldn't care any less. I wondered if she was a Sox fan or just didn't care about baseball. Mr. Markey took the last swig from his blue and white can, crushed it in his right hand, and threw it in the garbage can next to the refrigerator.

"Brickhouse drives me nuts," he continued telling his wife as he sat down at the head of the table. "His entire contribution to the game is saying 'Hey, hey!' and 'Wee!' every time Ernie Banks hits a home run. That's it. 'Wee' and 'Hey, hey.' That's his value to the Cubs broadcasts. He must go home to his wife at night and say 'I did a great job announcing the Cubs game today. Said three hey, heys! and two wees!'

"I wish they would just let Lloyd Pettit announce the games and tell Brickhouse to get lost."

"Brickhouse stinks, Dad!" Jimmy said, looking for his father's approval.

"That's right, Jimmy, he's horrible. Right, dear?" he directed to his wife.

"Right," said Mrs. Markey, who I am certain had no idea what her husband was talking about as she brought over a large square metal pan of something that had white cheese melted over red sauce.

"Here is the lasagna," she said, laying it in front of Mr. Markey, who still wasn't quite finished explaining the Cubs' woes to his uninterested wife.

"Kessinger has a 3–1 count and the pitcher is having trouble throwing strikes. All he has to do is take a pitch. One pitch! But no, not Kessinger. Struck out. Stinkin' bum!"

"Kessinger can't hit, Dad," chimed Jimmy, smiling at the recognition he was receiving.

"That's right, Jimmy, especially with men on base," his father agreed.

I thought about bringing up the fact that Mr. Markey and his son were living on the South Side of Chicago and were rooting for the wrong team, but I thought it better just to keep my mouth shut—at least until dinner was over.

Mrs. Markey cut the lasagna and placed a good-sized square piece on my plate. "My John says you have never had lasagna before," she said, bumping against me as she placed it on my plate.

"No, this will be my first time," I replied, quickly leaning to my right to give her plenty of room. Once everyone had been served a generous piece of lasagna, Mrs. Markey led us in prayer.

"Bless us, O Lord, and these Thy gifts which we are about to receive from Thy bounty through Christ our Lord."

"Amen," we all said, and Mr. Markey added, "And please help the Cubs start winning again."

"Amen," said Jimmy, obviously influenced the wrong way by his father. They would get no amen out of me for that portion of the prayer.

Mr. Markey wasn't done.

"And if you see Your way to helping the front office get rid of Brickhouse, that would answer many of my prayers."

"Amen," Jimmy said again. "Please God, fire Brickhead."

I noticed my friend John didn't say anything. And I knew why. He was a true Sox fan like me. He knew there was no helping his father.

I cut the lasagna, which took some work because it was so thick. Besides the pasta, it was a mixture of ricotta cheese, ground beef, and red sauce held together by large flat sheets of pasta.

I took my first bite, and *wow*!

This was good.

I mean, really good!

I looked up at Mrs. Markey, who could see I really liked it. She was smiling.

"Like it?" she asked me.

"Boy, this is great, Mrs. Markey," I said. "Really good!"

"Yeah, it's very good, honey," Mr. Markey said. "I wish the Cubs were as good as your lasagna. Brickhead! I'll never watch him again. Makes me mad."

"Makes me mad too, Dad," Jimmy blurted.

"That's right, Jimmy, he makes everyone mad," Mr. Cub fan said.

I ate bite after bite and could not get over its flavor. The wonderful blend of the cheese, meat, and sauce evolved into one very special taste. I couldn't get enough of it.

"Would you like another piece?" John asked.

"Is it okay?" I said.

"Sure," his mother said as she cut me another piece.

After finishing the meal that evening, John and I helped his mother clear the table. As I walked the dirty plates over to the sink, I thought the time had come to ask the question. Mr. Markey had just gotten up to get another can of Hamms from the refrigerator. He snapped open the pop-top can and took a rather large swig.

"Mr. Markey, can I ask you a question?" I asked, drawing the attention of not only Mr. Markey but John and his mother as well.

"Sure, John, anything," he said, turning in his chair to face me.

"I always thought that everyone on the South Side of Chicago was supposed to be a White Sox fan, but you are a Cubs fan," I said, going back to the table to collect the dirty glasses. "Why is that?"

A look of concern crossed my friend John's face.

Mr. Markey took another swig, cleared his throat, and smiled.

"Well, there is a simple explanation for that, John, and I am glad you asked," he said, standing to address his audience. "You see, I was raised a Cubs fan. My father was a Cubs fan, so naturally I too became a Cubs fan. When we moved into this neighborhood, I wasn't going to change my loyalty, despite the pleas of my wife and oldest boy."

"John is a big White Sox fan," I interrupted.

"Yes, I know," he responded, looking a bit disappointed. "I blame myself for that. John has watched me yell at Brickhouse on the TV for so long that I think it turned him against the Cubs."

"Everyone I know is a White Sox fan," John energetically piped into the conversation.

"Morons, all of them," his father retaliated. "Don't know what they are doing. They live out here on the South Side, downwind of the Stockyards, I'm sure their brains have been saturated with the stench and they can't think straight."

"Yeah, they have crap for brains, Dad," Jimmy said, laughing to himself.

"That's right, crap for brains, Jimmy," Mr. Markey agreed. "I learned from my mistake with John and brought Jimmy up the right way, letting him know immediately that my disgust for Jack Brickhouse doesn't reflect on the team. Plus they are winning this year, which never happens. Right, Jimmy?"

"Right, Dad, Cubs stink," the smiling young Cubs fan said.

"But we love them, right, Son?"

"That's right, Dad, love 'em," the little Markey chirped. "And hate Brickhead."

"Thatta boy, Jimmy." His proud father smiled. "See, Jimmy's got his head on straight. Smart kid."

I thanked John's mother for a very nice meal, maybe the best I had ever eaten, and promised myself I would only revisit their home when a Cubs losing streak coincided with a White Sox winning streak. That seemed to occur fairly often in September of 1969, as the Cubs fell apart and dropped out of a pennant race they thought they had in the bag.

My dinner with the Markeys was an interesting experience, providing insight into other people's lives, and it absolutely made me appreciate and cherish my time at home with my own family. It also made me feel real good about being a White Sox fan.

Chapter Eighteen

CONFIRMATION OF FAITH

Confirmation day is a very important and special day for every Catholic, as they become "soldiers of Christ." It is the day, in my mind, when I became mature in my faith. I was old enough to say "Yes, I do believe in one God, the Father Almighty, Maker of Heaven and Earth. I do believe in Jesus Christ the Most High. I do believe in one holy Catholic and Apostolic Church."

These are important declarations indeed.

When I was in second grade preparing for my First Holy Communion and the nuns told us what to say, no one gave it a second thought. The nuns told us what to believe and how to say it, so we did. But as a sixth-grader, we were old enough to start thinking for ourselves. That is why I think this is such an important day in the lives of Catholic youths.

Someone could argue a sixth-grader would never tell his mother or father he didn't believe in the declarations of the Nicene Creed and wasn't going to participate in the Confirmation. That's probably true. But I never heard any of my classmates rejecting the ceremony or commitment to the language of the declarations. As I prepared for Confirmation, I knew in my heart that I did believe.

The Church has a tradition in which each Confirmation candidate must select a sponsor. This is a person who would stand with the prospective soldier through the process. We were told it should be someone who is a good Catholic role model: a leader, a person to whom we looked up.

A good number of my friends chose relatives—aunts, uncles, older brothers. The only two relatives I had in the area never attended Mass, so they weren't a consideration. No, for me, there were only two choices. It would either be Johnny Mackey or Mark Janek, two older boys I admired. Both had been altar boys. I thought Johnny would be the best choice because his family seemed especially devout. His father was a member of the Pilgrim Virgin, the Catholic organization that brought the statue of the Blessed Virgin Mary into homes where friends and neighbors could honor Mary by praying together as a community for one week.

Johnny was the older brother of Tommy Mackey, one of my best friends when I was younger. Johnny and Tommy looked like brothers, both skinny boys and about the same height. Hanging around with the Mackey boys was always a hoot because of their older brother–younger brother "fight until you give" relationship. It seemed like Tommy and Johnny used to go at it all the time when I was at their house. Those two would get into fights for no reason at all. We would be sitting in their bedroom on a Saturday afternoon watching a college football game while their mother was in the living room, listening to the soundtrack from *West Side Story,* when a scene like this would occur:

Tommy and I would be talking about our favorite lunch selections when he would say something like, "My favorite sandwich is peanut butter and jelly."

"No, it's not!" Johnny interrupted.

"Yes, it is," Tommy said, standing up and getting right in his brother's face.

"Prove it!" Johnny said, pushing his brother.

"Make me!" Tommy said, pushing him back.

And the fight was on, even though neither one of them ever got hurt. Johnny would let his younger brother challenge him, but he never would let it get past a wrestling match. Their poor mild diminutive mother must have felt like Maria trying to stop the fight between the Sharks and Jets. She would come into the bedroom and plead with them, but she always had to rely on the magic words to stop it.

"Wait until your father gets home," she would say, standing at the entrance to their bedroom with her arms folded. "You'll be punished."

It didn't matter if they stopped right then and there, they would get punished anyway. But they always stopped, hoping their promise to never fight again would win their mother's sympathy and a stay of execution from their father. Their mother knew better. Five minutes later the fight was on again, and she was back at the doorway pronouncing "real trouble when your father gets home." I just sat there dumbfounded.

The Mackeys' father was typical of that era in that he believed in corporal punishment. At their home, a curtain rod was the tool of punishment against their respective bottoms for any breach of good behavior.

This became a topic of discussion one hot day during the summer of 1964 at the prairie next to the Mackeys' house where we were building a fort. Three of the Janek boys along with the four McGrady brothers were with us, nailing away at odd-sized scrap sheets of plywood when the subject came up. It was amazing for me to hear about the various punishment devices. Sure, the Mackey boys were given the curtain rod, but the McGradys' dad had an even more effective tool, a wide paddle that covered more rumpage and thus inflicted pain to a larger area. The Janeks' dad preferred a belt, which was probably one of the most popular choices of the day. It was quick, accessible, and painful.

Regardless of the severe punishment, these brothers never stopped battling each other and ended up on the wrong end of a curtain rod, paddle, or belt several times a week.

Both the Janeks and McGradys had four boys in their families. Any time I went over to either of their homes, there always seemed to be a boxing, wrestling, or shouting match going on. Unlike the Mackey boys, the McGrady brothers threw real punches at each other, which I found shocking. They would hit each other hard across the face and actually hurt each other. Any kid who showed up at their door to call them out to play learned to stay out of the way and let them kill each other. Whoever survived would be available to play that day.

Building that fort in the summer of '64 brought the brothers closer together because everyone was working as a team. The prairie next to the Mackeys' home, a lot full of weeds, grass, and dirt, was the last vacant one left on their block. We all knew that a house would be coming someday, but for the time being it was our playground.

Johnny Mackey and Mark Janek were like the foremen, our leaders directing us in the construction of this very important fort that, we hoped, one day would become our clubhouse.

"Get those two-by-fours and nail them together in a square," Johnny said, trying to form a base for the fort. "We should be able to finish the base and supports today. We'll start on the clubhouse tomorrow."

"We will need a lot more wood for that," said Mark, who was helping Terry and Pat McGrady hammer the nails into the wood of the base.

"We'll get it tonight," Johnny said.

As the sun was setting later that afternoon, a group of us walked over to a building site near the Mackeys' home. The real construction workers were already gone for the day. We needed enough light to see but, hopefully, not be seen. A huge private cop named Amos was responsible for watching this new building site at night. Amos scared the living daylights out of all of us. Just hearing his name struck fear into us.

Tommy, Johnny, Mark, and I decided we were going to get as much scrap lumber as possible to build the walls of the clubhouse. The pieces we took would be the ones the workers threw away.

The four of us nonchalantly walked north down the sidewalk on Kolin Avenue in front of John Crerar School, perusing the two bilevel homes being built right across the street. We all looked up and down 85th Street and then Kolin to see if any cars were coming, especially Amos's blue and white Cadillac resplendent with whitewalled tires.

"It's clear, let's go," said Johnny, our leader on this expedition because he was the oldest in the group. The four of us darted across the street, jumped over the piles of debris in front of the house, then disappeared into the framed wooden structure.

"Hey, I got a bunch of scrap lumber down here," yelled Mark, who quickly found his way to the basement.

"I have sawed plywood sheets," said Tommy, whispering far too loud to pass for a whisper.

"Here's a spilled box of nails," I said, seeing a completely untouched red carton of nails scattered all over the floor near the kitchen area.

"Just take the ones that are out of the box," Johnny said.

"Are you sure?" I asked, wondering if they qualified as garbage.

"Just pick 'em up," Johnny ordered. "I guarantee you they'll sweep those nails up and throw them away. We might as well use them."

I kneeled down and started stuffing them into the pockets of my blue jeans.

And that's when it happened. We heard the motor, then the car's squeaky brakes bringing a vehicle to a halt in front of the house. The four of us froze. We all could see each other in the dim light. Mark was still downstairs, I was in the front with Johnny, and Tommy was near the steps leading to the basement. Johnny tiptoed toward the front of the house and stopped dead in his tracks. We heard a car door slam.

"It's Amos!" yelled Johnny, not even trying to whisper. My heart felt like it shot up through my throat and my head started buzzing. I looked at Johnny and we both ran fast toward those basement steps with the sound of our feet hitting the plywood echoing off the walls. I could see Mark going out the back door with Tommy right behind him.

That's when I heard that deep heavy voice: "You damn kids are in trouble!"

It was Amos.

I ran down the steps as fast as I could. Johnny wasn't going to waste time going down the stairs. He ran and jumped from the kitchen through the opening into the basement and fell hard on his right leg just a few feet from me as I reached the landing. I quickly ran over to help him up.

"Go, get out of here!" he ordered me. "I'm all right."

I didn't listen and grabbed his arm to help him up. He limped in front of me toward the back exit. As we reached the door, I could see the big dirt hill behind the house. We were home free. Then I saw Tommy and Mark standing in the alley motioning with their arms, indicating to get down. They were trying to mouth something that I couldn't make out.

Then they yelled, "Look out, Amos!"

They both ran off fast. Then we saw him. The tall heavy black man came running around the back of the house just as we started up the steps.

"Get over here, you two," he yelled, speeding toward us.

I have run fast in my life but never as fast as I did that night. Johnny and I both turned at the same time and shot back into the house, up the stairs and out the front door. We bolted across Kolin, turning right toward Johnny's house. As we reached the cyclone fence at the corner of his red-bricked ranch home, we turned back to see if Amos was still chasing us. He wasn't. I could make out his car through the darkening night. We both stood next to each other, huffing and puffing, standing at the corner of Johnny's gate, peering over the cyclone fence. I could feel a pain across the top of my right thigh. The nails in my pocket had dug into me as I was running. I pulled them out and tossed them into the empty lot. I knew I was cut, but I would deal with it later.

Then we saw Amos walk out from the side of the house. All 250 pounds of him stood in front of the construction site and looked up and down the street for any sign of four kids interested in using his building scraps to erect a fort. We were nowhere in his sight. Then I saw Tommy and Mark hiding in the gangway of the two homes across the street from us. They were watching Amos too.

We all watched Amos trod over to his blue Cadillac, open the driver's door, and climb in. The car shook and sunk as he sat down. He started the powerful V-8 engine and drove straight toward us. For a brief second, I wondered if he had actually seen us run over to the Mackeys'. Or did he know where Tommy and Johnny lived? There was no way that could be possible. I was right. He turned left on 85th Street.

All four of us came out of hiding and ran toward 85th to make sure he kept driving away. We stood there together watching Amos's taillights get smaller and smaller as he drove past Tripp, Keeler, Kedvale, Karlov, past the water pumping station, and on toward Pulaski.

"Oh my God," Tommy said. "What happened to you guys?"

"It was my fault," said Johnny, sounding very much like a true leader taking the blame for the failure of our mission. "I fell trying to get out of there. We were lucky to get out."

"Johnny jumped from the kitchen area all the way to the basement," I told Tommy and Mark.

"Johnny, are you crazy?" his younger brother asked.

"No, I'm not crazy," Johnny said, getting right in Tommy's face. "Are you calling me crazy?"

Oh no, not now, I thought.

Then Tommy's head quickly turned toward the street as he heard a car approaching. We all looked. It was a white Pontiac. A sigh of relief.

"Hey, let's go inside," Johnny said, again taking the lead. "We can't go back in there now. It's too dark."

As we worked on the fort that summer, we all got to know each other very well. Although I had watched Tommy and Johnny fight with each other many times, I grew to believe that was the relationship they preferred. If anyone ever tried to pick on either one of them, the other brother would be there, ready to fight to the death. The same would be said about the McGrady brothers, as well as the Janeks. They would duke it out with each other, even drawing blood on occasion, but if anyone outside their family ever dared take a poke at one of them, the other brothers would be there to stop it and pummel the foolish aggressor.

I had just become a new older brother, because Danny had arrived on November 2, 1961. I accepted the way my friends fought each other, but knew I would never do that to my little brother. I guess I just didn't understand it.

To some people, Johnny Mackey may not seem like the best person to select as a Confirmation sponsor. Catholics are supposed to turn the other cheek rather than fight. But for me, I viewed him as a leader, a courageous role model. And because Jesus was the most courageous man to walk this earth, I felt courage was the right characteristic to follow for my confirmation of faith.

So five years after we built that fort together, I called Johnny and asked him to sponsor me. He was fourteen years old, which met the age requirement, and a freshman at Quigley South, a college preparatory seminary. I don't know if the priesthood was in Johnny's plans, but I thought it was a real plus to have a sponsor who was involved in such a serious religious educational environment. He seemed honored that I would consider him. His mother and father were delighted, as it gave their son a chance to be a Catholic role model.

The funny thing was that by sixth grade, I didn't really see Johnny or Tommy that often. So in many ways Johnny seemed a bit like a stranger to me. However, in the process of making my Confirmation, I actually got to spend some quality time with him, and I grew to like and respect him even more.

There were two Confirmation practice sessions we attended together in the evenings leading up to the big day. Although it was awkward for both of us in the beginning, slowly we began to get to know each other a little better. We talked about old times—building forts, running from Amos, watching college football games on Saturday afternoons, and trying to start our own band inspired by the Monkeys' television show. That was a joke. I used my father's drums. The other guys had regular guitars, no fancy electric ones. And we started singing "Hey hey, we're the Monkeys." We stunk. We knew it. And within a week, our aspirations to become the next Monkeys quickly ended.

As Johnny and I sat in the pew toward the middle of St. Bede's Church that Thursday evening during the first Confirmation practice, I looked around to see who the other kids chose as sponsors. There were a lot of older teens or adults standing next to the students. In some cases, it was an older brother, like Mike Hannon's older brother, Johnny. Ann Mallon was with her aunt Gerth, who was quite a bit older. Mary Therese, who lived down the block from me, had her aunt Sissy with her. My friend Eddie Crandell was paired with his cousin Leo Cliff.

I guess in some ways I felt a little strange because it seemed everyone else's sponsor was a relative. But that was okay. I knew Johnny was the perfect sponsor for me.

Father Griffin came out from those familiar plastic accordionlike doors to address the gathering. He told us how the Mass would be different from any other Mass we had attended, a High Mass celebrated by John Cardinal Cody with all four of the priests from St. Bede's assisting. The thought of Cardinal Cody saying the Mass raised the level of importance considerably higher. I had read about him in the *Daily News* and had seen him interviewed on television. Johnny and I both agreed Cardinal Cody was a real religious bigshot—just one rank below Pope.

When the big day finally came, Johnny arrived at my house just past five o'clock on that fairly warm Saturday afternoon. He was dressed in a nice dark blue suit, white shirt, and red tie. His black dress shoes were shined well and his hair combed neatly. That was a first! His mother must have made him use Vitalis or some other hair gook, because his curly brown hair was combed back like I had never seen it before. It actually looked neat. He didn't even look like the same guy.

I was dressed in my white Confirmation robe and red square-tasseled cap covering my crew cut with dress blue pants and white shirt underneath for the celebration afterward. My three sisters were all dolled up in their pretty colorful dresses, sitting on the gold-colored couch watching Mom give Johnny and me final directions.

"Now don't be nervous, Johnny," my mother said to me, then proceeded to give me a big hug and kiss. "Just because Cardinal Cody is the most important Catholic in the city and one of the most important Catholic leaders in the world, you don't have to think about that during the Mass."

Good thing she reminded me of just how important Cardinal Cody was to Chicago and the world. That's all I would think about for the next two hours.

Johnny and I made the one-block trek down the cement sidewalk along Kostner Avenue to St. Bede's. It was almost 5:30 P.M., the time we were told to arrive, and many of the kids in my class were walking in the front door of the church with their sponsors. As we entered the silver metal front doors and followed the crowd into the church, I could hear the resonance of the organ in the choir loft above me playing an unfamiliar hymn. It sounded awe-inspiring—like the kind of music you would want entering Heaven. Maybe that was the idea.

I looked toward the front to see the altar decorated differently than I had ever seen before. There were two identical large rectangular white banners with gold crosses hung from the ceiling on each side of the altar. Large pots of white lilies were placed along the sides of the altar. A white candle, much taller than usual, was placed near the center of the altar.

My robe-clad classmates and their semiformal-dressed sponsors filled the two center sections of the church, as family members made their way to the pews along the side walls.

Johnny and I made our way down the main aisle to the tenth row. The boys and sponsors were on the left side with girls on the right, just as in our First Communion ceremony. As I entered our row, I saw Mike Roar and Tom Rycheck in the two spots next to our open place in the pew: alphabetical order.

"Mike," I said, and quickly raised my chin up toward him, which is how boys said hello to each other back then.

"Scoots." He responded with my nickname, chinning hello back.

It seemed like only a few minutes later when the glass doors at the back of the church were closed and the organ began playing "Everlasting Is Thy Reign." The voices of a cantor backed by a large choir were heard behind us in the choir loft, filling the packed church:

Holy God, we praise Thy name;
Lord of all, we bow before Thee!
All on Earth, Thy scepter claim,
All in Heaven above adore Thee
Infinite Thy vast domain
Everlasting is Thy reign.

The moment sent chills down my spine as I stood with everyone else in the church. Then I saw him. John Cardinal Cody entered through the wooden doors to the right of the altar, following the four St. Bede's priests: Father Griffin, Father McInerney, Father Mockenhaupt, and Father Mollan. There were no altar boys at this Mass. The priests assumed their duties, and Cardinal Cody looked like Pope Paul VI himself. He was a bit on the pudgy side, with white hair seen along the sides of his pointed red hat. His black-framed eyeglasses rested on his fairly prominent nose but seemed to need adjustment from his right index finger every few minutes. He was adorned in special ornate vestments, as only a bishop can give this sacrament.

The solemn entourage made that familiar walk around the white marble altar rail and up the steps to the base of the green marble table, then turned in unison to face the gathering. The cardinal began Mass by making the Sign of the Cross and saying, "In the name of the Father and the Son and the Holy Spirit."

"Amen," the congregation responded.

For the next ninety minutes or so, I was entranced, breathing in the atmosphere and the strong scent of incense often wafting over the crowd while the cardinal and his four altar priests recited prayers. St. Bede's had a very different feel to it on this day. It just felt, smelled, and sounded so . . . holy, almost heavenly. It was the perfect atmosphere to make the next step in my commitment to God.

When my moment finally came, I was ready. The pipe organ blared and the choir sang, seemingly filling the church with the Holy Spirit. For each pair, the student went first, with the sponsor following behind. As I walked up the aisle, I thought about how this moment felt different than any other ceremony I had experienced as a student or altar boy. This indeed was special.

I watched the kids in front of me walk one by one directly up to the cardinal. The sponsor would stand behind the candidate, extend their right arm, and place their hand on the confirmant's right shoulder as a sign of support. The idea is that the sponsor will be there to support their faith. Then, for each of us, the cardinal stated the blessing, dipped his right thumb into holy oil, and made the Sign of the Cross on the forehead. To complete the ritual, the cardinal gave each of us a slight slap on the cheek as we became official "soldiers of Christ."

When Mike Roar in front of me had finished and walked back toward the pew, I looked the cardinal in the eye. I wanted to be sure he knew I was serious about my Confirmation. I was one of a couple of hundred kids. He never would remember me, but it was important I remembered the moment. I felt the weight of Johnny's right hand on my shoulder. Amos wasn't chasing us on this day, but we were there together, ready to face the challenges that lay ahead.

Cardinal Cody placed his right hand on me as he prayed that the Holy Spirit would come down upon those who already have been regenerated and "send forth upon them Thy sevenfold Spirit, the work of the Holy Paraclete," he said, while dipping his thumb into the holy oil. He drew the Sign of the Cross on my forehead, and at that moment I could feel the oil on my head and knew I was a changed person.

"I sign thee with the Sign of the Cross and confirm thee with the chrism of salvation, in the name of the Father and of the Son and of the Holy Spirit," Cody said, finishing the ritual by giving me a light tap on the right cheek. "Be sealed with the gift of the Holy Spirit. Peace be with thee."

I responded, "And also with you."

The door had opened to give me the opportunity to succeed or fail as a young adult Catholic. It was all up to me now. I was a confirmed Catholic—John Bernard Joseph Ruane.

As I walked back to my pew, I saw my family sitting together in the section to the side of the altar. My mother smiled, then lifted her hand to give me a small wave. Dad's new Polaroid camera flashed, and Maureen, Danny, Kathy, and Margaret smiled. It was a nice moment that reminded me of my First Communion.

Once in my pew, I knelt and prayed to God that I would live up to the expectations of the Catholic Church. I asked that God would help me be good and kind, and I would try very hard to live as close to the model that Jesus established on earth. When I finished my prayer, I sat back down and watched the few remaining kids complete the ritual. The choir finished singing, but the organist continued playing a more subtle version of the hymn as a backdrop. I looked around to see everyone in the church, their faces, expressions. I glanced up at the choir loft, then at the altar and the stained glass windows of the stations of the cross. I wanted to soak it all in and remember this moment.

When the Mass ended, I watched Cardinal Cody, led by the four St. Bede's priests, walk around the white marble Communion rail and out the wooden doors. I doubted I would ever see him again in person, but I was thankful he was the one to confirm me that day. It made my mother happy, proud.

Later, Johnny Mackey sat at our kitchen table eating a piece of the Confirmation cake Mom had ordered from Jewel's bakery. She always baked her own cakes, only ordering baked goods on special occasions. This definitely qualified as special.

We all talked about the big event and Cardinal Cody. When Johnny left our home that night, he wished me luck and shook my hand. "Hey, you're ready!" he said, assuring me that I would be a good Catholic. Maybe I would grow up to be like his dad and have a statue of the Blessed Virgin at my home someday. Maybe I would become a priest. I really didn't know what my future held for me that day. But I did know I was glad I chose Johnny Mackey to help me take the next step toward God.

Dad's siblings, 1941 (left to right): May with John (center) and Peter (right); Dotty in front of their home; and the youngest, Patrick, who eventually took over the farm.

Brother Robert with Ellen and Jack Naughton, the people who helped Dad come to America.

The Harry Boland Hurling Club. Dad is sitting first row center.

In the background: Dad (center) with Mick (left) and Jack Naughton (right).

Dad with his tank unit in Germany and visiting the homestead in Ireland.

The baby is Mom.

Mom with Aunt Marge.

Mom at a wedding (second from the right).

Mom's sister Ann, with Dad's uncle Tom Naughton, at my parents' wedding.

Dad and his family outside the church on his wedding day.

Mom and Dad. One of the photos that survived the fire.

Here's Mom with Maureen, Kathy, and me (left to right).

In the background: my parents' wedding.

Dad washing that memorable green Plymouth.

That's me on Dad's lap at a picnic in the late 1950s. Kathy is busy saving her seat.

Dad (far left) playing the drums for Tom Tracy's Irish Band.

A recent photo of St. Bede's altar.

The first St. Bede's. That became the Scottsdale Recreation Center.

Father Griffin in the center (below), blessing the new church.

Father Griffin is the second from the right.

This recent shot shows the doors (right) where the altar boys entered.

In the background: the church basement set up for bingo.

Me, Kathy, and Maureen.

Danny.

Margaret posing on her bed.

In the background:
Danny, Buddy Butz,
and Margaret.

The neighborhood when life was good.

In the background: Mom in a barn at Dad's homestead in Ireland.

A visit to Dad's home in Ireland sometime in April 1973. That's Essie, my dad's brother Patrick, Mom, and two of their kids, Johnny and Mary.

That's Maureen, me, and cousin Jeannie McInerney at her home on Kolin Avenue.

Danny, Maureen, and me (left to right) in our St. Bede's uniforms.

Margaret.

Danny, me, and Buddy, with
the mailman behind us.

In the front room with Mom. That's
Margaret and Danny in front of me.

Posing with Mom.

In the background: Maureen and me
in the backyard.

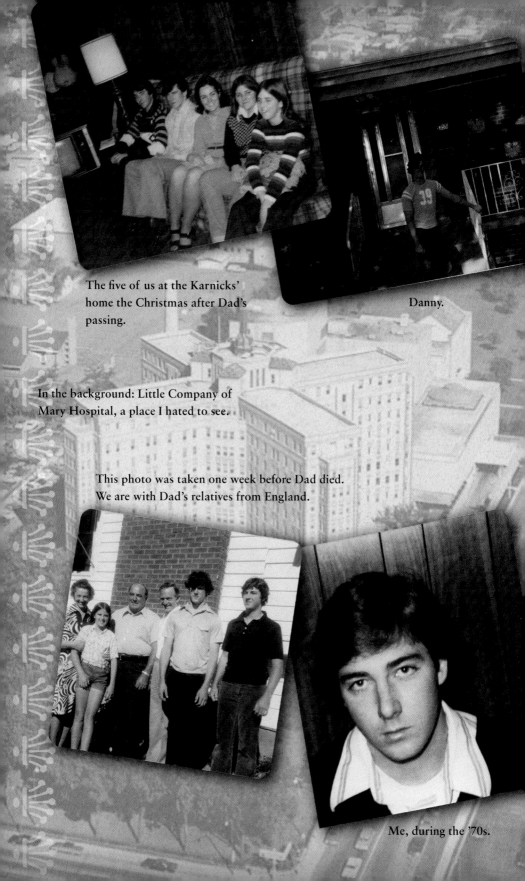

The five of us at the Karnicks' home the Christmas after Dad's passing.

Danny.

In the background: Little Company of Mary Hospital, a place I hated to see.

This photo was taken one week before Dad died. We are with Dad's relatives from England.

Me, during the '70s.

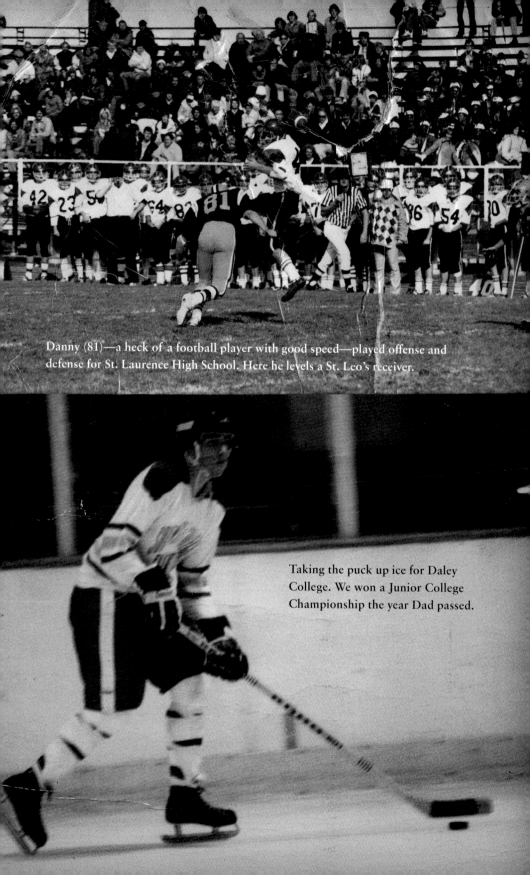

Danny (81)—a heck of a football player with good speed—played offense and defense for St. Laurence High School. Here he levels a St. Leo's receiver.

Taking the puck up ice for Daley College. We won a Junior College Championship the year Dad passed.

BENEFIT PARTY for the five Ruane children of 8355 S. Kostner is planned for Saturday by committee of friends, including (from left) Robery Hynes, 2529 W. 110th st.; Malachy Mannion, 9001 S. Richmond, chairman; Mrs. Betty McMahon, 10230 S. St. Louis, and Pat Hennessey, 6843 S. Pulaski.

Plan Benefit Party For Five Ruane Children

The five children of the late Bernard and Terri Ruane, of 8355 S. Kostner, will benefit from a party planned this Saturday at St. Bede's parish hall, 4400 W. 83rd st.

Following the death of Mr. Ruane last October at the age of 50, friends formed a committee "to help lighten the financial burden of the Ruane children."

The children are Maureen, 20; John, 19, a student at Daley college; Kathleen, 18, a college student in Iowa; Daniel, 16, a student at St. Laurence High school; and Margaret, 12, a student at St. Bede's Grammar school.

The committee wants "to help them keep their home, pay the bills and stay together," according to Pat Hennessey, 6843 S. Pulaski, a committee member.

mortgage and an unpaid loan taken out by Mr. Ruane to pay for hospital and medical expenses for his wife who died earlier last year after a prolonged illness.

"The oldest girl has a part-time job but her earnings do not even pay the weekly food bill," according to an appeal letter prepared by the committee.

"Bernie Ruane was an excellent provider for his family — often holding down two jobs," the committee said. He worked for the city water department for 18 years.

"After Terri's death, he tried to be both mother and father to his children, a task that proved too much for him," according to the letter. Mr. Ruane died of a heart attack.

"His death leaves the five Ruane children facing their tomorrows alone and afraid to carry burdens too heavy for their young shoulders," the letter said.

Food and refreshments at the party will be served free beginning at 8 p.m. Donations are voluntary. Music will be provided by the Chicago Irish Musicians association.

The committee noted that Mr. Ruane was the drummer for Tom Tracey's Band and played at benefits all over the city. He had been a member of the Harry Boland Hurling club and was a veteran of the Korean War.

The Bogan High school key club is sponsoring a benefit fashion show Wednesday at 7:45 p.m. at Himmel Furriers, 2201 W. 95th st., for the Ruane children. The donation is $2 and tickets may be purchased from Key club members at the school.

Char and I were married at the same church where I had served as an altar boy.

Father Frank McNamee, the pastor of St. Peter Chanel, doing the Lord's work.

The best work Char and I ever did—our four beautiful children: Maggie, Kelly, Megan, and Sean (left to right).

I'm holding Megan about the same time I returned to the Church.

The current St. Peter Chanel church.

The new St. Peter Chanel under construction.

The groundbreaking ceremony for the new sanctuary.

In 2003 we placed a new monument on our parents' graves to honor them.

Me, Maureen, Danny, Father Hyland, Margaret, and Kathy.

My parents' legacy: their beautiful grandchildren.

Chapter Nineteen

HOOP DAYS

St. Bede's Grammar School offered two sports programs for boys. I had no interest in football but was definitely eager to try out for basketball.

I had played basketball in the Durkin Park League for two years and became a pretty decent guard. In October of 1967, I attended tryouts for the fifth-grade team, hoping I could play well enough to make the squad.

The head coach was Mr. McDonald, a fairly tall man with an average build, featuring the seemingly standard protruding middle-age belly. He wore thick black-framed glasses, had short dark hair, and a heavy beard. I never knew if Mr. McDonald had any experience as either a player or coach, but I was aware he didn't have a son on the team, which I viewed as a plus. His tryout basically tested us on dribbling and shooting skills, with a scrimmage at the end to reveal who could play the game.

I would enjoy playing for Mr. McDonald because he had a good sense of humor and was positive. There must have been thirty boys trying out, and the best players were obvious to everyone in the gym. Tom Harlin was by far the best player on the court. Tom had a great nickname, "Tippy," and a distinctive look to him: a fairly tall boy with a medium build highlighted by red hair and freckles. When he dribbled quickly toward an opponent, his wavy red hair would bounce over his forehead, which seemed to help him as a player because it created the perception of extra motion.

Tippy was a quiet kid, with a couple of older brothers who kept him in line. It seemed like his entire existence was basketball. He was smart, a decent dribbler, exceptional shooter, and tall enough to help rebound. He was a positive leader on the court as well. Basically he had it all.

The other boys at the tryout said I was the next best guard, a good ball-handler and quick, but only an average shooter. My friend Eddie Crandell was a decent dribbler and shooter, but his strength and tenacity earned him a spot at guard as well.

Barry Hardin, a tall thin kid with a narrow face and big bulging eyes, was a deadly shooter from the corner and easily the best forward on the floor. Barry had several older brothers who must have taught him how to play because he was outstanding.

Billy Mittich won the other starting forward spot. Billy was fast, aggressive, and a decent shooter. With Billy and Barry at the forwards, we were tough to stop on a fast break. A boy named Mike Roar, a tremendous athlete, should have made the team, but Mr. McDonald made a mistake.

There was no contest for the center position. Wally Bronner was the biggest, tallest, strongest kid, and that would be his position for the next four years.

Even without such clearly defined positions, I ended up playing what is known today as point guard. I would bring the ball up the court and pass off to start the play. I rarely looked to shoot but most often tried to find an open man, mainly Tippy on the wing or Wally posting up in the paint. Barry Hardin was also a favorite target in the corner, because of his shooting skill, or Billy flying up the court on the break. When I wanted to score, I would drive the lane and shoot a runner, which looks almost like a layup, only from farther out. I would take a few shots from the top of the key, but mostly left the outside shooting to Tippy or Barry, the experts.

Besides our once-a-week practice in the gym each Thursday night, I worked hard to improve, practicing every day on my own at the St. Bede's parking lot, where four basketball goals were provided. Rain or shine, I loved going up there to work on my shooting and ball-handling.

It was in fifth grade that I met Eddie Crandell in Miss Pasco's class, and I really came to know him well playing on the basketball team together. Eddie was definitely different—more mature than the rest of us. He used to read Civil War history and would tell me about the battles and generals. Now, I was just an ignorant fifth-grader. I didn't care about the Civil War or the generals. Heck, that sounded too much like school to me, but Eddie was fascinated by it and would often talk about it. Hanging around and playing basketball with Eddie was almost like playing with a miniature adult.

He always was impressing me, like the night I stayed over at his house and was standing next to him in his bathroom brushing my teeth. Eddie used a lot of toothpaste, and I could see he was very thorough. As he finished brushing, he took a drink of water from a small plastic cup to rinse, I thought. He swished the water in his cheeks, then threw his head back and swallowed. I stopped and just looked at him in amazement.

"Don't ever try that," Eddie advised me. "That's just something I can do."

I was impressed. Eddie swallowed his toothpaste. By the fifth grade, I knew a lot of kids, but no kid I had ever met swallowed their toothpaste. No, Eddie was special.

During our fifth- and sixth-grade seasons, Eddie and I got plenty of playing time and we both contributed to the success of the team. One of us usually started at guard, and with Tippy on our team we won most of our games. Mr. McDonald was fair about playing time, making sure everyone got plenty of court action. In 1969 we finished second among all of the sixth-grade teams in the southwest conference of the Catholic Youth Organization and received a nice trophy for our accomplishment. That same year, I helped our "rec" team at Durkin Park to a first-place finish and received another nice trophy. By seventh grade, I was feeling pretty confident about my abilities.

When it was time for the seventh-grade tryouts, we learned Mr. McDonald would no longer be our coach. For some reason Mr. Hackel was named the new head coach. This was disappointing, because we all liked Mr. McDonald and had won under his leadership. I didn't know much about the new coach, except he had a son named Steve, an eighth-grader who was a good athlete. Mr. Hackel coached Steve's eighth-grade team as well, but he had no boy on our team. Unfortunately for me, he viewed basketball players differently than Mr. McDonald. His priority was height, not skill.

Jimmy Shobek and Mike Roar were two of the kids who benefited from Mr. Hackel's priority. Billy, Eddie, and I were three kids who suffered because of it.

At the first practice in November of 1969, Mr. Hackel set up the two scrimmage squads. Usually it was always the starting five versus the second team, or backup players. But when Mr. Hackel divided up the teams, he put Shobek at guard with Tippy, the spot either Eddie or I would normally play. I looked over at Eddie, who looked as stunned as I felt. Billy's starting spot was taken by Mike Roar, which was probably a little easier to swallow, since Mike was an exceptional athlete. But

Shobek was not a very good player, and that was difficult to accept. Tippy and Barry looked at the three displaced starters, wondering what was happening.

I thought about asking our new coach why he was putting Shobek in my spot. Instead, I decided to show him that I was the better player.

During the scrimmage that evening, instead of passing the ball off most of the time, I drove on Shobek a lot and blew right past him, either dishing to the center or putting up a runner. Every time I scored, I just looked over at the new head coach, who seemed disinterested. Shobek knew what was happening, but he never said anything. He was handed an opportunity to play on the first line with Tippy, and he took it. Who wouldn't?

Eddie and I both had a great scrimmage, but our team lost. I thought Mr. Hackel would be fair and put us back on the first squad. Didn't happen. The next Thursday night practice was identical to the first one. After drills, he put all three of us on the second squad again. This time I stood there and looked at him.

"Something on your mind, Ruane?" snapped the stocky, bulldog-faced coach with the slick-backed brown hair and prominent beer belly displayed in a tight blue short-sleeved polyester shirt.

I just looked straight at him as I jogged to my new squad. Billy, Eddie, and I worked very well together on the second squad in practice but barely got any playing time in the games. We had each contributed to two very successful teams and a sixth-grade squad that played for the championship, but we came up just a bit short for Mr. Hackel.

Throughout the entire season, no matter how well we played in practice, Hackel only put me and Eddie into games when he wanted to give Tippy or Shobek a quick rest, which wasn't very often. Billy was used the same way to give Mike or Barry a breather. I would watch Tippy come to the sidelines out of breath, red-faced, and dripping sweat, yet Hackel wouldn't sub us in and give him a break. He basically only played five boys.

This new role was disruptive. When I got into the games, I tried to do too much to take advantage of my playing time. I started making mistakes and had no rhythm with my teammates. I just never felt like the same player and never felt the support of the coach. I began losing my confidence, a mortal sin for an athlete. Once the confidence goes, the performance usually follows. It did.

It was a miserable year for me, and our team finished in the middle of the standings, behind schools we had creamed the year before. When eighth grade rolled around, I prayed we would have a new coach. No such luck. I walked into the gym for the tryout in October of 1970 and there was Mr. Hackel in his blue short-sleeved polo shirt with the whistle around his neck, talking to Mr. Bronner, his new assistant coach. I stood at the entrance to the gym pondering my next move. Billy and Barry saw me at the door. They knew what was going on. So did Mr. Bronner.

I should have turned and walked back home that night, but I wasn't smart enough to make that decision. I was stubborn and wanted to play basketball. Maybe he would give me a fair chance this year, I naïvely believed. After all, the team finished poorly last year. Maybe if he wants to win more games, he would put me back in at point guard. Never happened. The first month of the season was a carbon copy, with Eddie and I going in for only a few minutes at a time to give Tippy or Jimmy a much-needed breather.

I was ready to quit when something happened that changed my perspective. It was a cold Sunday afternoon in December of 1970, and we were playing against St. Bernadette, which had a pretty good team.

I was sitting in my normal spot on the last metal foldout chair, as far away from Mr. Hackel as possible. It had been a very tough game. Tippy was playing great, though, and he kept us in it. We were tied at halftime. Then in the third quarter, we had the ball in their end. St. Bernadette was playing a zone defense against us, and we moved the ball around the perimeter quickly. Mike was standing in the corner on the far side of the gym and passed it out to Tippy at the top of the key, who passed it across to Jimmy on the right side. He dribbled it, then passed to Barry, who threw it right back to him.

The boy defending Barry put his arms up to block the pass, but as he raised his arms he dropped straight to the ground, hitting his head on the white tile floor. The referee quickly blew the whistle and ran to the boy's side. Barry just stood there next to the fallen kid, not knowing what to do. The opposing team's coach jumped out onto the court.

"Are you all right?" he asked in a panic, as Mr. Hackel and everyone on our team rushed over. "What happened?"

The boy was not responding.

"Back up, everyone," the referee ordered, with his arms outstretched to give the fallen boy room.

Mr. Hackel, an ex-Marine trained in cardiopulmonary resuscitation (CPR), stepped through the crowd of players. The other coach had placed the boy on his back. I was standing about ten feet from him, watching his face. It was all white, and the boy was unconscious. Mr. Hackel knelt down next to him and could see he was not breathing.

"Back up," he yelled to the mix of maroon and red uniformed players that continued to creep up to get a better look.

I watched Mr. Hackel open the boy's mouth and pull his tongue out. With his right thumb and index finger, he pinched the boy's nose, then leaned over and started blowing into his mouth. He would blow, then come up and push against the kid's chest. He did it again and again. Nothing happened. No response at all. The boy's face began to turn purple, and it wasn't looking good. Mr. Hackel kept trying to revive him, pushing against his chest in short thrusts, then giving him mouth-to-mouth resuscitation. When he realized that he wasn't going to be able to save this poor kid, he glanced up at the ref and opposing coach, a look of frustration across his sweaty red face.

The ref and parents herded all of us to the other side of the gym, near the old stage. We all milled about, not quite certain what we had just seen.

"Is he okay?" Billy asked.

"I don't know," I said. "He turned purple."

"I know, I saw that too," Billy said.

It looked like Barry was going to cry. I'm sure a lot of kids in the gym felt the same way.

Then the ambulance arrived and two paramedics came running through the entrance to the gym with a rolling stretcher bed. One of them knelt down and put his right index finger against the boy's neck. He looked over at the other paramedic and grimaced. They picked the limp boy up and placed him on the stretcher, then quickly rolled him out the door.

It seemed like half the people in the gym tried to follow them out the exit, while the others, including me, ran to the other exit door closest to the stage. When we opened the door, we felt the blast of cold air. I could see the paramedics lifting the rolling stretcher into the back of the ambulance. The younger paramedic jumped in the back with the boy. Then he did something we all hoped he wouldn't do. He covered the boy up with a white sheet, pulling it all the way over his head.

The news of Michael Bloom's death quickly spread at St. Bede's the next day, and the entire school was led in prayer during the announcements that morning.

On Tuesday evening, my dad drove Eddie and me to the funeral parlor on Kedzie Avenue, where we met with the other kids on the team and paid our respects to the fallen basketball player. I don't think there was a kid on our team who didn't wonder if something like that could happen to one of us. One minute Michael Bloom was out there playing against us, and the next minute he was on the ground, dead. Mr. Hackel called us all together in the back of the funeral home to address us.

"Boys, this young man had a brain defect that went unnoticed," he explained, trying to make us understand that this was an unusual situation. "He could have been walking down the street or sitting in class and collapsed the same way he did on the basketball court Sunday. Playing in the game had nothing to do with it. None of you need to feel guilty about it. Unfortunately, this was going to happen to him. It was just a matter of time."

I think Mr. Hackel's talk made Barry feel a little better. We all filed into the room where the boy was being waked and went up to the casket two by two, knelt down, and said a prayer over him.

"Dear God, please bless this boy," I prayed. "I am sorry he had to die so young. Please look over him in Heaven."

I stood up and walked to the back of the room with my teammates. Barry was standing with Billy, who was trying to console him. Barry's eyes were all red again.

Mr. Hackel was the last one to pray, and he walked toward his team. I just looked at our coach, knowing how much I hated this man for being so unfair to me. But I couldn't help admiring his ability to try and save that boy's life. No one else in the gym seemed to know what to do when that boy went down. Mr. Hackel jumped right in and tried to breathe life into him. He didn't save that boy, but he tried. I have never seen anything like it before or since. It was a heroic act.

After that experience, I decided to stay on the team and make the best of my situation. I would try to have fun where I could, which meant during the scrimmages. I looked forward to Thursday night practice because we scrimmaged so much. We were playing basketball and I loved it.

Upon arriving home from practice around eight-thirty, I'd wash up and plop down on the green living-room rug to watch *The Dean Martin Show* while eating my mom's chocolate brownies. This was my favorite night of the week. Basketball followed by Mom's brownies surrounded by my family as we enjoyed a consummate entertainer. It couldn't be beat.

My season would have ended that way, riding the bench, if it had not been for an unexpected turn of events and an angel in a black and white striped shirt. On a Friday afternoon in early January we were scheduled to play against Stevenson Public School at the Hancock Park gym.

By 4:20 P.M. there was no sign of our coach. The referee, who looked like a college-aged kid, was sitting on the sidelines, watching us warm up. Somehow with Mr. Hackel not around, I felt great. Our assistant coach, Mr. Bronner, directed our warmups, having us do layups along with shooting and one-on-one drills. After warmups, we were milling about our bench when the referee approached me.

"What grade are you kids in?" he asked me.

"Eighth," I said.

"No kidding? Where did you learn to dribble like that?" he asked.

"I just practice all the time." I smiled.

He laughed. "I played high-school basketball and we didn't have kids who could dribble like you," he said. "You're really good. You're going to be a great player."

"Thanks," I said, and I laughed to myself, feeling some of my confidence return.

Mr. Bronner called us into a team huddle. "Okay, give me the starting five up here," he said, reading his clipboard. "And Ruane, you'll start at guard with Tippy."

I just looked up at him, stunned.

"Mr. Bronner, I usually start at guard," Jimmy said, trying to defend his position.

"Not today, Jimmy. John, you'll start."

I looked at Jimmy, who just turned and walked back to the bench, throwing his white hand towel against the brown metal chair he would sit on that afternoon.

As I walked out onto the court, all of a sudden I felt incredibly motivated by the ref's comments and Mr. Bronner's decision to put me back into the starting lineup.

"Let's go, Scoots," Tippy said, shaking my hand. "Just like old times, right?"

"You bet, Tippy."

I then proceeded to have the best game of my life. I drove the lane and dished to Wally, who laid in two easy points; drove the lane and took runners, never missing. I dribbled around their guard easily and kicked it out to Barry, who drained his shot from the corner. I dribbled around Tippy's pick at the top of the key, then passed it back to him as he rolled out and nailed a beautiful shot. I pulled up at the top of the key and hit my shot, all net. I was on fire. At halftime, the ref came up to me as I was sitting on the bench.

"I told you that you were good," he said, chuckling.

"Thanks," I said, thinking how lucky I was to have this playing opportunity and that ref all on the same day. "You have no idea how much I needed to hear that."

The ref gave me a puzzled look.

"Just keep playing hard. You'll be great!"

For the first time all season, everyone on the team played. Billy and Eddie were having great games, running the floor, scoring, passing, and defending well. This was the game all three of us needed.

At the start of the fourth quarter, Billy replaced Mike again at forward. I saw Mr. Hackel walk into the gym as Billy prepared to inbound the ball to me. I tried to stay focused on the game, but as I brought the ball up, I kept watching him as he walked up to Mr. Bronner. He probably was going to take me out. Jimmy stood up, smiling.

The muscular, brown-haired guard on Stevenson, Mike Bern, must have noticed

I wasn't focused on the game, and he darted at me to try and steal the ball. I made a quick crossover move to my left, going around him, then drove right up the middle of the lane and shot a runner off the backboard for two points. I turned to run back upcourt and saw that Mr. Hackel had watched the play.

"Tippy, get a timeout when we get possession," he yelled across the floor to my teammate.

Tippy just looked at me. He must have known what I was thinking. A smiling Jimmy Shobek was already standing next to our head coach.

Up to this point in the game, I had already scored 12 points and had 7 assists. If he took me out of the game, I had made up my mind to leave the team.

Bern, Stevenson's talented guard, in his blue hightop Chuck Taylor Converse sneakers, came up the court hard and fast. They were down by six points. I saw him glance over at the other guard, who cut to the middle for a pass. I stepped in front of him, stole the pass, and dribbled upcourt like my life depended on scoring the basket. The brown-haired guard tried to catch me, but I had four steps on him and made an easy layup. We were up eight points.

Again I looked at Mr. Hackel, who was standing in front of our bench. Shobek turned and sat down.

"Forget it, Tippy, keep playing," Mr. Hackel instructed.

This was progress. He was actually going to let me play. This was the opportunity I had been waiting to get for two years. Stevenson's other guard, realizing the clock was running out, came down quickly and tried to hit an outside shot but missed badly. Wally came off the boards with the rebound and made a quick outlet pass to Tippy on the left wing. I quickly cut across the middle, caught Tippy's pass, and dribbled up the left side. Spotting Billy sprinting toward the basket, I led him perfectly with a long bounce pass that he caught in stride and made the layup. Up 10!

"This is fun, isn't it?" my smiling friend Billy said, giving me five. "Why haven't we been out here more?"

"Ask Mr. Hackel," I said. "Nice layup, Billy."

I had been shooting great all afternoon but Hackel hadn't seen any of it. Stevenson put on a press to try and get the ball back. Wally came up the middle for the inbound pass, then hit me breaking up the right side. I could have driven the lane against their two defenders, but I pulled up at the top of the key and took a shot, all net. We were up 12 and as they came down one more time, the buzzer went off. Game over.

I finished with 16 points and 10 assists. After we shook hands with the opposing team and gathered up our bags, Tippy walked up to me.

"Scoots, that was a great game!" he said. "I'm sorry it hasn't worked out for you with Mr. Hackel. We could have used you."

"Thanks, Tippy," I said, realizing he had not said anything to me earlier because it might have caused dissension on the team.

As I grabbed my duffel bag of clothes, the ref jogged over to me.

"Hey No. 6, what's your name?" he asked with a big smile on his face.

"John Ruane," I said, wondering why he wanted to know.

"Well, John Ruane, that is one of the best games I have ever seen a kid your age play. Outstanding! Nice job," he said, shaking my hand.

"You can't imagine how grateful I am for your encouragement today," I said. "I hope you become a coach. You'll be great!"

"Thanks," he said. "I actually do plan to coach someday."

"Well, if you do, make sure you apply at St. Bede's," I said, then spotted Mr. Bronner headed for the exit. I ran toward him. "Mr. Bronner!" I said, waving to him.

He stopped, and a big smile crossed his face.

"Mr. Bronner, I can't thank you enough for giving me a chance to play today," I said, shaking his hand.

"Well, you deserved it, John," he said, smiling and patting me on the shoulder. "And you might as well be the first to know. I just spoke to Mr. Hackel and he would like me to take over the team as head coach for the last few games of the season. So as far as I'm concerned, you're back in the starting lineup."

My jaw dropped. I couldn't believe it. My fortunes had changed. As Mr. Bronner walked out the door, I said a quick prayer, thanking God. As I made the Sign of the Cross to finish, I felt a warm hand on my right shoulder. I looked up to see the referee.

"Keep up the good work," he said, looking as happy as I felt. "And remember, sometimes you just have to be patient and get through the bad times. Better things are ahead."

"Thank you, I will," I said, so grateful he came into my life that day.

I caught up with Billy and Eddie, who were also very happy about their performance on the court. All three of us would end our season on a positive note. Everyone on the team did. We all played.

We learned weeks later that Mr. Hackel had some type of medical problem. We were never informed about the nature of the problem, but we did learn he returned to coach the basketball team the following year.

The major lesson learned from my basketball experience is the importance of a good head coach in youth sports. The coach makes all the difference to the success or failure of a team and the individual players on that team. A good coach will get the best out of each player. And in each player's case, the production will differ depending on their talent and abilities. But I know for certain that a positive coach will help all the young players improve and progress to the maximum of their capabilities. Whereas a coach like Mr. Hackel will benefit only a few and destroy the others. So who are they in it for? Themselves? There are too few good coaches and too many Mr. Hackels.

I pray that all the kids who have to deal with coaches like Mr. Hackel can find the patience to get past the emotional strain of such a bad experience and move on to a better coach and playing experience.

Chapter Twenty

FIRST LOVE

I n my eyes, Janie Falco was the cutest girl to walk the halls at St. Bede's, which is exactly where I first saw her and fell in love at first sight.

Janie was petite, not too thin, perfect. Her long shimmering brown hair ran down to the middle of her back and her clear olive skin made her stand out among the many fair-skinned, freckled Irish kids at St. Bede's. A wonderful bright smile lit up her brown eyes and accentuated all her most attractive features.

One day in eighth grade, I passed a note to one of her best friends, Catherine Finn, so she would forward it to Janie. Word of mouth and passing notes was the main means of communication in those days. My goal was to let her know I "liked" her and to find out if she "liked" me. "Like" was a big word in those days.

You couldn't participate in a conversation, nor overhear one, without hearing the phrases "Does she like him? Does he like her? Who does he like? I hear he likes her. Is that right, well I'm not sure if she likes him. Can you ask her if she likes him, because I'm pretty sure that if she said that she likes him, he might like her. At least that's what I've heard."

The word "love" was never used at this age. Certainly not! That was for high-school kids and married people. The furthest anyone would go at this age was to emphasize the attraction by saying "He doesn't just like you. He *really* likes you!"

or "He likes you, likes you, if you know what I mean." For an eighth-grader those words carried heavy commitment and led to going steady.

Up until this point, my only attempt to enter the world of girlfriends was in sixth grade when I found out that the ponytailed Colleen Bannon communicated through three of her friends to my best friend, Marty Durks, that she "liked" me. Well, neither Marty nor I had a girlfriend then, so it seemed like a good idea for one of us to take a crack at it. I had only talked to Colleen a few times in class up until that point—important conversations like "May I borrow a pencil" or "Would you pass this Fluffernutter sandwich to Eddie." Given that extensive experience, Marty and I decided the time had come to get a ring for Colleen to let the world know we were going "steady."

So one afternoon after school, we rode our twenty-four-inch banana-seat bikes up to Kresge's dime store to purchase a ring. Standing over the valuable glass-enclosed jewelry, we agreed the clear red-stoned golden ring that was on sale for a whopping one dollar was perfect. I was now fully ready to ask Colleen to go steady. I wasn't actually planning on spending any time with her. Heck no, I would just get the "steady" commitment from her and be on my way back to the basketball court or baseball diamond where I belonged. I'm sure Colleen felt the same way.

Soon afterward, Marty and I washed our bikes for the special occasion and came upon Colleen with two of her friends at the corner of 78th Street and Kenton Avenue.

"Hi, Colleen," I said, smiling and pedaling just enough to maintain my balance.

"Hi, what are you guys doing?" the always-bubbly and curious girl said.

"We were just up at the store," I informed her, as I pedaled even slower, turning the handle bars quickly back and forth so I wouldn't fall. "And I was wondering if you would like to go steady."

Her face lit up, happy to be asked the big question.

"Yes!" she said, almost giddy.

"Great!" I said, reaching into the front pouch of my hooded blue sweatshirt, taking out the ring.

"Here you go," I said, tossing the ring about ten feet toward my new official girlfriend. She caught it with both hands, which was pretty impressive, and made the moment that much more romantic in my eyes.

"Hey, we'll see you later," I said, pedaling off with my pal Marty, while watching Colleen put the seemingly valuable trinket on her left ring finger and show it to her equally excited friends.

"Bye!" she shouted, unable to contain her excitement. "See you at school tomorrow."

I believe that sixth-grade love affair lasted just about three weeks, which was a heck of a long time in my opinion.

But in eighth grade, I really was interested in Janie Falco, so I was ecstatic when Catherine returned my note with one that read, "Janie likes you." Wow! This really pretty girl actually liked me. And heck, she didn't even know me. Plus I wasn't Mike Hannon or Mike Roar, the two boys all the girls swooned over.

Once I knew she was interested, it was time for the next major action. But what would I do? Would I ask her to meet me outside after school? Or just go to the next major step: make a request through Catherine to walk her home from school. I chose to use both strategies, to give her options and reduce the chance of a "shoot down." I had come this far; I wasn't going to get shot down.

When I arrived at school one Wednesday morning in late October of 1970, I went straight to my desk in the far right corner at the back of the classroom. I plunked my math and history books onto the floor next to me and reached into my desk for my 8x11 blue spiral notebook. It was placed carefully between several broken crayons, a crumpled piece of construction paper from the previous week's failed art project, and my English and science books. I yanked the notepad out, slapped it on my desk, opened it, zipped out a piece of paper, and grabbed my blue Bic pen from my shirt pocket and began writing. I only had five minutes before the other kids would start piling into the classroom, so I had to work quickly.

Dear Janie,
Can I meet you outside the front doors after school today? I'd like to walk you home.
John

Was this good enough? Should I write more? I looked up when I heard a noise at the front of the classroom. The other kids already were streaming in.

I quickly folded the paper with the tattered edge six times until it was a small square. After everyone was seated, I knew it was time to get that note to the messenger, who sat in the next row, three seats up from me.

"Pass this to Catherine," I said, loud enough for several students around me to hear clearly. This blatant note pass was an acknowledgment to my classmates that things were going well for me in my quest for the "walk home." The note had to be passed to Mark Leko, then Anita Carick, and finally to Catherine. And nothing was going by Anita Carick without the entire eighth grade hearing about it. Any time a kid passed a note through her, the rumors flew. What's that all about? Hey, what's in the note? He's giving it to Catherine, Janie Falco's friend. He thinks she's the cutest girl in the eighth grade. She must like him. Really, do you think he's going for the "walk home"? The "walk home" is pretty gutsy, but I'll bet you're right. Catherine's not opening it. It must be for Janie. It's a secret note. Oh my goodness, it's a love note!

When Catherine got it she turned and silently mouthed, "For Janie." I nodded. She smiled at me, then winked. I guess the wink meant the mail would go through. Sure, but when would I receive a letter of confirmation? That was the key to this entire event. I saw Anita leaning across the aisle to whisper something to her two good friends, Ann Mallon and Mary Caravan. There was a lot of whispering!

Sister Pelagia entered the class, which now was abuzz. I was the one responsible for a good deal of that chatter.

"Good morning, children," she said in her quivering seventy-year-old voice, as she walked to her desk with the labored stride she always exhibited.

"Good morning, Sister," rang out in unison.

"Now, we have a lot to do this week," she explained as she stood in front of the class. "We need to go over some grammar, especially about when to use the comma and semicolon."

Ah yes, the semicolon. How exciting!

Sister Pelagia wasn't two minutes into her detailed explanation of the comma when the chatter began again. The rumorfest was taking place right in front of her, but she was too wrapped up in commas and semicolons to notice. I felt a bit guilty but also proud. I would know in a short time if this cute girl would let me walk her home.

All at once Anita, Ann, and Mary stopped talking. Their mouths seemed to drop simultaneously and they turned to look at me. Then a large knowing smile crossed their respective faces and they nodded. Oh, they knew all right. This would be front-page news at St. Bede's even though we didn't have a school newspaper. Nonetheless, the Anita Carick Hotline would spread this news faster than Western Union.

After English finished, we changed classrooms for history. This was the opportunity for "the exchange." We formed a line and made our way along the wall toward room 105. I stared at the cinder blocks along the top half of the wall, trying to think about what I would say if I saw her in the hall. The green tiled hallway was about ten feet wide, but that space was cut down by the students along both walls. Catherine was about five students in front of me. Anita, Ann, and Mary were only a few feet behind her.

Then I saw her. Janie's class was passing along the opposite wall just as it did every day. This is how she first caught my eye, and I used the opportunity each morning to trade a smile with her. With Sister Pelagia at the front of the line guiding our class into the next room and Janie's teacher nowhere in sight, Catherine quickly jutted out of line.

I could see a wide-eyed look on her face, like she was committing the crime of the century. She slapped the note into Janie's right hand and jumped back into line. None of the teachers observed this, but none of the students missed it. What a reaction this generated from the three eyewitnesses behind Catherine.

"Did you see that?"

"Yeah, I saw it."

"Was that a note?"

"I think so."

"Wonder what it said."

"I don't know, but I'll find out," Anita said. And I knew she would do just that.

I looked at Janie as she quickly placed the note into her book. She seemed a bit embarrassed by all the attention and looked straight ahead with a somewhat painful smile on her face. This wasn't good, I thought. I've embarrassed her. Oh, maybe I was thinking too much. She doesn't know what's in that note. It's just her friend Catherine jumping out in the hallway with a wide-eyed, crazed look on her face, giving her a note. What's the big deal?

All I had to do was be patient. I likely would get my answer after history. This subject was taught by my least favorite teacher at St. Bede's—Mrs. Consentino, whose eyebrows looked like they were drawn on with Magic Marker. She always seemed unhappy, and her attitude was reflected toward the students and the subject matter. I hated her history class, hated history, and hated her. It was painful sitting in the class each day looking at the mean-looking freak yelling at kids because they didn't know the date of the Boston Tea Party.

As I sat at my desk that morning listening to her, all I could think about was Janie and that note. Would she have read it by now? Did she make up her mind? Would Catherine get a note back after class? That's when I was startled by a familiar piercing voice.

"And who were the Minutemen, Mr. Ruane?"

Startled, I know I jumped a bit when I looked up to see the Cruella de Vil of St. Bede's. "I'm sorry, what was the question?" I asked, feeling the rush of embarrassment fill my face. Then I watched Ann and Anita turn toward me simultaneously and nod. They knew what was going on.

"The Minutemen, who were they?"

Your first three husbands, I thought. No. I couldn't say that to her. My face grew warm, and she leaned in toward me to embarrass me further. From a distance, her face looked scary. Up close, it was horrific. Before she got any closer, I blurted out,

"The Minutemen were the farmers who formed the militia to support the United States army in the Revolutionary War against the British." I had no idea where that came from, but I knew I was right.

"That's correct, Mr. Ruane," she said, pulling her head back and away from me. Thank goodness. I hoped I could sleep tonight without seeing her face in my dreams, which certainly would turn into a nightmare. But she wasn't done. She was sure I wasn't paying attention.

"And what was the first capital of the United States, Mr. Ruane?"

As I sat there for a second thinking about it, Anita and Ann began giggling. As I opened my mouth to answer, Mrs. Consentino put her hand up to stop me, then turned toward the gigglers.

"Anita Carick, what was the first capital of the United States?"

She didn't know. She didn't have a clue. She knew about the note. She knew young love was in the works between Janie and me. But she sure didn't know the first capital of these United States.

"Ann Mallon, do you know the answer?" the teacher asked sharply.

Ann took a shot at it, "New York?"

"Yeah, nice try, Ms. Mallon," the evil one smirked. "Wrong!"

Oh boy, this was getting bad. All of a sudden, the note and Janie were a distant memory. I had been thrown into an educational whirlpool with no way out, except to answer the question. It was my only hope. Then it popped into my head.

"Philadelphia," I blurted. "The site of the first Continental Congress in Carpenters Hall."

Anita and Ann looked back at me quickly and nodded a sigh of relief. Slowly, Mrs. Consentino turned around toward me.

"Very good, Mr. Ruane," she said, a look of surprise crossing her frightful face.

At once, my head stopped buzzing and thoughts of Janie reentered my mind, taking me back to daydream land, a place I used to love spending time in. When class ended, everyone shuffled into the hall toward our next class. Anita stopped me and whispered in my ear, "I know." Then she looked me right in the eyes as if she knew the secret of life.

When I entered math class, I could see Catherine sitting down already. And the second I walked through the door, she spotted me and a big smile crossed her face. I could see Anita, Ann, and Mary watching the show. The teacher, Sister Ellen, hadn't come into the classroom yet. As I sat down, my eyes were glued to Catherine, who stood up quickly and walked directly to my desk. She smiled wide as she handed me the familiar-looking tattered piece of paper folded six times. I just held it and looked at it. This was it. I would either be walking Janie home or rejected, sent directly to the greatest embarrassment of my life.

As I unfolded the note, fumbling to open it, I could feel the eyes of several students around me watching.

"Mr. Ruane!" Sister Ellen said.

I nearly jumped out of my seat.

"Philadelphia!" I yelped.

"What?" she asked.

I composed myself and stood. "Oh, nothing, Sister. I was just going over some information from our history class."

"Oh well, you're probably going to need this then," she said, handing me the history book I had left in Mrs. Consentino's room.

"Oh, thank you, Sister, I'm sorry," I said, stuffing the note in my pants pocket and walking up to the front of the room to collect the book.

"I saw that," Anita said as I passed her desk.

When I returned to my desk, I placed the history book on the floor and opened my math book. I reached in my pocket for the note and placed it in the middle of the book. I looked up to see Anita peaking back every few seconds, then looking at Ann and Mary, who were giggling again. Oh, brother!

I opened the note, now more determined to find out the answer. And there it was in beautiful black ink handwriting:

Hi John,
Yes. Meet me in front of school. I'd love to have you walk me home today.
Janie

Wow! That was it. I felt a burst of energy come up from my stomach through my chest and into my head. Wow! Janie said "Love to have you walk me home." This was big. I was excited. I looked up, and there was Anita grinning at me. She may not have known the first capital of the United States, but she was an expert at reading people's hearts and minds.

In seconds, she was whispering to Ann, then Mary. Like a string of dominoes the entire class was finding out about the affirmation of the "walk home" without even seeing the note. Sister Ellen started the math lesson, but only a few seemed to be paying attention. Most were whispering. Sister Ellen noticed the disruption and said, "Okay now, let's stop the talking and pay attention. Class already has started."

Order was restored quickly. Thank goodness, I thought. All were quiet except for Ella Ronan, a thin Irish girl, with long pretty brown hair and freckles. She was the girl in class whose uniform skirt was hemmed several inches above her knee. It made her stand out, even in the 1960s, when miniskirts were the rage. The dress was only the start for her. She was not shy about letting a boy know when she liked him. I never knew how to react to her flirting, so I just kept a friendly and cordial classmate relationship with her. And maybe that was the problem.

"Ms. Ronan," Sister Ellen scolded. "I said we are starting class. What is so important that can't wait until class is over? Why don't you share it with everyone."

This wasn't good! She stood up with a big smile across her face. She looked over at me with a wicked "I'm going to get you" look. I was dead.

"John Ruane just found out that Janie Falco is going to let him walk her home from school today."

The entire class burst into laughter. Wow! I looked down at my desktop with my hand over my head, trying to hide. I was angry. I looked up at Ella Ronan. She was laughing.

"Mr. Ruane," Sister said in a direct manner. Everything became quiet.

"Yes, Sister," I said, as I looked up at her. I knew I had an angry face. I hoped I wouldn't be sent to the principal's office.

"I teach Janie math as well. She's very cute. Congratulations!"

A total of twenty-eight mouths seemed to drop simultaneously. No one, especially me and Ella Ronan, expected that reply. I could have been the butt of jokes for the rest of the school year, but Sister Ellen's quick reaction turned me into more of a hero. I'll never forget her for it. Sister Ellen, one of the new breed of nuns wearing a skirt and the new headdress, handled the situation adeptly.

During the final two hours of school, all I heard about was what the nun had said to me. And was I walking Janie home?

During the last period, I don't think I heard a word that Sister Pelagia said during religion class. All I could think about was what I would say to Janie. I never had spoken to her before—just hello and a smile in the hall.

At 1:25 P.M., Sister Pelagia told us to get our books together and prepare for dismissal, just as she did every day. The good news is, I only had math homework, so I had just one book to carry home.

The final bell startled me. I stood and walked toward the door when Anita stepped in front of me with a devilish grin on her face.

"So, are you coming to my party Friday night?" she asked.

"Sure."

"Don't forget to tell the other guys."

"I won't."

"And you can bring Janie if you want."

I hadn't even walked her home yet, and all of a sudden I'm receiving a couple's invitation.

As I walked out the door, I overheard some of the kids talking about me and the strange events of the day. I turned right out of the classroom and walked down the hall toward the gym, quickly exiting the building. A group of eighth-graders were standing outside talking, as was the case each day. I turned left and walked toward the main entrance to the school, where the note indicated I should meet her. I looked for Janie in the wave of kids exiting the building. As I drew closer, there she was, standing there with her two good friends, Tammy and Catherine.

"Hi," I said to her, suddenly not feeling nervous at all.

"Hi!" she said back, flashing her beautiful smile.

"It's nice to finally meet you."

"You too!"

"Can I carry your books?"

"That would be nice, thank you."

"Where do you live from here?"

"It's a pretty good walk. You sure you want to walk me all the way home?"

"I'm sure."

When she handed me her books, I could smell Janie's hair—a fresh, peachlike aroma from her shampoo. She told her two friends she would call them later and we began walking down the sidewalk past the rectory. As we began to cross Kostner Avenue, a busy street, I wondered if I should hold her hand. No! No way! She probably would scream if I pulled a stunt like that on the first walk home.

After we crossed Kostner and turned left down Tripp, I asked her all about herself and her family. She had one older brother, Curt, and they lived on the 8100 block of South Tripp. I knew the area, because it was close to Hancock Park, where I had played baseball and basketball. She asked about my family and I filled her in about my brother, three sisters, and where I lived. She seemed to know all of this already and finished some of my sentences.

She had heard I was a good athlete, a basketball and baseball player. She said her brother, Curt, played baseball as well. As we walked down Tripp, I realized that not only was she pretty, she seemed nice and had a good sense of humor. I really liked her. Truth is, I fell for her that afternoon walking her home. That's right. I didn't just like her. I liked her, liked her.

Every day after school, I walked her home and we really got to know each other. During the second week, I decided it was time to take the relationship to a much higher level. It was time to try to hold her hand. When we walked home that bright sunny Friday afternoon, thank goodness neither of us had many books. That was the key. As we passed the rectory, I tried to think of how I would take her hand. With the books in my left hand, we waited for a gap in the traffic, and as we stepped into the street, I took her hand in mine just before we crossed. It felt so right, so natural. This wasn't like I was holding her hand as much as I was assisting her crossing the street—like a young gentlemen, which is what my parents expected of me.

Her hand was small and soft. From the corner of my eyes, I saw a slight smile cross her face. After we crossed Kostner, she squeezed my hand. I think it meant don't let go, so I didn't. I looked at her, and she smiled. I smiled too. This was wonderful. I was walking a nice, cute girl home. I was holding her hand and she was smiling. Life couldn't be any better.

When we reached the easement on Tripp near her home, she stopped and thanked me for escorting her home once again. I guess she didn't want her mother to see me holding her hand.

It was a long walk each day, almost a mile, but I didn't care. And nearly every day, when I walked in the door about two-fifteen, the phone would ring and it was Marty calling to find out how the walk home had gone.

He seemed to be as excited about me and Janie as I was. There was so much talk at school about it, I'm sure he felt he was in on the big news story for St. Bede's that month. I'm sure he took a certain pride in being an eyewitness to the romance, someone who could provide insight to the other nosy students about this great love affair and the odds of it lasting.

"I asked her if I could meet her tonight," I informed him about my next bold move.

"You're kidding," he said. "Kind of quick, isn't it?"

"I don't think so, especially since she suggested I meet her at Tammy's house at seven o'clock."

"Scoots, you're in! Are you going to try to kiss her?"

I knew my best friend had my interests at heart, but all of a sudden I felt like he was intruding on my new friendship for the purpose of school gossip.

"I'm just going to go meet her at Tammy's house. No big deal."

"Hey, I can walk over there with you," Marty suggested. "We can go to my cousin's house, the Drissells'. It's only a couple of blocks over and you can cut through the easements to get to Tammy's."

Marty had a good idea. I could walk over with him, go see Janie, and catch up with him at his cousin's house afterward. A base of operation, nice!

It was a little chilly that Friday evening in October. The skies were overcast as the sun was close to setting. As usual, we were wearing blue jeans, flannel button-down shirts, and blue hightop Chuck Taylor Converse shoes, the most popular footwear in our neighborhood. Marty wore a red and white plaid CPO (Chief Petty Officer) jacket, a pullover wool coat that was most definitely the fad of the day. Mine was blue and white.

We spent the fifteen-minute walk from my house trying to prepare for what might lie ahead for me this evening. It could be one of the biggest nights of my life, Marty informed me. I thought he might have been right.

I left my friend at his cousin's house and headed toward Tammy's home, using the easements, the cement walkways that ran between the homes at the midpoint of the block, so it was easier to get from block to block.

As I came out of the easement at Tripp, I turned right toward Tammy's house. Tammy was a tall redhead, taller than most boys our age. She had grown and matured quicker than the boys, which I think made her feel a bit awkward.

"Hello!" I said to Tammy and Janie, sitting on the top step of the front porch.

"Hi, John," said Tammy, who had a kind face and seemed like a really nice girl.

"Hi!" said Janie, with the smile I had fallen in love with at first sight.

I sat down next to Janie, who also was dressed in blue jeans and was wearing a bright yellow wool coat that zippered up in front. This was not a CPO but a much nicer coat. Her beautiful long brown hair was draped over her shoulders. As she talked, I noticed her lips were glossy with a clear lipstick, and her cheeks and ears were a bit rosy from the cold weather. Every time I looked at her face, I had the same thought. She is beautiful! And I couldn't get enough of her. I loved every second I was with her. I felt close to her.

About half an hour later, Janie said she was supposed to be home by eight.

"Can I walk you home?" I asked.

"I was hoping you would," she said coyly.

I took her by the hand and said goodbye to Tammy, who was grinning from ear to ear at the sight of two eighth-graders holding hands on a cool Friday night in the fall of 1970.

As we approached the easement, I knew that was the stopping point for me. It had become the end of the walk since the day we started holding hands. Janie wasn't ready to let her parents see her holding hands with a boy. I couldn't contain myself any longer.

"Janie, I have to tell you something," I said, and I watched a look of concern cross her face. I took her other hand and looked into her eyes.

"I want you to know that I really like you."

She looked surprised. I think she knew it, but she was probably surprised to hear me say it so soon.

"I think about you all day long. I think you're wonderful."

There it was. I said it. Her eyes grew wide, and without even thinking, my head started moving toward hers. Before I knew what I was doing, my lips were pressed against hers and we were kissing. Her lips felt so soft against mine. I could smell her hair, and now I knew the lip gloss she was wearing must have been some type of cherry flavor. After a few seconds, I slowly pulled my head back and looked into her beautiful brown eyes. I was absolutely in love with her. Eighth-graders aren't supposed to fall in love, but I did. Head over heels. Knocked off my feet. Hit by a ton of bricks. Colleen Bannon may have received my first ring, tossed from my bicycle in sixth grade. But Janie Falco was my first kiss and, without question, my first love.

A smile grew on Janie's "oh so pretty" face. The gloss from her lipstick was no longer noticeable.

"C'mon, I'll walk you home," I said, not wishing to have her walk the remaining two houses by herself.

"Okay."

I didn't care if her parents saw me holding her hand, and apparently neither did she at that point.

"I'll see you Monday at school," I said, standing in her driveway on the side of her house.

"See you Monday," she said as she entered her house. She raised her hand with a polite wave before closing the door.

Feeling an incredible surge of energy, I turned and ran right past her neighbor's house and darted right down the easement toward the Drissells' house. I flew across one empty street through the next easement past the next empty street and turned right into the Drissells' yard. I stopped for a moment to catch my breath. I didn't want Marty to think I was an idiot, walking in his cousin's door panting after just meeting with my girlfriend.

And that kiss officially made her my girlfriend.

Chapter Twenty-one

ENTER FATHER RICHARD

H e was the light at the end of the dark tunnel. He represented the future of the Catholic Church. His name was Father Richard Kawczynski, and when he arrived at St. Bede's in July of 1968, the first thing parishioners noticed was how young he was: twenty-five years old.

Serving ten o'clock Mass on the second Sunday of July, I was seated behind the kneelers on the altar following the homily. Father Griffin told the congregation that a new priest has been assigned to the parish. He described him as young and energetic. The pastor explained that he would be working with the teen club, senior citizens club, and men's club. "Please welcome to our parish Father Richard Kawczynski," he announced, extending his arm out toward the brown folding door leading to the sacristy as the parishioners politely clapped.

The doors opened and out bounced a young, short bundle of energy wearing his priest's cassock and Roman collar. Father Richard was about 5 feet 6 inches, with a medium build and light brown hair, which was rapidly leaving his scalp. It wasn't his appearance that got our undivided attention that day as much as his energy and enthusiasm.

He approached the lectern on the other side of the altar from Father Griffin, who turned and walked back to sit in his red thronelike chair.

"Thank you, Father Griffin," said this fresh-faced priest, who had been warned about Griffin's temper before coming to his parish. "I am Father Richard and have been lucky enough to be assigned to St. Bede the Venerable. I am from the Southwest Side and attended St. Mary of the Lake Seminary in Mundelein. I spent four months at St. Brendan's Parish on the far South Side before receiving this assignment."

As he talked, I could feel a difference in the church that day, like a bolt of lightning had hit our sanctuary, a shot of energy, new life.

"I will also be responsible for the youth ministry here and will announce plans at Mass and in the bulletin each week to get our youth involved in their faith. We are at a point in our Church's history where we are coming together more as a community, and I embrace this new opportunity and hope to be able to share it with all of you."

Pope John XXIII wanted to "open the windows of the Church" and let in the fresh air. At St. Bede's Parish on the far Southwest Side of Chicago, that fresh air came in the form of Father Richard. The parish, like all parishes across the country, was trying to deal with the changes in the church after Vatican II. Whereas our pastor was reluctant to make the reforms to bring the community into the celebration of the Mass, Father Richard embraced them, truly representing the new Church.

Father Richard's approach represented a serious break in the priestly tradition that had dominated the Church for a thousand years. This priest didn't separate himself from his flock, stand above us and talk down to the kids in the parish. He became our friend. He was positive, supportive—a good mentor for all of us at St. Bede's. He was the early model of the new priest now present at Catholic churches across the country. He was one of the young priests of the 1960s, breaking ground for the Church of today.

When Father Richard took over the teen club there were only a hundred kids involved. He created a teen board and adult board to help manage the youth organization. Teens were registered at dances every Friday night in the darkened school gymnasium, the dimmed lights making the atmosphere *cool* for us kids. Local bands were hired to play the popular music of the day, while the kids danced and were served soft drinks. One of the teens on the board had a connection to the American Breed, an established rock group at the time, best known for their hit "Bend Me, Shape Me." Normally, the group charged $5,000 for a performance, but it agreed to perform at St. Bede's for $1,600. The teens who attended the dance that night were awestruck to see a famous band playing in their school gymnasium.

Besides dances, Father Richard organized hay rides and field trips. In the winter the teen club would go skiing at Wilmot Mountain in Wisconsin. During the summer, buses were loaded for a day at the beach along the Indiana sand dunes. The word was spreading about the teen club and in a relatively short time, he built the club up to a thousand Catholic teens. Good work by this young priest. He was making a difference.

Although Father Richard had done great work with the various clubs, which was a traditional assignment for a parish priest, that was not his major contribution to St. Bede's. After arriving in July and meeting with Father Griffin, the new priest made an appeal to introduce a "guitar Mass." Father Griffin vehemently opposed this idea, but after much discussion and weeks of debate with the old-style pastor, Father Richard was allowed to introduce one experimental "guitar Mass" during the ten o'clock service, considered the children's Mass. Father Griffin believed this idea would fail, that Father Richard would fall in line and life in the rectory would return to normal.

I was lucky enough to be serving the Mass that day with my best friend, Marty Durks. The guitar Mass was never announced in the bulletin. Father Griffin probably figured he would let Father Richard surprise the parishioners, and the shock waves in the parish would be so overwhelmingly negative that he wouldn't be able to do it again.

He was wrong.

Marty and I lined up with Father Ralph Mollan outside the wooden doors, ready to begin Mass. When we opened the doors, that's when we heard it. Four guitars strumming in unison with an upbeat song. We both stopped dead in our tracks for a second, having no idea what was taking place.

"Let's go," said the impatient priest behind us. He obviously knew the guitar Mass was scheduled. No one else did. Marty and I both looked up at the choir loft, where Father Richard and two teenage boys and a girl were strumming their guitars in unison and singing "Glory and Praise." It seemed every person in the church had turned around and was looking up at the priest and his young Catholic musicians.

As we drew closer to the altar, the sound of the song became louder and clearer, and the energy filled me. This was a different feeling in church as we walked around the altar rail. It almost felt like we should be dancing toward the altar. I looked at Marty, who raised his eyebrows, perhaps feeling the same thing. People seemed to be trying to follow along in their missals, which did not have this song printed.

As Marty and I walked up to the altar and stepped behind our kneelers, I looked out to see heads bobbing with the music, mostly teenagers. The older people in the church looked a bit unsettled. Their collective faces seemed to say "What in God's name is this about? This isn't church!"

But the youth of the parish were on the other side of that opinion. For us, this was fun! All of a sudden, Mass had a new appeal for us.

Father Richard and his young trio played and sang several songs that morning. He was a good musician, and the teens joining him did a great job harmonizing the vocals and strumming their six-stringed guitars. A chill shot up my spine more than once that day, my reaction to the wonderful melodies produced from that choir loft.

The Mass was ended with a very upbeat tune that had the kids in the pews bouncing and tapping their toes to the beat. Walking around the altar rail, it was difficult to contain the energy I was feeling from the music. Marty and I talked about it later. We laughed about how we felt like dancing right out the door that morning, but we didn't think it would fly with Father Mollan.

As we cleared the altar table, preparing for the next Mass, we could hear the buzz Father Richard had instigated. I looked out to see groups of kids still milling about in the aisles, obviously talking about this new guitar Mass. The adults seemed to have cleared the church already.

When I stepped back into the altar boys' room, I could hear someone talking to Father Mollan.

"No one said anything to me about a guitar Mass," said the irate, middle-aged woman, whom I recognized immediately from her active involvement in the parish. "I don't like it. I don't like it one bit, and I'm going to talk to Father Griffin about it. Disgraceful! Guitar music in a church. It's bad enough the kids are listening to the Beatles and all of those other hippie groups. Do we really have to bring it into our church?"

She stormed out, and it looked like she was headed for the rectory. After that display, I was certain the guitar Mass at St. Bede's was history. That lady, who thought she ran the parish, would put a stop to it.

At school the next day, everyone was talking about the guitar Mass. Some of the kids had heard Marty and I were the altar boys, so we were besieged with questions and opinions about it.

"How come they didn't announce it?"

"Father Richard is really talented!"

"Will they do it again this Sunday at the ten o'clock Mass?"

"It was great!"

"I play the guitar, can I be in the band?"

"No!" Marty said, taking advantage of the power he possessed. "No, you can't. You stink!"

He laughed and told our classmate he was just kidding.

It must have been quite a scene at the rectory that week, with calls coming in from angry adults, while the nuns and teachers at the school passed along the positive reaction from the students. Father Griffin thought he had won, and he stubbornly told Father Richard his guitar Mass days were over. Stick to the teen club.

The next Sunday, I was scheduled for the 8:30 A.M. Mass, which was usually attended by a good number of the elderly in our parish, along with many families. Father Richard was the scheduled priest, and I wondered if he was assigned to this Mass so he could play the guitar at the ten o'clock service. As the church cleared out and I began setting up the altar with my friend Kevin Fox, who would be serving the next Mass, I couldn't help but notice large groups of students from St. Bede's entering the church early. They wanted to get a seat for the guitar Mass. By 9:45 A.M., the church was packed with kids from our school as well as high-school teenagers from Bogan, St. Rita, St. Laurence, and Brother Rice.

I saw Father Griffin peaking out of the doors at the back of the altar. He must have been utterly disappointed at the now-visible reaction to the guitar Mass. The kids loved it, and they showed up early at church to make certain they got a seat. That was unheard of back then. Sure, the responsible adults always arrived at church ten to fifteen minutes early. But kids? No, they would walk in the door five minutes before Mass at the earliest.

I tied together the laces of my white Converse shoes and slung them over my shoulder, making my way down the brown steps and through the doors on the west side of the church. I walked up the aisle and could see the church was completely filled. Some teenage kids were standing along the wall. People being forced to stand during Mass because all of the seats had been taken only occurred at St Bede's during midnight Mass on Christmas Eve, when the twice-a-year Catholics made an appearance. I looked up to the choir loft but didn't see Father Richard. There were only a few minutes before Mass would start. I wondered if he would be ready in time.

I stood at the back of the church to watch the reaction. I could see kids turning around and looking up at the choir loft, trying to spot Father Richard. When the doors opened and Kevin and an older altar boy emerged with Father Griffin behind them, the loud pipe organ in the choir loft above bellowed out the familiar tune. A commotion followed, with nearly every kid in the church looking back up to the choir loft, disappointed that Father Richard was not up there playing his guitar. By the time the opening hymn concluded, Father Griffin was standing behind the altar, looking out at his congregation as more than a few high-school kids walked right past me and out of the church. I turned and left as well, having already served my Mass for the day. The show was over.

At school the next day, I learned that halfway through the ten o'clock Mass, the church was nearly half empty. I thought about how that must have disappointed Father Griffin, receiving a lighter collection. Then again, it was the kids that left, not the donating adults.

The guitar Mass was once again the main topic of conversation, only this time Kevin Fox was getting all of the questions and comments.

"Why didn't they have the guitar Mass yesterday?"

"I hate that old organ."

"I got to Mass twenty minutes early for the guitar Mass. What happened?"

Kevin, like Marty and I the week before, had no answers for them. He was just the altar boy, doing his duty. Nobody asked the altar boys their opinion about guitar Masses.

Two days later, before serving the 7:30 A.M. Mass, I heard two of the eighth-grade altar boys talking about the situation. Apparently more than a few parents had called the rectory, asking why there had been no guitar Mass on Sunday. These were the parents who had pleaded with their teenagers to attend Mass but could rarely convince them, even with threats of eternal damnation. They had found the answer to their prayers: Father Richard and his guitar-playing trio of teens. Why was Father Griffin not helping them? I imagined how some of those phone calls must have gone.

"Father Griffin, why was there no guitar Mass Sunday?" one angry parent would ask.

"Well, as you may know, we tried it one week, but we received a number of complaints from some of our longtime parishioners and didn't feel it appropriate," he would reply.

"I haven't been able to get my son to go to Mass in three years," the angry parent would counter. "He heard about the excitement of the new guitar Mass and went to church expecting a guitar Mass. But it was cancelled, so he left."

"Yes, I see," Father Griffin would say, trying to consider an alternative method to encourage the boy to start attending Mass again. "Have you threatened eternal damnation?"

"Twice, but it never works."

A different kind of savior had arrived at our church, a guitar-strumming priest with energy, and all the kids wanted to be part of it. On Wednesday afternoon during the final announcements of the day, we learned from our principal that Father Griffin had caved in.

"And finally," said Sister Rita as the kids in our class sat, eager to leave school for the day, "this Sunday, at the ten o'clock Mass, Father Richard will lead a guitar

Mass!" The classroom exploded with cheers, clapping, and howling. I could hear the same coming from the rooms next to us. This was exciting! And I was scheduled to serve that Mass with one of my other good friends, Mike Hannon.

That Sunday, the church was filled again, standing room only. A buzz bounced off the walls, as 1,300 kids sat holding the music handout, ready to join the celebration of Mass. When we walked through the doors with the reluctant Father Griffin behind us, the four guitars kicked in, strumming the upbeat tune "Go Up to the Mountain," and smiles filled the pews. Once again walking around the altar rail, the urge to start dancing filled me as I watched the heads in the pews bob and feet tap with young voices singing along with Rich—Father Rich.

Happy days had arrived at St. Bede's, and the pews for the ten o'clock Mass were packed every Sunday for the next four years.

Chapter Twenty-two

BAND OF BULLIES

It was eighth grade and they were bullies. Their leaders were Dave Dazzo, a small pudgy kid whose father was the head football coach at St. Bede's, and his two lieutenants. Jim Gallon was a fairly tall, heavyset boy with brown curly hair over his massive melon-sized head. Jimmy Shobek, who played on the basketball team with me, was a skinny, blond-haired boy with freckles surrounding his constant smirk. He was believed to be the instigator behind most of the trouble.

These three were the main thugs, but Dazzo also dragged in a couple of guys who weren't normally bad kids. My baseball teammate Keith Cereno somehow got involved with these goofs, as did Mike Lock, the strongest kid in the eighth grade. Keith and Mike were two of the biggest boys in our class and generally were considered decent guys. But they both played on the football team with Dazzo, and they must have felt some peer pressure from him.

On the other hand, Gallon, like Shobek and Dazzo, was a first-class jerk, and his crimes fit his disposition. Looking back, it's hard to believe kids could act so evil—especially at a Catholic school—but those three set the standard for wickedness at St. Bede's.

Our teacher was Sister Pelagia, a seventyish nun dressed in the required new style of blue or gray knee-length dress and vest and short blue head garment.

The trouble started right after we returned from the Christmas break, during the bitter cold January of 1971. On our second day back, Sister Pelagia closed her history book around eleven o'clock and announced it was time for a bathroom break.

"But Sister Pelagia, couldn't you teach us more about how the 'EARLmen' who were drilling for 'EARL' in Texas and how the poor 'IN-DINS' were treated by the settlers?" wiseguy Shobek said, successfully trying to get a rise out of his bully crew as he made fun of the nun's accent.

Dazzo was not to be outdone. He stood up, pointed at the wall behind her, and yelled, "Sister, quick! There's a prick on the wall. Kill that prick, Sister!"

Well, the class went up for grabs, laughing at Dazzo's vulgar antics in a parody of Sister Pelagia referring to spiders as pricks. A few weeks earlier, she had spotted a spider on the window and actually did yell out, "There's a prick on the window. Kill it!"

As everyone stood up, still laughing from the smart-aleck show, I could see the two punks conspiring with Gallon and Lock. The show was just beginning.

We walked out of room 103 and turned right down the hallway. All the boys lined up in single file along the cinder block wall on the right, leading to the boys' restroom, while the girls did the same on the left. Sister Pelagia paced back and forth between the two lines to maintain proper decorum.

The one thing I knew about bullies was that they never pick on anyone who fights back. Thus skinny, smiling Joe Dalton was a prime target. On this day, Dazzo and his gang made a noticeable effort to move to the front of the line, right behind Dalton, who smiled as if he was being admitted into this contemptuous committee. Poor Joe had no idea what lay in front of him. Neither did the rest of us. Mark Leko, the smartest boy in the class, and John Harey, a small, fairly thin boy, stood in the line behind them.

Sister Pelagia instructed the first eight boys and six girls to enter their respective restrooms. In went Joe Dalton along with Dazzo's entire gang. The next two boys in line, Leko and Harey, followed them in. My friend Kevin Fox was behind me and must have noticed something unusual as well.

"Hey, what's Dazzo doing?" he whispered.

"I don't know, but he cut to the front of the line for some reason," I said, looking at our teacher, who seemed oblivious to the impending doom of smiling Joe Dalton.

Then a few seconds later, we heard it.

Everyone heard it.

"Hey, what are you—" came echoing out of the boys' bathroom. This was followed by a gurgling noise and muffled laughter. Even Sister Pelagia could not avoid hearing it.

"What's going on in there?" she called.

Silence. Then a few laughs. Whispering.

The nun could not see past the brown metal partition at the entrance to the restroom, even when the large wooden door was wide open.

"Nothing, Sister, everything is fine," bellowed a familiar voice—Dalton's.

I looked at Kevin. He and I both knew something was amiss. That had been Joe's panicky voice we heard echoing down the hall just a few moments before.

"Okay, but there had better not be any horseplay in there or you will all stay after school today," the kindhearted nun said, visibly shaken.

Silence.

A few seconds later Dazzo, Gallon, and Lock emerged from the bathroom trying to contain a laugh. Sister Pelagia grabbed Dazzo's right arm and pulled him toward her.

"What happened in there?" she demanded directly in his face.

"I don't know, Sister Pelagia," the young thug replied innocently.

The nun stood up straight and perused the faces of the other hooligans. They appeared dumbfounded, one demeanor that actually fit them.

"Go back to the classroom right now," she ordered the three of them, a stern look across her pale, wrinkled face. As they walked back to the classroom, the other two in the bully band emerged from the washroom: Cereno with a straight face and a smirking Shobek.

"Mr. Cereno, what's going on in there?" the sister asked in a quavering voice.

He just shrugged his shoulders and walked toward the classroom behind Shobek. They quickly scooted into the classroom and, cackling, escaped into the hall once again. Sister Pelagia stood between the two lines of students with her shoulders slumped, looking defeated. She stared down the hall, probably wondering why she was still teaching at her age. Why put up with a bunch of punks who had no respect? Did the nuns in Peru receive this kind of disrespect from the poor starving kids they helped to feed and clothe? Did the kids in India show such disrespect to their elders, to their teachers?

Kevin and I stood there watching her bottom lip grow stiff while her face flushed red with anger.

The tension broke temporarily when Dalton staggered out. He always looked neat in school, with his blond hair combed to the side, held perfectly in place with some hair gook. His shirts and pants were always ironed and his shoes shined. But here he was, drenched and disheveled. The poor kid's hair looked like he had just walked out of a shower. Joe's eyes were red, and he was crying. He tried to walk to the classroom with his head down so no one would see him, but everyone—boys and girls—couldn't take their eyes off of him.

"What in the world?" Sister Pelagia exclaimed. "Why, you're all wet!"

Joe couldn't even look at her—or any of us. He turned and ran straight out the exit near the gym.

"He must be going home," I whispered to Kevin.

"Yeah, those jerks!" Kevin said.

Dalton lived right across the alley from my house, so it was a short run for him. Everyone was somewhat befuddled, but they all knew who was responsible. Sister Pelagia was going to get to the bottom of it.

When we returned to the classroom, the gang of five was seated with hands folded on their desks and wiseguy grins across their mugs. We all glared at them.

Sister Pelagia didn't make a scene but sternly instructed each of them to follow her into the hallway. She asked Leko and Harey, the other two witnesses, to step into the hall as well. A few moments later she returned with Leko, who walked straight to his desk. Sister Pelagia knew her best student was an unlikely conspirator.

"Class, I would like you to take out your lunches. I will be back in a few minutes," she said, confident order would reign because the miscreants had been removed. The moment she stepped out, everyone turned toward Leko, and half the class circled around his desk.

"Mark, what happened?" asked Anita Carick, the lead busybody of the eighth grade. "Why was Joe Dalton all wet and crying?"

Leko adjusted his glasses, just as he always did before speaking.

"Well, as soon as I walked toward the urinal, I saw Dazzo grab Dalton by the back of his collar and walk him over to the first stall," he explained. "Joe was laughing, trying to be a nice guy, and probably thinking it was all just some fun gag. Then Dazzo told Shobek and Gallon to give him a swirly."

"What's a swirly?" asked Anita.

"Just listen," said Leko, who still looked a bit shocked. "The two goons laughed and turned Dalton upside down and shoved his head into the toilet. I came around to wash my hands, and Dazzo looked at me to see if I was watching. He didn't realize I saw everything in the mirror. Shobek used his foot to flush the toilet with Dalton's head in it. That's a swirly."

Anita's hands shot up against the sides of her face in disbelief.

"They stuck his head in the toilet and flushed it?" she exclaimed.

"Then they lifted Dalton up and he struggled to catch his breath," Leko said.

"Dazzo was standing outside the stall, giving the orders, and told them to do it again. And they did. I thought they were going to drown him. The worst thing was when Gallon peed right on Dalton's head. Those guys are demented. Totally sick. I hope they get thrown out of school."

"Gallon peed on his head?" Anita said, her jaw dropping.

"I can't even think about it," Leko said, lifting the palms of his hands up in front of his face as if to deflect the horrible image from entering his head again.

"Hey, why didn't you say something or try to stop them?" yelped Tim Barnes, one of Dalton's friends. "What if they drowned him?"

"Yeah, and then they would do the same to me," snapped Leko, a mild-mannered kid who avoided confrontation.

"Well, you are going to tell Sister Pelagia, right?" Barnes said.

"And get beat up after school?" Leko replied. "I don't think so."

"Well then, I'll tell her," Barnes said boldly.

"Go ahead. Then they'll beat you up and stuff your head in the toilet."

"Was John Harey helping them?" Anita said.

"No, Dazzo told him to stand in the corner facing the wall, which he did. He had nothing to do with it."

"That's good," Anita said. "I'm going to make sure Sister Pelagia finds out about this, even if I have to tell her myself. They can't touch me. They know my older brother is in the Ma Beefy Boys gang and what will happen to them if they try something."

Everyone went back to their desk feeling somewhat threatened at their nice parochial school, where the worst thing we previously had to fear was Mr. O'Connell smacking bad kids across the knuckles with his ruler. This was hooliganism. Gang stuff. It shouldn't happen at a Catholic school, but it did.

A few minutes later, Sister Pelagia reentered the classroom with John Harey, who walked with his head down, embarrassed, to his desk. All eyes followed him. He had the scoop, and we wanted it.

"Students, we had an incident that we are working to resolve," Sister Pelagia said, looking much more relaxed than when she had left the classroom. "Our principal, Sister Rita, is handling it so you don't have to be concerned about it. Okay?"

Anita raised her hand.

"Are they going to be suspended?" she said before she could be called on.

"I don't know what Sister Rita will decide, but it's nothing for any of you to be concerned about," she said. "Now finish your lunches and we will begin our reading lesson in five minutes."

The dismissal bell couldn't come fast enough for any of us that afternoon. We all knew the second we got outside, we would pin down John Harey. Every one of the twenty-nine remaining kids in the class surrounded him outside the gym to find out what happened in the principal's office.

"They had already gotten a call from Mrs. Dalton, so Sister Rita knew what happened and who did it," said Harey, who didn't seem fearful of retribution for describing the scene. "But they didn't tell us that right away. Sister Rita tried to see who would confess, tell the truth. No one would say anything. I certainly wasn't going to say anything. So when she described exactly what happened, they knew they were in big trouble. She told me I could go back to the class, while she started calling each of their parents. And that's all I know."

The next day Joe Dalton arrived at school looking like his usual neat self, but he didn't say a word to anyone. He just sat at his desk with his nose in his books. All morning, everyone stared at him.

There was no sign of Dazzo or his gang. They must have been suspended. We all knew Dazzo was a jerk, but we also knew his dad was a tough, demanding football coach. Somehow the idea of his father finding out his son had caused trouble at school and was being suspended wouldn't sit well with him.

"Shooter, what do you mean you stuffed a kid's head in the toilet?" I imagined the short, muscular father screaming at his portly son, to whom he always referred as "Shooter."

"He didn't wash his hair, Pop," the kid would explain. "It was dirty. Me and the guys were just helping him with his grooming, that's all."

Whatever happened between Dazzo and his dad didn't seem to change his attitude when he and the rest of them returned to school two days later. No, he still had a cocky smirk on his chubby-cheeked face. I never could understand why Sister Rita didn't put him in Mr. O'Connell's class. He would have straightened Dazzo out quickly.

That first morning back, Sister Pelagia walked gingerly into the room carrying two books behind her desk, which she slammed down on the desktop to announce her arrival. She wanted to let Dazzo know she meant business.

"Now, listen to me," she said loudly, to get everyone's attention. "Regarding the incident a few days ago, the students involved have been dealt with by the principal. However, this is my classroom, and this is a Catholic school. We do not allow fighting or bullying. If I even so much as suspect a student has been picked on, beaten, or bullied, it will cause immediate dismissal of the students responsible. There is no more second chance here. I want to be perfectly clear about that."

Dazzo, his hands folded at his desk, trying to look like a perfect angel, responded, "Yes, Sister."

Everyone, including Sister Pelagia, knew he was being sarcastic, but she let it go. That was a mistake.

Over the next couple of days and weeks, it seemed only half of our attention was on the lessons while the other half focused on Dazzo, Dalton, Leko, and Harey. Every so often, Dazzo would turn sideways in his desk, like sitting sidesaddle on a horse, so he could stare down his perceived enemies. It didn't take much—a quick glance would send Dalton's eyes straight into his book, away from the bully. Leko and Harey had the same reactions. Gallon and Shobek chuckled each time it happened. Cereno and Lock didn't pay any attention. Their parents must have really punished them.

But Dazzo's fun was over, even if he didn't know it. He stood up in the middle of English class one day, pointing at the window and shouting, "Sister, there's a prick. Kill it, Sister! Kill it!" Shobek and Gallon laughed, but no one else saw the humor any longer. Dazzo just looked around the room and sat down. He must have understood then he had lost his support, and most of the kids in the class disliked him.

Throughout the month of February, during bathroom breaks, Dazzo was not allowed into the washroom at the same time as Dalton, Leko, or Harey. When March rolled around, however, Sister Pelagia stopped dictating who Dazzo's company would be in the bathroom. I believe she was trying to test him.

On the fourth day of this experiment, Dazzo was in a group that included Dalton and me. He didn't have his cronies with him, so if he was going to try anything, he would be alone. As we walked into the bathroom, I stood next to Dazzo at one of the six long urinals along the back wall. To my amazement, he never looked at Dalton, who was at the urinal farthest from him, although Dalton couldn't help peeking over at Dazzo every few seconds to make sure he wasn't coming up behind him.

It had become obvious that the principal's threat, along with Sister Pelagia's terse statement and perhaps something Mr. Dazzo told "Shooter," resulted in the end of Dazzo's bully days.

At least that's what I thought until the last Friday in March, when Harey and Dalton walked into the boys' restroom followed by Shobek, Gallon, and Dazzo.

Keith Cereno was next in line, with Kevin Fox and me right behind him. The second Dazzo disappeared into the washroom behind Dalton, Keith turned to us and said, "This is not going to be good. I'm just glad I'm not in there."

He looked back at Lock, who was farther back in line, and they nodded to each other. They both knew what was coming.

While Sister Pelagia patrolled between the boys' and girls' lines, we heard a small shriek. She stopped dead in her tracks. Her face dropped. Not again!

She quickly walked over to the boys' restroom and yelled inside, "There better not be any horseplay going on in there."

Then she looked up.

"Mr. Harey, stop your fooling around and get down from there."

Keith, Kevin, and I scooted up to see what she was looking at, and there was John Harey, hanging by his pants belt on the hook at the top of the washroom door. He was struggling to boost himself off of it.

Then Dazzo emerged from the bathroom.

Before Sister Pelagia could say anything, the sound of a toilet flushing and a gargling noise reverberated.

She looked at Dazzo, who shrugged his shoulders and said, "Couldn't have been me." As he walked past her, all the boys and girls in line watched his crooked smile grow wider. He was like a gangster who had ordered a hit and was safely away from the scene of the crime so no one could pin it on him. He had an alibi.

Sister Pelagia wanted to know what was going on, and she turned to the first boy in line.

"Keith, you go in there—"

Then she realized who she was talking to and stopped herself.

"John Ruane, you go in there and see if everything is all right."

"Yes, Sister," I said and quickly ran into the washroom, where I saw Shobek and Gallon at the urinals, while Dalton was drying his head with white paper towels. His face and eyes were bright red.

"Joe, Sister Pelagia sent me in to see if everything is all right," I said.

"I'm fine," he lied in embarrassment.

"You sure?" I said, glancing at Shobek, who was looking over his shoulder at me. I scooted over to John Harey, who was still struggling to get off the hook, and I lifted him up enough to free him. He came down quickly, but I caught him so he didn't hurt himself.

"How did that happen?" I asked him.

"How do you think," he said, looking over at Gallon and Shobek.

I just glared at both of them and walked out.

"I think everything's okay," I told the irritated nun. "John Harey is down and Joe Dalton's okay."

When Dalton emerged, his hair was combed and the top of his shirt was only a little damp along the top of his collar—nothing like the first time. Shobek and Gallon walked out together with John Harey right in front of them. They weren't going to let him say a word.

"Mr. Harey, I better not see you fooling around like that again, do you understand?" Sister Pelagia scolded him.

"Yes, Sister, I'm sorry," Harey said, remaining tight-lipped about the real cir-cumstances.

Shobek couldn't let it go at that.

"I'll try to watch so he doesn't do that again, Sister," he said in his smarmy way.

She just glared at him, knowing this jerk was totally worthless and shouldn't be at St. Bede's. He should have been in reform school.

For the next two weeks, Dalton was swirlied every day by Shobek, Gallon, or Dazzo. This was easy to identify, because his head and collar were always wet. But no noise or chaos was being created, so Sister Pelagia was unaware of it. Dazzo probably threatened Dalton with greater torture if he made a sound.

The following week, I was sent in with the group of thugs. When I walked in, Gallon, Shobek, and Dazzo were standing with arms crossed, waiting for Dalton, who walked in behind me.

Before they could grab him, he threw his arms up and said, "Wait a minute. I'll do it."

Then Dalton walked into the first stall, stuck his head in the toilet, and flushed it.

The three punks burst out laughing, Shobek actually falling to the floor and holding his stomach from laughing so hard. Dalton went over to dry his head off with the thin paper towels. I just stood there amazed.

Gallon wasn't satisfied, though.

"Hey, let's put Ruane up—"

I quickly turned toward him and glared, making a fist, ready to let him have it if he took a step toward me.

"Or not . . ." he finished his sentence, laughing to himself, then turned away to use the urinal.

Dalton repeated this act of self-swirlying for the next week. I just couldn't understand how a kid could accept this kind of degradation. Why not fight back? Even if you lose, you still have your pride. No, Dalton chose to be passive, and soon large red pimples began to appear on his face. Within ten days he had the worst case of acne I had ever seen. It was actually hard to look at him, his face had become so gross looking.

"Joe, why are you letting them do that to you?" I asked him in math class one afternoon.

"Hey, they're not doing anything to me now," he responded, sounding somewhat triumphant. "I do it to myself so they can't do it to me anymore. I win!"

I guess people can justify anything, but with that defeatist attitude I stopped paying attention to his problem. I guess he really did sort of beat them at their own game, because they let him flush his own head down the toilet for the next week, not bothering him further.

There is an existing image that sums up the impression Dazzo, Shobek, and Gallon made on the eighth-graders at St. Bede's in 1971. During our sixth-grade year, each classroom had a photo taken with all of the students in the class pictured. Shobek's class photo shows him sitting at his desk with his arm extended across the desktop and his middle finger straight out. That picture reveals the true character of Shobek and his two pals, as well as what they thought of St. Bede's.

I'm glad I never had to see them again after eighth grade. After interviewing so many others from our class for this book, most feel exactly the same way.

No one likes bullies!

Chapter Twenty-three

HANCOCK HILL

I t seemed that nearly every day, after having just walked my new girlfriend home from school, my mother would ask me why I was so late. Finally one day, I asked her to come into my bedroom. I closed the door and asked her to sit down on my bed.

"If I tell you, please do not tell anyone else—Dad, Danny, you know . . ." I paused as my mother smiled. She seemed to know what was coming.

"Okay, but this has gone on long enough," she said. "What's going on here?"

"I met a girl at school and I walk her home each day, carrying her books."

My mother's eyes lit up as she stood, grinning. Somehow I could tell immediately this was exciting news for her.

"Do you promise not to tell anyone?" I insisted.

"Okay, I promise, but who is she?" she asked, trying to contain her happiness. This was dangerous territory. Do I give out this vital information?

"Janie Falco," I decided to admit. "I had never seen her before this year. She lives over on Tripp near Hancock Park."

"That's pretty far from here, almost a mile. You must really like her." She grinned. This was obviously a wonderful moment for Mom, her son's first girlfriend.

"You have to promise me that you won't tell anyone."

"Not even your father?"

"I'll tell Dad and the others when I'm ready. I don't feel like being made fun of 'cause I have a girlfriend."

"Girlfriend! She's your girlfriend!" She chuckled slightly, placing her right hand over her mouth to hide her amusement.

"I think so. I mean, I walk her home every day. I think that makes her my girlfriend, right?"

"Okay, I won't say anything."

"You promise?"

"I promise."

Just then, my brother Danny's voice could be heard from the front room.

"Johnny, Marty's here!"

Mom and I walked out of the back bedroom, down the hallway to the front room, where Marty Durks was standing with my brother, Danny, and sister Kathy.

"Hi, Marty," my mother said.

"Hello, Mrs. Ruane," he politely replied. "So, did you tell your family about your girlfriend yet?"

My brother and sister burst out laughing. So did Mom.

"Girlfriend!" Danny yelped.

"Johnny's got a girlfriend, Johnny's got a girlfriend," Kathy sang, skipping around the front room.

I just looked at Marty, wondering what possessed him to expose me so blatantly.

"Sorry, was I not supposed to say anything?" Marty said, laughing at the response to his announcement.

Marty was on a roll, and he wasn't about to stop.

"Should I not have mentioned that you have had a girlfriend for a few weeks now and her name is—"

I put my hand over Marty's mouth. "Don't even think about it."

"Who is it?" Danny shouted.

"You'll never know, moron," I said, taking my hand off Marty's mouth.

"I'm sorry I said anything, Scoots," Marty said, oozing sincerity. "It would take an army to pry the name out of me."

"Thanks, Marty."

"I could have a gun pointed at me and I wouldn't give up the name," he continued.

"Thanks."

"You can sleep easily knowing I will keep the secret. And you can let Janie Falco know that as well."

"Janie Falco!" my brother screamed. "Her name is Janie Falco!"

My mother had to sit down in the armchair in the corner of the living room, she was laughing so hard. Marty bent over laughing, knowing he had just set me up and knocked me out.

Danny decided it was time for a song.

"Johnny and Janie, sitting in a tree, k-i-s-s-i-n-g, first comes love, then comes marriage, then comes Johnny in the baby carriage. Ha! Ha! Ha!"

For the next few minutes, my brother found himself facedown on the living-room floor with me on top of him, holding his right arm behind his back to make my point until he said the magic words.

"Okay, uncle, I give," he said, still laughing.

"Promise to give up your singing and teasing career?" I pressed.

"Yes." He grunted, and I let him up.

Just then, Dad arrived home from work and sat on the top step of the stairway leading to the basement. Even though my brother had just surrendered, he wasn't going to let this opportunity go by. As my father sat there taking off his worn brown work boots, Danny flew across the yellow linoleum kitchen floor with the evening news: "Dad, Johnny's got a girlfriend!"

"What?"

"Johnny's got a girlfriend! And he just beat me up!"

"What?" My father stood up quickly. "Johnny's got a girlfriend?"

"And he just beat me up."

"What's her name?"

Like my mother, a silly smile crossed Dad's face.

"So, did you kiss her?" he asked, knowing that would upset me.

"Bernie!" scolded my mother. "That's his business."

"Thanks, Mom," I said. "C'mon, Marty, let's go outside."

"Dad, did you hear me, Johnny beat me up. Look at this!" Danny pleaded, lifting his shirt to show his stomach.

My father turned toward him. "Rub it up, it'll be fine."

"Rub it up?" Danny said in disbelief, holding his stomach in a failed attempt to have me punished.

My dad turned back toward me. "So, did you kiss her?"

"Mom!"

My brother fell on the floor laughing, and my father made kissing noises, smacking his lips together.

"Kissy, kissy, kissy."

Marty couldn't help laughing either.

"You're dead, Danny!" I said, staring daggers at my brother, then ducked out the back door, purposely letting it slam into Marty, who was following right behind me.

"Is she pretty?" I could hear my dad continue his barrage from beyond the door.

My mother must have talked to my father, because after that day, he completely stopped teasing me. My brother, on the other hand, felt my sensitivity to this issue signaled a weakness in me that required a full attack, daily teasing. He tried to sing his silly little song, but the second I heard "Johnny and Janie, sitting in a tree . . ." that's as far as he got before I pummeled him to the ground, and the fight was on. I loved my brother, but even as a cute little fourth-grader, he had a knack for getting on my nerves.

I wish I had Marty's attitude toward teasing. When his sister Gerry decided to tease him about a girl, he responded proudly, describing his girlfriend and leaving his attackers frustrated. They couldn't fluster him. He enjoyed having a girlfriend and the status it brought him.

And Marty had just found a pretty new girlfriend, Susan Meltee, a tall, slender, pretty girl with olive skin and long, beautiful brown hair. Like Janie, she didn't hang around with any of the cliques.

"Scoots, what do you think about going by Sue's house Friday night?" Marty asked, throwing a football to me as we stood on opposite ends of my front lawn, playing catch.

"Sure, okay with me," I replied, knowing full well that he was hoping we could walk by her house and see her, the same way I rode my bike by Janie's house with the same purpose.

"We can walk by Janie's house if you'd like as well," he offered.

I hadn't considered that idea. The surprise walkby. Sure, it had worked for other guys in our class. But I knew Janie pretty well by this point. What if her parents were out in front? I didn't think she would appreciate me walking by unannounced.

"Hey, that's okay, Marty. We can just go by Sue's house."

About seven o'clock that Friday night, we trekked all the way down Kostner Avenue, across 79th Street, past Hancock Park. Sue lived only a few short blocks north of the park on the same street as Anita Carick, so we knew the neighborhood pretty well. We walked by the well-kept brick ranch. On the first walkby, there was no sign of Sue or her family. Maybe they had gone out to dinner?

"I know she's home," said Marty, who was always a stickler for preparation. "I asked her today at school what she was going to be doing tonight."

We stopped walking when we were five houses past Sue's.

"C'mon, let's go by one more time," Marty said, determined to see Sue that night.

As we approached her house the second time, we both saw a hand move the white sheer drapes in the front picture window.

"Someone's looking out the front window!" Marty noticed.

"Should we run?" I asked.

"No, we're going across. I'm going to see her tonight."

As we drew closer, the hand pulled back and the sheers swung together. Would we walk right by again? I wondered.

"Hold it," Marty said, stopping us right in front of her house. "Got to tie my shoe."

Oh, this was bold! He was using stall tactics, a sure invitation for her to make the next move. Nice! We both knew if he came up from the shoe-tie stall with no sign of Sue, our night was over. All of a sudden, down the side driveway, Sue walked by with a rake. She was obviously walking out front that late to rake the fourteen or fifteen scattered leaves on her front lawn. It was obvious those leaves couldn't wait to be raked until the next morning. Still, an acceptable cover move on her part.

"Oh, Marty, John. Hi!" Sue said, in her very soft, pleasant voice, trying to look surprised. "I didn't know you were out here."

"We were just walking by," Marty quickly replied. "I didn't know this is where you lived."

They could both count on seeing the inside of a confessional the next day.

"Yeah, I've lived here my whole life," she giggled.

"Pretty far walk to school," Marty said, smiling.

"My parents give me a ride."

"Yeah, I remember you telling me that when I asked about walking you home last week."

Feeling very much like three was a crowd, and I was most definitely the crowd, I told Marty and Sue I had to head home. I was supposed to rake the leaves as well, and I had to hurry since it was already getting dark. Guess I would have to visit the confessional as well.

When I left Sue's home, I cut through the easements. This led me to Hancock Park, where I walked up that oh-so-familiar hill. As I stood at the top, looking at the red and white lights from the cars moving east and west on 79th Street, I realized I was only about a block from Janie's house. Could I walk by? Would I be so daring? As I thought about it, I found myself walking toward Tripp. I crossed 79th Street at the light and could see Janie's house. No one was out in front, so, somewhat disappointed, I kept walking.

The next day I called Marty to see if he wanted to get Eddie and Mike together to play football. No, he was going over to Sue's house to help her rake the leaves.

"You're kidding me, right?" I asked. "She had fifteen leaves on her lawn last night."

"They don't like leaves on the lawn at the Meltees'," he laughed. "Got to help her get 'em up. I'm pretty sure at one point we may be standing out there with bushel baskets trying to catch the leaves as they fall off the maple tree."

With nothing to do on this unusually warm Saturday in November, I thought I would ride my bike up to Hancock Park, which would take me past Janie's house. The idea of calling Janie on the phone was never an option. As I pedaled my bike, I saw her in the driveway, washing her parents' green Volvo. Success!

"Hi!" I said, startling her a bit. She laughed, embarrassed by her reaction.

"Hi!" she replied.

"Need some help?" I offered.

"Oh, that's okay. I'm nearly done."

"Hey, do you want to ride up to Hancock Park?" I suggested.

"For what?"

"I like sitting on the hill. You can see everything from up there. And it's such a nice day."

She smiled and thought about it for a few seconds.

"Sure. I don't have a bike though."

I left my bike in her driveway, which I knew was risky for her, because it meant she might have to explain the boy with the bike to her parents. I held her hand as we walked south on Tripp toward Hancock Park.

When we crossed 79th Street, I could see the park was fairly empty. It was a big park, covering the two blocks north of 79th and about three blocks east of Kostner. Hancock Park Grammar School, a gray-bricked building with a fenced-in asphalt playground in front, stood at the corner of 79th and Kostner. East of the school were tennis courts, a big grassy hill, and four baseball fields. I had played basketball at the grammar-school gym, hockey on the tennis courts frozen over in the winter, and baseball on the largest of the four baseball fields during the summer.

This was also the field where the St. Bede's football team practiced and played their games on Sunday. The park held many athletic memories for me, but the hill was even more special. It was unique to the area and rose about thirty feet high in the middle of the park. For me it became the place to see the realities of our world, to express the truth.

A few years earlier, I sat on that hill with my friend Jimmy Daul after having just fled the nearby White Hen on 79th west of Pulaski, where he had convinced me to join him in the theft of a Milky Way candy bar. It was the first and last time I had ever stolen anything, but I learned that day that Jimmy was just starting down the wrong path in life and trying to take me with him. Sitting with me on the hill, he broke down crying, telling me for the first time about the day his mother hung herself in the basement of their home. Everyone on our block had known about the suicide, and we felt so badly for the Daul family. Jimmy and I had never talked about it until that day—a year after his mom's death—but he spent about an hour heaving his anger and confusion about the traumatic event. It was obvious that he was never the same kid after his mother's passing, as he began wearing a leather greaser jacket, smoking cigarettes, and stealing from stores. I had no interest in joining his personal rebellion, but we parted as friends.

On the same hill, a short time later, my friend Lenny, who lived right next door to Jimmy, informed me about his mother's mysterious absence from their home. All the kids who played with Lenny wondered why she was never around anymore. I found out on Hancock Hill. One night, she attacked Lenny's father with a butcher's knife and had to be sent to a sanitarium for help. Lenny seemed so sad and confused by the violent incident, but at the same time relieved that no one was hurt. He had to learn to live with the idea that his mother would need psychiatric help to find her way back to South Kostner. Unlike Jimmy, Lenny didn't take a rebellious path but just continued on with his life, which seemed so lonely without his mother around. After that day, I tried hard to be a better friend to him.

There were good stories traded on that hill as well. Many a day, Marty and I sat on the very top waiting for our buddies Mike, Eddie, and Kevin to join us as I listened to Marty create silly stories, mimicking the voices of teachers or fellow students in his tales. This was a boy with a very creative mind and tremendous oratory skills. He was hilarious, and I always looked forward to his fables of fantasy and fun. And I think he always enjoyed the fact that I was a good audience, laughing at every punch line.

As Janie and I climbed up Hancock Hill that bright, warm Saturday afternoon, I hoped this would be a memorable day as well. We sat down at the top facing east, overlooking the baseball fields.

"You ever come here and just sit on the hill?" I asked.

"No, this is the first time," she said with a smile.

We sat there looking at each other as the rumble of the traffic along 79th Street filled the air. A couple of younger boys, probably third-graders, were on the baseball field in front of us playing catch with a football. It was peaceful on that hill. Somehow, sitting above it all with the fresh air blowing in our faces, made life seem so wonderful.

"I told my parents," Janie said.

"What?" I said.

"I told them about us. That you are my boyfriend."

I was stunned. This made our relationship very real for the first time, not something I had cooked up in my own daydreaming mind. She was really my girlfriend. I gazed into her brown eyes and was overcome by the moment.

"Janie," I said, ready to make the statement of my life.

"Yes," she said, lifting her head up to look at me.

"I know we are only in eighth grade."

"Yes."

"I don't just like you."

Her eyes grew wide.

"Do you know what I mean?"

A smile crossed her face. "I feel the same way."

I leaned in and kissed her. It all felt so right. She laid her head on my shoulder and I stroked her hair. I could feel the warm breeze across my face as it blew her hair. Once again, this hill proved that anyone climbing its grassy slopes would find the truth.

When we left that afternoon, we walked down to the White Hen to get a soft drink. This was the same store from which Jimmy Daul and I had stolen candy bars four years earlier. Since then, I always felt uncomfortable walking in there because of that experience. Janie and I both got a Coke and added a pack of Wrigley spearmint gum. I handed the money, plus an additional quarter, to the lady behind the counter known as Ma Beefy.

"I think I shorted you on a candy bar a while ago," I explained to the thirty-something blonde whose nickname was derived from her well-developed bosom, which always seemed to be on display in a very low-cut blouse.

"Well, thank you," she replied, winking at me with my girlfriend standing right next to me, making it a bit uncomfortable.

Ma Beefy could wink at whomever she pleased, though. She was famous in our area, earning the distinction of having a neighborhood greaser gang label themselves the Ma Beefy Boys. Once immortalized by a gang, she knew she could wink at whomever she pleased, whenever she pleased. Out the door we escaped the discomfort of the moment, walking down the sidewalk along heavily trafficked 79th Street.

"I told my parents how hard you used to work on your paper route," Janie said, holding my hand once again. "In the heat and cold. My dad thinks that's great. Then he yelled at my brother for not having a job."

We laughed. When we arrived back at her light brown–bricked house on Tripp, Janie's mother was doing some gardening in the front of their home.

"Mom, this is John," Janie said, looking somewhat proud to make the introduction.

"Hello, Mrs. Falco, it's nice to meet you," I said, reaching out to shake her hand.

"Hello, John," she said, and she extended her hand and smiled a familiar smile, just like her daughter's.

"Thank you for walking Janie home after school, John," she said.

"It's my pleasure, Mrs. Falco. Well, I probably should head home since it's getting close to dinnertime and my mother gets mad if I'm late."

"See Janie, I'm not the only one," her mother said.

Janie rolled her eyes as I walked up her driveway to retrieve my Schwinn.

Riding home that afternoon, I couldn't help but think about how much my life had changed that afternoon. I really had a girlfriend—a very pretty girlfriend who liked me so much she introduced me to her mother. This was a girl with whom I spent the entire afternoon sitting on my favorite hill.

Then a thought occurred to me. After all of this, what comes next?

Chapter Twenty-four

MAKING MONEY

Growing up on the Southwest Side of Chicago during the 1960s, I was like most kids in my blue-collar neighborhood whose parents expected us to make our own spending money. In my case, five dollars a week would suffice and be enough to help Mom and Dad. With five kids, every few dollars helped.

Whereas my sisters would babysit to make money, I chose to pursue the newspaper business—delivering them, to be specific.

I took my first paper route when I was in fifth grade during the fall of 1967, delivering the *Southtown Economist,* which is still around today. Back then it was published only twice a week, so it wasn't as demanding as the kids who were delivering the *Tribune, Sun-Times,* or *Daily News.* Sure, they made more money in tips, but I made enough to go up to the Scottsdale Shopping Center with Marty, Mike, and Eddie and buy a chocolate shake at Talley Ho restaurant, or candy and baseball cards at Kresge's—all the necessities for a fifth-grader.

A two-day-a-week route was perfect for me, Wednesdays and Sundays. For Sundays, we received the newspaper late Saturday afternoon so we could deliver them early that evening if we preferred.

Mr. Janek, the father of the Mark and Greg whom I had known since kindergarten, was the man in charge of all the paperboys in the neighborhood. It was his job to find kids desperate enough to do this work for nothing except tips. There seemed to be plenty of takers. He dropped the newspapers on our porch each delivery day, and on Friday nights he picked up the blue zipper pouch filled with the money collected from customers.

After a few weeks of delivering the *Southtown* in wonderful fall weather, I was fairly certain I could continue doing this until I had graduated from college. Heck, I only had to walk a few blocks east to 84th and Kildare, reveling in the cool breezes and admiring the colors of the leaves falling off the trees. The pleasant smell of burning leaves was in the air on many days. What could be better than this? A couple of days a week, I would take a nice stroll with my wagon full of newspapers, tossing the news onto porches. I didn't even have to walk up the steps and stick the paper in the door, like the other paperboys. Poor saps! And I was making about five dollars a week in tips, depending on how many subscribers I could collect from.

My route was the 8300 blocks of Kildare, Tripp, and Keeler. Piece of cake. If I hurried, I could actually deliver all thirty-two newspapers in an hour. But why run, when it's so nice out? I knew I had the golden route, and I wasn't going to let anyone take it away from me.

Then it rained. After coming home one Wednesday in November drenched from delivering thirty-two damp newspapers into the doors of my customers in an effort to keep them dry, I felt a little less optimistic about making it all the way through college with the route. I mean, what if it rains all the time? Fortunately it didn't, so I remained optimistic.

Then December came and it snowed. Sure, in the past I had gotten cold playing ice hockey outside at Durkin Park, but delivering newspapers in the snow and cold wasn't the same. To put it bluntly, it was lousy! Still, by then I had been delivering the *Southtown* for almost three months and I knew I could get through the winter.

Then January came. And unfortunately, that month was followed by February. In Chicago, that is when life becomes a major challenge. I would compare having subzero wind blasted against my face for two hours with sticking my face in a bucket of ice water. The cold was relentless.

As a typical hardy Chicagoan, though, I held my "can do" attitude. On the early evening of Saturday, January 13, 1968, there was a foot of snow swirling on and above the ground as I determinedly pulled my wagon along the plowed streets with the temperature hovering near zero. About halfway into my deliveries, with my feet becoming colder, my "can do" attitude became my "maybe can do" attitude. About half an hour later, with my face burning from the whipping wind, it became my "hope I can do" attitude. I tried all kinds of tricks to warm myself up, like pulling my wool hat over my face, running in place, kicking my feet, shaking my hands, jumping up and down—anything to generate warmth. These tricks would work for only a few seconds, but the wind never seemed to stop and neither did the painful feeling of the cold.

I finished around seven o'clock and trudged through deep snow to my house and finally my bedroom. I sat on my bed feeling a burning sensation across my face, feet, and hands as they thawed out. I thought about how much I liked earning my five dollars a week in tips and how nice it was only delivering newspapers twice a week. But I thought about how selfish it would be for me to keep this route until I was in college. No, I decided I would only keep it through high school and then give someone else a chance. It seemed like the right thing to do.

Four days later, the cold front had not broken. It was ten degrees that Wednesday afternoon, warm enough for a blizzard to hit the city. Upon my arrival home, having endured another freezing and snowy delivery experience, I sat on the top of the steps leading to the basement as my mother made me a nice cup of hot chocolate. I could smell the Hershey's in the air. That would help.

"Mom," I said to her as I tried to wrestle the black snow boots off my frozen feet. "I think the time has come for me to give someone else a chance to take my paper route."

"Take your paper route?" she repeated, sounding surprised. "I thought you loved your route—two days a week, five dollars in tips."

"Yes, I do love it, Mom, but what about all the other boys out there who haven't had a chance to deliver newspapers in January and earn some money?"

"But you said you wanted to try and keep the route away from them."

"Yes, I know, but somehow over the last few days, I have had a change of heart. I think it was selfish of me, and I will contact Mr. Janek to let him know that I will be quitting as of today."

"Johnny, you should give him at least a week's notice," Mom said, making it sound like I was leaving Mr. Janek in a tough spot.

"I think there are boys right now who will take this route. They're lined up, Mom, just waiting."

"What if they are not lined up?

"Well then, Mr. Janek can deliver these stupid papers himself, because I am not going out in that subzero weather one more time to give those ungrateful customers their newspaper when they are only giving me a ten-cent tip!" I confessed, making Mom realize I was not real keen on frostbite.

It was that January experience that made me realize that being a paperboy was not easy work. As a matter of fact, it was a grind that ate up two solid hours after school on delivery days, not counting the three hours a week I spent trying to collect money from customers. Not only did I have to put the time in to deliver papers, but I had to contend with the weather, which could really make life tough on an eleven-year-old kid.

As it turned out Mr. Janek was able to find someone right away to take the route, one of his four sons—whoever had gotten into the most trouble with him that week. That was only until he found a replacement, which took about a week. I had come to the conclusion that Mr. Janek had all boys just for this reason—to fill in when paperboys quit their routes. And I learned later that happened all the time, so the Janek boys were busy helping out their dad quite often.

Over the next few weeks, I thought about how lucky I was not having to deliver newspapers in that cold weather anymore. Yes, I returned home from school on those wintry days of 1968 and sat in my warm home looking out the window at the two feet of snow on the ground and two-foot-long pointed icicles hanging from our roof. I appreciated our house like never before.

As I sat there, however, I realized one negative aspect was not having any money. Yes, this was a problem that really seemed to curb my lifestyle. I couldn't just go up to Scottsdale Shopping Center and buy a milkshake anymore with Marty, Mike, and Eddie. I couldn't buy a pack of baseball cards whenever I wanted to, like when I was a working boy. Of course, I wouldn't want to go out in this weather, but what about when it warmed up a bit?

I had to find a way to make some money to return to my expensive lifestyle. Marty, Mike, and Eddie would shovel snow to earn their money. That sounded like a good idea to me. They charged three dollars per home to shovel the porch, front walk, and gangway. The backyard was an extra buck.

Shoveling snow. Sure, I could offer my neighbors a deal—two dollars to shovel their walk. They would go for that. So after the next big snowfall, I bundled up, grabbed our large red snow shovel from the garage, and started knocking on doors to line up my customers. I was prepared to take only five homes because that would earn me ten dollars. Plus I didn't want to be shoveling snow all day long.

"No, but thank you," said Mrs. Lewen, closing the door on me as quickly as she opened it. Never liked her, mean!

I walked next door to the Russells' home. No answer. I wondered if they were ever home. The only time we ever saw them was when their college-age son, John, was in the backyard looking through a telescope at the moon. But that Johnny Russell sighting occurred only twice a year.

The next home was the Festerhouse family. I wasn't knocking on their door. He probably would yell at me for shoveling the snow onto his lawn, which already was covered with snow.

I passed Lenny's and Jimmy's houses. I knew their dads would make them shovel their own walks. The Toney family was next. I'm certain they would need my help. Their little curly-haired nine-year-old Maureen certainly wouldn't be able to shovel the snow. No answer. That's strange: I could have sworn I saw someone move the drapes.

Oh well, off to the Lashers' where I hit paydirt. My first customer, hurray! The snow was about half a foot deep and powdery, so it wasn't too difficult a job. I shoveled their front walk, gangway, and porch in about twenty minutes. This was great, I thought. I am working up a sweat shoveling the snow, so I stay warm. Plus it only takes me twenty minutes and I earn two dollars. I could do this all the way through college.

"Thank you, Johnny," the kind-faced Mrs. Lasher said in her colorful housedress. "You did a really great job. Would you like to come in and have some hot chocolate?"

"Oh thanks, Mrs. Lasher, but I have other houses to do," I said. "I'll just collect my two dollars and be on my way."

"Okay," she said with a big smile and returned a few minutes later digging through her massive black leather purse. "I'm sure I had money in here somewhere."

Uh-oh!

"You know what, Johnny, why don't you come back tonight when Mr. Lasher is home and he will be able to pay you, okay?"

"Okay, Mrs. Lasher. I'll see you later."

I left their home and continued down to the end of the block to the home of Mrs. Weeks, a widow who always gave out popcorn balls at Halloween. She was a very nice lady, but no one ate her popcorn balls. Our parents just were not certain they were safe. Too many stories about apples or popcorn balls with razors in them. I'm sure no-one thought Mrs. Weeks would ever do that to a kid, but just to be safe, right?

"Yes, I would like you to shovel my walk, Johnny," said the short, plump, kind-faced woman. "The last time I tried to shovel it, I fell and hurt my back very badly. Ended up in the hospital for X-rays."

"Well, I'll shovel it for you, Mrs. Weeks, don't worry," I reassured her. "And I'm only charging two dollars for the entire walk."

Her smile dropped at the cost of the job.

Uh-oh!

"Well, what would it cost for just the porch, steps, and front walkway because I really don't have two dollars."

I stood there confronted with a moral dilemma. Here was a nice lady who passed out popcorn balls at Halloween who couldn't shovel her own walk because she might fall and hurt her back again and end up getting X-rays at the hospital. I didn't want that to happen. Yet she wanted to hire me to shovel her walk. I wanted that. But she didn't have the money to pay me. I didn't want that.

"Mrs. Weeks, I am very sorry to hear about your back," I told her, as I bent over to start shoveling off her porch. "Don't worry about the money, I'll shovel your walk free. I'd hate to see you get hurt again."

"Thank you so much, Johnny," she said, her smile returning to her plump face like she had just been given a wonderful gift. "I may not have money to give you, but would you like some popcorn balls?"

I stopped and looked up at her.

"Popcorn balls? No thanks, I only like to get those on Halloween, but thank you."

I finished shoveling the snow from Mrs. Weeks's porch, steps and front walk and was ready to call it quits for the day. On the way home, I saw that Mr. Lasher's car was in front of his home.

"Oh, hello, Johnny," said Mr. Lasher, one of the few white-collar workers on our block, still dressed in the suit he wore to his accountant's job at the steel company.

"My wife said you had stopped by to shovel the snow, but I have to tell you, two dollars sounds a bit high."

Uh-oh!

"That is what I am charging everyone, Mr. Lasher. It's a dollar less than the other kids are charging."

"Still, two dollars is a little high for me," he insisted.

As I walked home with one dollar in my pocket and the sun setting, I made a mental note to cancel the Lashers from my client list. I sat in my front room after dinner that evening, watching television when my dad entered looking quite unhappy.

"Johnny, why isn't the walk shoveled?"

Uh-oh.

Some kids might have a hard time admitting they may have made a mistake giving up a paper route. But in September of 1968, with school just beginning, I thought it was time to take another crack at it.

"Yes, Mr. Janek, I realize I didn't give you any notice before quitting," I groveled over the phone, pleading for a chance to redeem myself. "If you can just give me one more chance, I will do a good job for you."

Mr. Janek informed me that my *Southtown* route had been through two other paperboys in the past six months. I was sure the kid who had it wasn't about to give it up during the beautiful fall months.

"We have a daily route if you are interested," Mr. Janek informed me, pointing out that his son Greg was now delivering those papers until they could find a new paperboy. I heard stories from other kids who had taken a daily paper route. It was not easy. The worst route was the *Tribune,* which meant delivering papers early in the morning. My friend Eddie Crandell and his brothers had been delivering the *Tribune* for years, getting up at five o'clock, delivering the papers, then going to St. Bede's Church to serve the early Mass. I would never even consider that insanity. This opportunity to deliver the *Daily News* each weekday afternoon seemed perfect. Our family subscribed to the newspaper, so I was very familiar with it. Mike Royko was the main columnist, and the sports section had Ray Sons reporting on my favorite teams.

"I'll do it, Mr. Janek," I said, ready to jump in with both feet. And I did. Unlike the *Southtown,* the *Daily News* was a real Chicago newspaper, reporting all of the important events that took place in the city and around the world. Reading the newspaper as I walked along my route was one aspect of the job that really appealed to me. I became enamored with the news, anxious to see what was being reported on the front page. The newspaper was far more informative than the reports I watched Walter Cronkite deliver on the *CBS Evening News,* because it was so much more in-depth. This paper route was really my entry into the world of news, in which I would later make my living and end up working with the great Royko and Sons at the *Sun-Times.*

Getting back into the grind of delivering papers was all too familiar. Each day when I arrived home from school at approximately 1:40 P.M., I would see the two bundles of newspapers on my front porch. I would race into the house, grab a snack of Oreo cookies and a glass of milk, change my clothes, put on a pair of jeans and a T-shirt, and out the door I went.

The walk to and from the route always seemed the longest part of the job. My route contained six city blocks, including the 8500 and 8600 blocks of Kildare, Tripp, and Keeler. I was literally on the other side of the park from my old *Southtown* route.

I was determined to keep this route, and I made it all the way to Christmas, my favorite time of year because I received much bigger tips, which I used to buy Christmas presents for my family. In a normal week, I would make about ten dollars to fifteen dollars in tips. When Christmas came in 1968, I made thirty-five dollars, which made me feel rich. Customers were giving me dollar tips. Unbelievable!

Saturday, January 4, 1969, is the day I most remember as a paperboy. When I woke up, I could feel the chill in our home. I looked out the window to see two feet of snow on the ground, and the temperature had plunged to five below zero, not counting the wind chill that brought it down to minus-fifteen. Dad was already up and had the coffee percolating on the stove, filling the air with that wonderful fresh-brewed aroma.

"Johnny, I don't want you going out in this weather," my dad said to me as I sat there drinking a cup of hot coffee mixed with cream and three teaspoons of sugar, trying to psyche myself up for the day ahead. Yes, I began drinking coffee far too young, age twelve. The wonderful smell and sight of Dad drinking it every day was too much for me. I had to have it.

"Dad, I have to deliver the newspapers," I said to him, wondering how else the weekend edition of the *Daily News* would get delivered that morning. My father tried to talk me out of it, but I was stubborn. I think he appreciated my willingness to go out in that weather. After all, he had to do it for us every day working for Chicago's Water Department, regardless of weather conditions.

I bundled up with a sweatshirt, jeans, warm socks, boots, my green parka, a wool hat, and a good pair of gloves. When I walked out the door that morning, the cold smacked me right in the face. It was really cold!

I wouldn't be able to use my wagon to deliver the papers on this snowy Saturday. I walked to the garage, listening to the wind howl through our gangway, and struggled to get the door open. The doorknob was frozen. With all of my might, I worked to turn the knob and at the same time used my right shoulder to bang against the door several times until it finally opened. Once I closed the door, the howling of the wind stopped. Although it was freezing in the garage, the silence and privacy felt wonderful, secure. Our blue '67 Chevy was parked there, with large chunks of gray ice stuck to the bottom near the tires. A sled was standing in the corner, next to the workbench my father had built after Danley Lumber put up the garage in 1965.

I took my cleanly varnished sled with red steel runners and walked back outside into the howling wind and swirling snow. At the front door, I found three bundles of newspapers placed in the middle of what used to be a snowdrift on our front porch. Mr. Janek had wrapped plastic around them so they wouldn't be ruined. And because it was Saturday and the weekend edition, the papers were much thicker than the weekday version. It was a very large stack of newspapers for me to haul. It seemed like it took twenty minutes to organize this, and I had no idea how I would be able to deliver them. I was only going to make one trip, so I tied the papers against the sled with kite string we had in the garage. They weren't held on perfectly, but I was going to make it in one trip no matter how many times I had to tie them back on the sled.

I pulled the sled past the Romes' house, down 84th Street. With each step, my boots plunged through the icy surface of the snow, sinking down into the white powder. The same sound was heard with each step. First the explosion through the hard layer, then the squeezing of the rubber from my boots into the softer snow beneath. I listened to the symphony of my own steps against the howling wind and my own heavy breathing as I trudged through the deep snowdrifts across the fields at Durkin Park. I could feel my face getting colder, with the wind whipping against it. This was far worse than my experience delivering the *Southtown* a year earlier.

The two stacks of newspapers only fell off the sled twice by the time I had reached 85th and Kildare and my first customers. I viewed that as a major accomplishment. But I really didn't want to be doing this. I had no choice. The newspapers had to be delivered. Despite my efforts to bundle up, my feet became very cold very quickly; so did my hands. And there was no sparing my face either as the harsh cold wind burned my cheeks, just like the sandblaster feeling of a year before. I knew this feeling. It was painful!

I went from house to house feeling colder with each passing minute. I could deal with the pain across my face but my feet were really cold. There was nowhere I could go to warm up. None of the customers seemed to be up at seven o'clock, the one morning a week the *Daily News* was delivered. No, they were all warm in their beds, waiting to wake up and have their coffee, then stroll to the front door where they would find their newspaper. Then they would stroll back to their couch, where they would sit and read their favorite sections. Did I think they cared that I was the one who had delivered it on this cold snowy day? I'm sure they didn't.

I tried my old *Southtown* tricks, kicking my feet, jumping up and down, shaking my hands. The warm relief was too short. I trudged through the snow from house to house, sticking the thick newspaper between the storm door and wooden front door to each home. The good news was that with each delivery, I had fewer papers to pull. Plus the apartment customers were at the end of each block and I could warm up a little in the entranceway. That kept my spirits up, and I fought through the pain of my cold feet and kept walking as fast as I could. I was actually starting to sweat a little, which I couldn't understand in such cold weather. But this had to be a good sign.

When I reached the apartment buildings at the end of Kildare, I walked inside to feel the warmth of the entryway. I closed the door and could feel the silence surround me. I dropped newspapers on the ground for each of the three customers and stood there kicking my feet to get the blood circulating. They stung so badly! I kept kicking my feet, shaking my hands, and then my face felt like it was starting to thaw out. After about five minutes, feeling somewhat rejuvenated, I went back out the door to make the trek across the alleyway to the apartments on Tripp. I must have gotten used to the cold a little, because this time out it didn't seem to hurt as much. I was able to deliver the newspapers to the three apartment buildings on the west side of the street without the need to warm up. Then I crossed the street to 8655, the familiar yellow and orange–bricked apartment building that no longer housed my fifth-grade teacher, Miss Pasco. The Collettis now lived in the apartment. But every single time I walked into that entryway, I thought of Miss Pasco and missed her. On this Saturday, I stood there a few minutes longer, kicking my feet, knowing that I would have to go all the way down Tripp and back up Keeler before I could warm up in another apartment building.

I psyched myself up and shot out the door, trudging through the snow even faster, tossing each newspaper to the door, my load getting lighter. This was good. I could make it. Down Tripp I went, delivering all seventeen newspapers in what seemed like only five minutes. I was now feeling very optimistic. My face was still incredibly cold, my feet in horrible pain, and I kept opening and closing my free hand, the one not pulling the rope on the sled. Along 85th I tugged the sled with only ten more papers to be delivered. I had my sights set on a quick delivery, warming up in the apartments at the end of the block, and then the walk home.

I reached the apartments and had no more newspapers to deliver. I had made it. I kicked my feet, opened and closed my hands, and could feel my face melting again as I stood there knowing I still had to walk home in this cold. But the sun had come out, so it had to warm up a little, right? Walking down Keeler back toward Durkin Park didn't seem too hard, but once I hit the open fields of the park, the cold wind slammed against me, nearly killing my spirit. My feet stung. My face felt numb. But I was pulling an empty sled and I had no choice. I had to get home. I tried to run in the deep snow. I would make it about twenty yards, then have to walk because it was too hard to keep going. I could see my next-door neighbor Mrs. Rome's house through the swirling snow. I felt an energy burst. I ran the last half block into the alley, through my back gate, and into the back door, letting go of the sled just before stepping inside. Ah, warmth! Thank God, I thought. I could feel it surround me.

My dad was sitting there in the kitchen waiting for me, and he jumped up once he saw me enter.

"Thank God you're home," he said, helping me off with my hood, parka, and boots. "Sit down here. I'll get you a cup of coffee."

Dad brought me over a cup of hot coffee, just the way I always liked it, three teaspoons of sugar and plenty of milk. As I sat there sipping that delicious coffee, my feet began to burn like never before.

"They will be all right in just a few minutes," he said, rubbing my feet with both his hands to get the circulation going again.

"Johnny, that's enough of the paper route, okay?"

He didn't have to twist my arm. I had made up my mind to quit halfway across Durkin Park. When I called Mr. Janek that afternoon, he said I was the fifth paperboy who had quit that day. I knew that meant it was going to be a busy and rough winter for his sons.

Chapter Twenty-five

A PERFECT CHRISTMAS
EVE

I t was Christmas week, 1970. The weather had been cold for two straight weeks, and there was a foot of snow on the ground. So many kids were sick and had missed school that I wondered why they just didn't close it down for a few days.

I luckily had dodged the bug until Tuesday, December 22, when I woke up feeling horrible. I had the twenty-four-hour flu. Somehow getting sick as a kid seems like the end of the world because it stops your entire life. Sure, it's the golden ticket to get out of going to school. But I couldn't play with friends, couldn't play sports, couldn't see Janie.

I had bought Janie a large expensive box of Fannie May chocolate candy. I prayed that I would recuperate by Wednesday, so I could go to school on the last day before the Christmas break. No such luck. When I woke up the next day, I still felt horrible, and Mom wasn't letting me go anywhere. Janie would just have to understand.

Marty called later that day to let me know he had spoken to her. She wanted to see me on Christmas Eve, because she had a present to deliver. The plan was to meet her at the easement by her house at 7:00 P.M. If I wasn't there, she would understand.

I was determined to see her, but when I woke up that next morning, I still felt lousy. The recuperation seemed to take forever. All day long, I just stayed in bed. My chances of seeing Janie weren't good. I heard Dad come home from work at about four-thirty, just like normal. My head felt dizzy as I strained to hear my mother talking to him.

Christmas Eve was a huge occasion in my house. It was absolutely the best day of the year for all of us. When we were younger, the ritual consisted of going to bed at eight o'clock, then being woken up by my father around ten to tell us Santa had just left our home. All five of us bolted out of our bedrooms to the living room, where the decorated silver Christmas tree with the spinning colored light underneath was surrounded by piles of beautifully wrapped presents. It must have been quite a sight for my parents to watch their five kids tear through those presents, searching for the tags with their names on them and then ripping open each present as quickly as possible. Once the present was opened, the general procedure consisted of yelling out a description of the gift, followed by half a second of joy, and then quickly moving on to search and tear into the next present. It always seemed to be a race: who could open their presents the fastest to find out what great gifts Santa had brought.

This Christmas Eve my mother carried in another bowl of chicken soup around five o'clock, dinnertime for us.

"Mom," I said meekly, trying to work up the courage to tell her of my intentions. "I'm supposed to meet Janie tonight at seven and give her the Christmas gift I bought her."

Mom's smile dropped and she sat down at the foot of my bed.

"Johnny, you're really not feeling well enough to go out, and the weather outside is miserable. I think you had better plan to see her after Christmas."

I turned and stuffed my face into my pillow, trying to contain my frustration and hold back the tears as my mother left the room. As I lay there I could hear my family sitting down to dinner.

Around six my father and mother walked into my room. They turned the ceiling light switch on, and the bright bulbs immediately stung my eyes. I sat up, squinting toward my parents, and reached up with my left arm to block the light.

"Johnny, do you want me to drive you over there?" my father offered. "I don't really want you walking outside in this weather."

I thought about this for a second as I sat upright in my bed. At that moment I realized that I was actually starting to feel a little better. Plus, maybe my dad's idea gave me a lift.

"Okay," I said, and I slowly made my way out of bed. "Thanks, Mom and Dad." I hugged them both and went into the bathroom for a quick bath. I had to hurry if I wanted to be on time. My adrenaline began to take over. My mother laid out my clothes, a red and white checkered flannel shirt, blue jeans, white socks, underwear, and my trusty rubber boots, the ones I always wore during my paper route days. I was feeling grubby from lying in bed for two days. The bathwater felt so warm and cleansing. This too gave me a boost, and I dressed quickly, then put on my heavy green parka, gloves, and boots. With the snowy weather outside, I had to wear a hat, so I grabbed my blue knit Bears hat, which would pass any "cool hat test" among eighth-graders in Chicago.

My dad was already in the garage, warming up our '67 Chevy. I grabbed the gift-wrapped box, kissed my mother on the cheek, and ran out the door. As I jogged toward the garage, all of a sudden my head felt a little woozy. Maybe I wasn't feeling so great! Nonetheless, onward I went into the side garage entrance, around the front of the running Chevy. I opened the passenger-side door and jumped in, closing it behind me.

As we backed into the alley, the snowflakes pelted our windshield. This was a blizzard, and I could hear the sound from the tires grinding into the snow on the cement alleyway. My father had shoveled the alley clear that morning, but the snowstorm filled it in again. As we drove slowly down Kostner, a few of our neighbors without garages were out shoveling the street in front of their homes, so they could park their cars without fear of getting stuck. The loud sound of the city snowplows could be heard in the distance, which I knew meant at some point my neighbors' shoveling efforts would be in vain. When those city plows arrive, they don't care how hard a person worked to clear a spot on the street, with two kitchen chairs reserving the space. They have blocks of snow-filled streets to plow, so they need to keep moving, even if that means pushing the snow from the middle of the street into a just-cleared parking space.

I guess I never really knew how angry our neighbor Mr. Festerhouse could get until the day I heard him express his disapproval to a snowplow driver one winter's day. In his address to the city worker, Festerhouse uttered a two-word term that referenced the driver's affection for his own mother and the idea that he may have engaged in inappropriate relations with her.

These were new words for him, because up until that point the only thing I had really heard him say was "Get the hell off my grass!" or "Stay off my grass!" or "If you step on my grass again I'll have to call your parents!" Mr. Festerhouse was very fond of his grass, even with the snow covering it.

Checking my silver-banded watch, it was 6:55 P.M., and Dad turned left down Tripp.

"Can you drop me off here and just wait?" I asked, hoping he would stay a good block back from my meeting point.

"That's fine, Johnny," he said, turning on the radio and dialing to WGN-AM 720. "I'll be fine right here. I want to hear Lloyd Pettit on the Blackhawks pregame show to find out if Bobby Hull is playing tonight."

I climbed out of the car and heard my rubber boots make that all-so-familiar sound as they plunged into the deep snow, each step leaving a deep imprint. Obviously the snowplow had not made it down Tripp all day. It was deep.

The wind and snow whipped against my face as I trudged on, trying to protect the present under my coat. It was a struggle to walk, and I could feel myself getting a little weak as I crossed the street. Thank goodness everyone on Janie's side of the block had shoveled the snow off their sidewalks. It was such a relief to walk with a normal gait along the path. I passed Tammy's house, which was dark. I looked up the street to see if Janie was at the easement. The snow was coming down so thick, I could barely see twenty feet in front of me. The streetlamps illuminated the large flakes as they streamed pristinely down to earth. I glanced back at my father, who waved his encouragement.

When I reached the easement, no one was in sight. I wondered if she just assumed I was sick and wouldn't be stupid enough to go outside in this blizzard. No, she knew me better than that. Janie knew I would do something that stupid—and probably something even dumber—if it meant seeing her.

Although the Falco home was only twenty yards away from where I was standing, I could barely make out the side entrance. There didn't seem to be any lights on at all, just like Tammy's house. Hey, maybe everyone on the block went somewhere. Sure, Johnny Ruane is home sick, we can just go out and have fun. We don't have to worry about him coming over to the easement tonight to give his girlfriend, Janie, a box of Fannie May chocolates. Sure, that's what they were thinking. I guess the fever from the flu really did affect me.

Then all of a sudden, I saw a light above the side entrance of her house. I squinted to see better and thought I watched the white wooden door open. I squinted harder through the falling flakes. The outside aluminum door opened. And there she was, all wrapped up in her blue winter coat with white mittens and a white fuzzy knit hat. Girls always looked good in hats, especially pretty girls.

I watched her make her way across her driveway, which had about four inches of snow on it. She was carrying something, a present. As she drew closer, I could feel my adrenaline begin to pump again.

"Merry Christmas!" I said, loud enough to be heard over the whipping wind.

"Merry Christmas to you! How are you feeling?"

"Better, thanks."

I wrapped my arms around her and gave her a hug. Standing there, holding her in my arms, she felt so good. It made my efforts in the miserable weather completely worthwhile.

"I don't want to give you anything," I said, backing away from her. "I mean, I don't want to get you sick. But I do want to give you this."

I handed her the red-and-blue–wrapped gift, now wet in several spots.

"Thank you," she said, smiling. "And I have this for you."

She handed me a small square gift wrapped in green, red, and white Christmas paper. She opened her gift first and her eyes opened wide.

"I love Fannie May chocolate! I absolutely love them! Thank you."

I opened my present next, and there was a small golden ring. This looked very familiar. I looked up at her, wondering if she had gone to Kresge's.

"One-dollar ring," she laughed. "I would have thrown it to you from my bicycle, but, as you know, I don't have a bike. And if I did, I couldn't ride it in this blizzard."

We laughed and embraced, holding each other tight in the blizzard, swaying ever so slightly. We were draped in silence, with only the wind filling our ears as the snowflakes melted on our heads, faces, shoulders. It felt so wonderful to hold her.

"Thanks for coming all the way over here. I was hoping to see you," she whispered, sounding relaxed, happy. "Now you have to wear that ring, so everyone knows you are my boyfriend."

"Oh, I'll wear it, all right. Proudly! I would kiss you, but I really shouldn't . . ."

Janie leaned in and kissed me on the cheek. I gazed into her beautiful brown eyes, feeling so blessed to have her in my life.

"Now you need to get back home into bed." She smiled in a sea of snowflakes. "I will talk to you when you are feeling better. Have a great Christmas!"

She turned and walked back to her house in the driving snow. Once again a surge of energy filled me. I turned and ran full speed down the snow-slicked sidewalk, past all of the darkened homes, past Tammy's house, past the streetlamps and across Tripp, through the deep snow to our '67 Chevy with my dad in the front seat listening to Lloyd Pettit on WGN.

"Why are you running?" he asked as I sat down in the passenger's seat, huffing and puffing.

"I just felt like it," I said, taking off my hat and gloves as he pulled away from the snowdrift along the curb. "Can't wait to get back home and see Bobby Hull play."

"And he is playing. He only had ten stitches from that Ferguson fight and can skate tonight."

"That's great! Hey, thanks for driving me over here tonight, Dad."

"Did it go okay?"

"Fine. It's really snowing out, though."

"Perfect weather for a perfect Christmas Eve!"

"That's right, a perfect Christmas Eve!"

Chapter Twenty-six

THE WAR HITS HOME

D elivering the *Daily News* in 1968, I couldn't help but keep up with the events in Southeast Asia. The Vietnam War was on the front page every day, dominated by news of fierce battles, body counts, and ongoing protests in the United States, demanding that President Lyndon Johnson get us out of a war that a growing number of Americans had lost interest in fighting. Too many American boys were dying for a "Domino Theory," the fear that if Vietnam fell to the Communists, the other countries in Southeast Asia would follow.

In my neighborhood, some may have believed we were untouched by all of the violence and protesting. But we were not. The residue of war was right in front of us. A blue service star was placed in the front window of each home that had a soldier serving our country. Gold stars signified boys who had sacrificed their lives. There were plenty of stars in my neighborhood and on my paper route. When I entered a home to collect, I never would ask about the brave son in Vietnam, but I could see how that fact dominated their lives.

That newspaper I delivered every afternoon was their best source of information to learn if the fighting was taking place in the region to which their sons were assigned. Many an afternoon, I would find the mothers of those sons waiting on the driveway for me to hand them the paper. They had to know what had happened.

Most of these homes received two newspapers a day, the *Tribune* in the morning and *Daily News* in the afternoon. If something happened, they wanted to be sure they knew about it, reading the latest reports in each news cycle. There was no cable television and twenty-four-hour news like today.

Most star families on my route would display a photo of their uniformed warrior proudly on the end table closest to the front door. Many of those pictures were adorned with rosaries, St. Christopher medals, holy cards, and other religious objects. The brave sons in those pictures were mere boys fresh out of high schools like Bogan, St. Rita, and St. Laurence, forced by fate and the fortunes of war to ride to the sound of the guns in the hellish place at the opposite end of the earth.

Thrust from high school to boot camp to Vietnam, often in a matter of months, they stood tall and answered their country's call. And back home their families watched, waited, and prayed for their safe return. In our parish, the war was omnipresent because it was our brothers and sons fighting and dying.

My friend Eddie Crandell's brother was in the navy and fortunate to receive an assignment away from Southeast Asia. Nonetheless, the Crandells worried greatly about him. And it made Eddie that much more sensitive to the families in his neighborhood with boys in Vietnam.

Eddie, who was a history buff, was also a paperboy. Many a day, we sat at the counter of the Tally Ho Restaurant in the Scottsdale Shopping Center, drinking chocolate malts and commiserating about our customers with sons in the war.

"Every week I enter a home with a soldier, I know instantly when good news has been received," he said, explaining his collection experience. "Even before the moms can tell me that the family had received a letter or a rare phone call from their sons assuring them that all was well, I could feel the relief in the air. When those sons returned home on temporary leave or for good, the homes remained decorated for weeks announcing the homecoming."

Those were happy days for the service star homes.

Eddie had a neighbor, Timmy Smith, who was wounded severely in Vietnam. His mother traveled to the Tokyo hospital where Timmy was being treated. The doctors wanted to amputate his legs because of the severity of his wounds, but Mrs. Smith persuaded them not to operate. She lived with her son in that hospital for more than a year, nursing him back to health. Timmy never fully recuperated, but when he returned home, a number of the police dads in the parish helped him get on the police force, somehow passing the physical exam.

As an altar boy at St. Bede's, I constantly checked the large brown board that hung on the wall just to the right of the two glass entrance doors of the church. The board was filled with brass nameplates listing the parish sons fighting in the war. A star on the nameplate was bad news, representing a fallen American hero.

On my route, five families had boys on that board, including the Staminskys. Each time I approached their home, I checked for that blue service star with the red border in the front window representing their son Ronny. I hoped that star never would be gold.

Ronny was on his second tour of duty in Vietnam. Mrs. Staminsky, a kindhearted woman who always wore knee-length flower-pattern dresses, would often invite me in from the cold. Almost without exception, I would find Mr. Staminsky sitting on their living-room sofa reading the *Daily News* that I had delivered earlier that day. Their pretty teenage daughter Kim would be sitting on the carpet two feet from her father, watching newsmen Chet Huntley and David Brinkley reporting on the war for NBC News. WBBM-AM radio, one of Chicago's all-news stations, usually was on in the background, and everything would become silent when a news report on the war was read.

One evening while collecting, I was made aware of how upset they were by the words and actions of the protesters, one of whom lived right down the block from them. Michael Phillips, who had been a childhood friend of Ronny's, went off to college at Michigan State. After graduating and returning home to Chicago, he received his draft notice. In the summer of 1968, Michael Phillips refused to go. He had a scruffy beard, and his brown hair touched his shoulders. He wore the hippie outfits of the day, tie-dye shirts with yellow peace symbols, bell-bottom blue jeans, and a jean jacket with a large yellow peace symbol on the back. He was one of the multitude in Grant Park during the summer of '68 protesting against the war. I listened to the Staminskys talk about him and how disappointed they were in him.

"I can't believe what has happened to Michael," Mr. Staminksy said to his wife in the kitchen, who was retrieving the $1.50 from her purse to pay me for the past week's newspapers. "He was good friends with Ronny. He knows he's over there fighting for our country—for him. I just don't understand it!"

Yes, the war was taking place on South Keeler Avenue, just as it was in many neighborhoods across the country.

We lived twelve miles from downtown Chicago, which, as a kid, seemed like a very long distance. In August of 1968, the hippies and yippies from all over the country invaded Chicago to protest the war during the Democratic National Convention at the International Amphitheater, located next to the old Chicago Stockyards. Fahey Flynn and Joel Daley reported from their WLS-TV studios in Marina Towers on State Street and the Chicago River. I read the details in the *Daily News* about this invasion of long-haired protesters.

The hippies would gather in Lincoln Park, where they were confronted by the police. Marty's uncle Francis Drissell was one of those cops who provided us with great insight about the hippies and their peace movement.

"Those freaks with their long hair and smelly clothes stand there and call us *pigs!*" he told us a few weeks after the convention. "They stood up on bridges and threw baggies filled with feces and urine at us. They spit on us and threw rocks at us. Some of these guys put razor blades in their shoes, trying to kick the cops and seriously hurt us. But all you see on the news is cops beating hippies with billy clubs. People wouldn't be so quick to blame us if they knew the whole story."

Uncle Fran's account put me squarely against the protesters. Like everyone I knew in my neighborhood, we were angry about this attack on our city by a bunch of freaky-looking protesters. That was without question the overwhelming sentiment on the Southwest Side of Chicago during the summer of '68.

Yes, we were shocked when Mayor Daley ordered the police to "Shoot to kill" when the rioting broke out on Michigan Avenue just outside the Conrad Hilton Hotel, the Democratic party's headquarters. Most people on our side of town loved the mayor, who had put his heart and soul into his city, building it up into a world-class metropolis.

Even though several months before the convention, President Johnson announced he would not seek reelection, the protesters wanted to be sure they sent a clear message to the Democratic party's presidential candidate, Hubert Humphrey.

"Hell no, we won't go!" was their chant outside the amphitheater. The peaceniks burned their draft cards. The hippies and yippies climbed atop the huge sculpted horse of the Logan Statue, positioned atop a fairly high hill in Grant Park across from the Hilton and chanted, "The whole world is watching!"

Even Walter Cronkite called for an end to the war, saying the United States should negotiate "as an honorable people who met their obligation to their allies and did the best we could."

One night during the summer of '68, my friend and neighbor Lenny Michaels got into an argument. I couldn't understand why we were fighting a conventional war. We were the ones with the nuclear weapons.

"Why don't we tell the Communists to get out of South Vietnam or we will be forced to drop a nuclear bomb on them," I argued to my know-it-all friend, who was double-promoted twice. "It's exactly what Harry Truman did in 1945."

"Yeah, and the Russians will drop a nuclear bomb on us," said Lenny, causing me to jump up off the porch, irritated by his support of the cat-and-mouse game the Communists were playing in Asia.

"Well, at least let's get it to that point," I argued. "Let's quit playing games and at least have the real enemy come out of the bushes. And if Russia and China are the real enemies, then why are we getting boys killed in Vietnam? Let's take on the real enemy or bring our boys home."

Attitudes were changing in America, but most kids in my neighborhood still went off to fight, while fewer boys, like Michael Phillips, protested. And for the next five years, I continued to watch blue stars placed in neighbors' windows and brass nameplates added to the large wooden board at St. Bede's Church.

Chapter Twenty-seven

DEVOTED
TEACHERS

I can look back on my Catholic school education at St. Bede's and appreciate it far more now than when I actually was going through the experience. Most of my teachers cared about how the students progressed. We weren't just a number. And much like the salaries Catholic school teachers receive today, the payback then was far less than their public school counterparts. So for most, I'm sure the job was more of a vocation than a method to make a living.

Although there were many good and dedicated teachers at the school, the first stories students usually relate are the bad ones. I've heard horrible stories about nuns who smacked misbehaving students with rulers across the knuckles, a nun who wouldn't let a student come back to class because she forgot her lunch; mean teachers, mean nuns.

Like every child that has attended any school in the country, I had my share of bad teachers. But the good ones are worth gold.

My fourth-grade teacher was a good, hard-working woman named Darlene Lausus. Many students who attended St. Bede's rank her as one of the best teachers at the school. By her approach, it was evident she was intent on teaching us. She wasn't going to just stand in front of us talking and hoping we were paying attention. No, she was going to keep our attention. Every time she finished a sentence, she always said "Hmmm?" as almost a question to us to make sure we heard it and understood it.

For example, during history class: "President Franklin Roosevelt suffered from polio. Hmmm?" she might say, looking at us to make sure it registered. "But that didn't stop him from running for governor of New York State. Hmmm? Or go on to run for president of the United States like his cousin Teddy Roosevelt. Hmmm?"

Her intentions were good. But young boys are born with the smart-aleck gene, and any time something strikes them funny, they must identify it and incorporate it into their comedy act. We must have been only two weeks into our fourth-grade year when Mike Wendell, a smart-aleck supreme, recognized the "hmmming," and that was the beginning of it.

During math class, when Miss Lausus said, "The square root of 4 is 2. Hmmm?" she was joined by another "hmmm" from somewhere else in the class.

I thought I heard it the first time.

"The square root of 9 is 3. Hmmm?"

Another "hmmm" echoed in the class. This time I most definitely heard it. So did several other kids as we began looking around for the "hmmm" mimic. We all had a pretty good idea who it would be.

"The square root of 25 is 5. Hmmm?" again echoed by "hmmm," and there was Wendell with his lips pressed hard together.

He was the culprit. Within five minutes, it seemed most of the boys in the class were aware of his joke and joined in with him. Every time Miss Lausus said "Hmmm?" she was accompanied by Wendell and his chorus of "hmmms." By the time she got to the square root of 100, it sounded like the St. Bede's Boys Choir backing her up.

"The square root of 100 is 10. Hmmm?" Hmmmmmmmmmmmmmmm!

She paused for a moment, wondering if there was a loud echo in the room, then repeated herself.

"The square root of 100 is 10. Hmmm?" Hmmmmmmm!

This time she realized what was happening.

"Okay, who is humming? Hmmm?"

She crossed her arms.

"Hmmm?" she repeated.

The boys in the class couldn't contain themselves. There was too much "hmmming" going on. Several burst out laughing.

"Oh, so you think this is funny, do you? Hmmm?"

The laughing grew louder.

"Would you like to go down to the principal's office? Hmmm?"

And louder.

"Take out some looseleaf paper and write a thousand times, 'I will respect my teacher at all times.' Hmmm?"

Silence.

"You idiot, Wendell," Kevin Fox whispered. "Now look what you did."

An hour later, when we had completed our assignment, Miss Lausus addressed us again.

"Now I hope you have all learned your lesson. Hmmm?"

We did learn our lesson that day, but we had to be reminded of it four more times during the school year as the urge to "hmmm" was too overwhelming for a bunch of ten-year-old boys.

Another great teacher was Sister Linda, one of my seventh-grade teachers. She was a member of the new, hip nuns resulting from Vatican II. Both she and Sister Ellen had just been assigned to the school, and they didn't wear the long black dresses with the white penguin bib typical of a nun's habit. They wore nice conservative blue dresses with a white shirt and blue or gray vest. Instead of the long black veil, Sister Linda wore a lighter blue babushkalike head garment with the white strip across the front to make sure we all knew she was a nun.

Sister Linda was a short, fairly thin lady with a narrow face and buck teeth. During religion class one day, she decided to teach her thirty students the correct way to stand. Didn't matter that she was a buck-toothed nun living in a convent. She had cornered the market on "hip" and was going to pass along her trendy knowledge to the thirty dorks in her classroom. During this time period, *The Flying Nun* was a hit TV show, so I think we all bought into the idea that the new younger nuns could be more modern.

"Okay, you put your left foot a little bit ahead of your right foot, bend your right knee to let your weight rest on it, and place your right hand on your hip," she said, standing in front of the class to demonstrate the correct standing posture. "Keep your head tilted upward just a bit and smile, always smile. This is the cool way to stand."

It may have been the cool way to stand, but I can promise you I never saw any kids trying to stand that way when we were milling around outside the school. If someone had tried it, others would have recognized the "attempt to be cool" and laughed them off the school grounds.

We all liked Sister Linda, though, very much. She was positive, energetic, and she had a good sense of humor. Her class was not drudgery like so many others. It was fun! I looked forward to my two classes each day with her because she was so upbeat. In my pecking order of great teachers at St. Bede's, Sister Linda finished right behind Miss Pasco.

I think that the hardest aspect of being a teacher must be bringing that enthusiasm to the classroom every day. It's probably why so many educators are young. The burnout rate must be high. I have seen some schools retain older, frustrated teachers who are obviously teaching for a paycheck, which is a crime. I know adults all have to make a living, but teaching is one of those special professions, because we ask more of our teachers than the rest of us. We really do want them to come into that classroom with great energy and enthusiasm, a positive attitude. Once they lose that, they should move on to something else and give some other teacher the opportunity.

Maybe this is one of the reasons that nuns have such a poor image. For many, their job is teaching. So when they become tired, impatient, and frustrated with the kids, they can't just quit and get another job. Perhaps that's why there are so many stories of nuns taking out their frustrations on kids with rulers, yardsticks, and anything else they can get their hands on to serve out some punishment. It doesn't excuse it, but it may explain it.

The one older nun I had at St. Bede's was Sister Pelagia, my eighth-grade teacher who looked to be around seventy years old. She was a very good person up against a group of wiseguys who had no respect or consideration for her. It was obvious the school should not have assigned her to an eighth-grade class where smart-aleck boys are the norm, not the exception.

Regardless, I would have to count myself as one of the lucky ones to attend St. Bede's. Of my twelve teachers, nine were good and three were pretty bad.

And I'm certain that my math teacher Miss Lausus would say "That's a pretty good ratio. Hmmm?"

Chapter Twenty-eight

TOUGH TIMES

As I knelt on the altar that cold Monday morning in February of 1971, watching Father Griffin recite the opening prayers, I was very aware of just how badly I was feeling—horrible! A pain ran through my entire body like I had never known before. How could she break up with me? *Why* would she break up with me?

Two days earlier, Saturday night, I was standing with her, holding her in my arms at the easement when she broke my heart.

"We're getting too close and I just think it's a good idea that we start seeing other people," Janie said to me, not looking completely committed to those words.

Stunned, I could hardly open my mouth. I just looked at her. Was this a bad dream? We were so happy together. The other kids in the eighth grade thought we were such a great couple.

"Why?" I asked. "I thought you really liked me."

"I do. Very much," she said. "But as hard as this is right now, I just think we are too young to get this serious."

"That sounds like something one of our parents would say," I snapped.

She paused. Oh, so that was it.

"Your mother?"

"I just think . . ."

"Your father?"

"I'm sorry."

I just looked at her, hurt, trying to hold back the tears that were building up quickly.

"We can still be friends," she offered, and she began to cry. "I have to go."

She turned quickly and started to walk toward her home.

"Janie!" I said, stopping her and approaching, taking her in my arms one last time. The wonderful scent of her beautiful brown hair filled the air. I would miss it. I looked into her brown eyes. "I want you to know that I will always love you."

I could see her eyes beginning to fill with tears. This was not easy for her either. She hugged me, then quickly turned and ran to her home. I realized I had never seen her run before. I had always been the one to run home after saying goodbye, filled with the energy and excitement from our time together.

I watched her disappear into that familiar white wooden door with the framed glass window. I saw the drapes in her front picture window move. Her mother was obviously making sure the breakup was final.

Just then, I heard a loud cough. Father Griffin was looking at me. I was supposed to bring the Bible up to him for the reading. I hurried to the altar boys' table, picked up the book, and hustled up the three red-carpeted steps, nearly tripping over my cassock. The priest wasn't happy. That made two of us.

The entire Mass, all I could think about was Janie and how lousy I felt. I took a Bayer aspirin that morning, but it didn't seem to help. I could feel my emotions rushing up from my chest. I wasn't going to let myself cry.

I remember my mother telling us about Mark Janek, my friend from younger days of building forts in the prairie next to the Mackeys' house. Mark was a junior in high school when his girlfriend broke up with him. He was so distraught that he went into his garage, took a can of gasoline, and drank from it. He was only sixteen years old, but he killed himself because a girl he obviously loved very much broke up with him.

As badly as I felt, I couldn't understand Mark's actions. I couldn't even understand consideration of such a tragic self-inflicted act. Mark's experience made it clear to me just how much love can hurt, even at a young age.

If Mrs. Falco was the reason for the breakup, why didn't she just wait until school was over in June? We were going to different high schools. Janie was scheduled to go to Bogan and I was hoping to attend St. Laurence, an all-boys' Catholic high school.

Regardless, I had to deal with it. I didn't say a word to anyone about the breakup, not even Marty. I was too depressed. That morning as I sat at my desk in school, it seemed like a normal day. If anyone knew about my troubles, there would be whispering, pointing, and peeking at me. There was none. When I passed Janie in the hallway, she wouldn't even look up from the floor as she walked past me. Her eyes were a bit swollen, as if she had been crying. Maybe she was struggling too.

The breakup would be big news on the Anita Carick news service that week, if she had been aware of it. That definitely wouldn't help my frame of mind. But I knew everyone would find out. It was inevitable.

Would Janie's mother issue a press release to let everyone know? What would the headline say? "Janie Falco breaks up with John Ruane. Mother says it's time to move on." Would Janie be quoted in it? "Sure I was hurt, but I can see my mother's position here. I'm only thirteen. Lots of fish in the sea. Can't just catch the first one and give up. No, got to get out there, play the field. Why settle with a halibut when you can catch a trout?"

About two weeks after the breakup, it was obvious the word had gotten out. Anita approached me at my desk before the second bell rang. She wanted the exclusive.

"Hi, John," she said, with her thin-lipped, sloppy red-lipsticked smile. "I'm having a party again Friday night. Are you interested in coming?"

"Thanks, Anita," I said. "I'm not sure."

"You can bring Janie," she said, watching to see my reaction.

"Thanks. I'll think about it."

Anita's face dropped a bit, having failed to receive the information she was seeking. She didn't give up.

"So how is Janie?"

"Good."

That didn't do it for her.

"I didn't see you walking her home after school yesterday."

"I have to go straight home from school this week."

"Oh!" she muttered, now completely confused. "Well, let me know about Friday."

"I will," I said, not wanting to go any further with the conversation. It was none of her business. Puzzled, she walked back to her desk. Anita had failed to get the scoop, a first for her.

Throughout the day, no one else mentioned Janie to me. I saw her pass in the hall each day, and each day she continued to stare at the floor as she walked past. Her eyes weren't swollen anymore. Guess it took two whole days to get over me. As I walked home that afternoon, I still felt horrible and wondered how long it would take to start feeling normal again.

Just when things seem really bad in life, sometimes they get worse. Three weeks later, I had just arrived home from school on a Wednesday afternoon to find no one home. I wondered where Mom had gone. My sister Maureen came through the front door a few minutes later, followed by Danny, Kathy, and Margaret.

"Where's Mom?" I asked.

"She had a doctor's appointment this afternoon," Maureen said. "She'll be home by three o'clock."

No big deal. Mom's at the doctor's for her normal checkup, I'll just make myself a snack, call Marty on the phone, and find out who's blabbing about me and Janie.

"Everyone knows," said Marty, who sounded like he was eating potato chips while talking on the phone. "The thing is, no one knows why. Not even Anita! So what's the story and how come you didn't tell me?"

I filled Marty in on the entire story and how badly I felt. He offered to approach Janie to confirm that her mother made her break up, but I asked him not to.

"Well, how about asking Anita to talk to her? She'll get it out of her."

"No, I think Janie feels bad enough as it is right now. I would rather just put it behind us and move on, for both of our sakes. It's too bad, I really liked her."

All five of the Ruane kids sat in the living room watching *Gilligan's Island* on television when Mom walked in the front door about 3:45 that afternoon. She didn't look well. We all noticed it. Mom went into her room, the middle bedroom along the hallway, and closed the door.

Something was wrong. Maureen stood up and walked to the bedroom.

"Mom?" she said, knocking on the door, which opened a few seconds later. Maureen walked in and the door was closed behind her. Maureen was only a sophomore in high school, but she was very smart and very mature for fifteen.

Kathy and I knew Maureen would find out what was going on, so we returned our focus to the Skipper and Gilligan. Four o'clock came and went with no sign of Maureen or Mom. About fifteen minutes later, we heard the back door open. Looking down the hallway, we could see our father in his green work pants and heavy coat sitting down on the top step of the stairway to take off his work boots. He was always tired and dirty when he got home from work each day with the Chicago Water Department.

All of a sudden, my mother's door opened and out stepped Maureen, who walked directly to my father and said something to him in a low tone, which seemed to alarm him. He stood up and walked into Mom's room. Maureen followed him in.

Kathy, having watched everything that was happening, stood up and turned off the TV.

"Hey, what are you doing?" Danny bellowed.

"Be quiet, Danny! Something's wrong!"

Danny's face dropped, as he now realized he had missed something important. We could hear them talking in the room, but the voices were too muffled to understand. Kathy walked right up to the door. With the TV off, her footsteps on the creaking wooden floor under the green carpet could be heard easily. The voices went silent as she reached the door. I think they heard her, because a few seconds later the doorknob began to turn. Kathy reacted quickly and darted back into the living room, leaping onto the couch. At the same time, Danny shot up and turned on the TV. My father walked out of the room first, followed by Mom and Maureen.

"Hey, kids, we need to have a quick family meeting here," announced Dad, as he turned off the Zenith, which was still warming up, the picture just beginning to appear on the screen.

Maureen sat next to Kathy and Margaret on the couch, while Mom walked to the brown armchair to the right of the picture window. Dad stood in front of the TV to address us.

"Mom just got back from the doctor, and she's going to have to go into the hospital for a few days to get something fixed," he said.

As each of our heads turned toward our mother simultaneously, he continued. "Dr. Fitzgerald can take care of it on Friday morning, but Mom will have to stay in the hospital for a few days until she is ready to come home. It's nothing bad, just something they have to take care of."

Somehow, I think my mother hearing my dad downplay her situation inspired her a little. "I will be fine," she assured us. "This is just something some mothers have to go through when they are my age."

"Well, what is it?" Kathy asked, not satisfied with the lack of information.

"They found a small lump in my chest and they just need to take it out," Mom explained. "It's done all the time. It will be like when you got your tonsils out, Kathy. You remember how you had to go into the hospital for a few days, but you were fine. Same thing."

That seemed to relieve Kathy's worries. She understood the tonsil analogy. It sounded simple enough, and my mother wasn't showing any signs of fear. She goes to the hospital where Dr. Kenneth Fitzgerald, our longtime family physician, would help perform the operation, and she would be home in a few days to recover. No big deal.

My father woke us all up early that cold Friday morning. The smell of bacon and percolating Hills Brothers coffee filled the air, while Dad stood at the stove cooking for all of us. Maureen and Kathy were setting the gray Formica-top kitchen table as I walked sleepily toward my chair, rubbing my eyes.

"Where's your brother?" Dad said.

"Still sleeping," I said, plopping down into my gray-cushioned, round metal-framed chair at the kitchen table.

"Well, wake him up!" he demanded, as I popped up and awoke completely, scampering back into our back bedroom, where Danny lay on his back, open-mouthed and sound asleep.

"Danny, wake up," I said, shaking my brother, who quickly woke up to see me holding his shoulders and then just as quickly closed his eyes to pretend he was sleeping in order to drive me crazy. "Okay, that's it. I'm getting a bucket of water."

Danny jumped out of bed.

"I'm up, I'm up," he said, making a beeline to the kitchen and his chair to the left of mine.

Mom came out of her room with a smile on her face. There was no sign of any problem. But Maureen knew better. She was smarter than me and fully aware of the circumstances.

"Did Dr. Fitzgerald say how long you would be in the hospital?" she asked.

"About a week," Mom replied. "After the operation, they just want to keep me there to make sure I am getting the best care."

No one was talking at the breakfast table that morning, which wasn't that unusual. On any normal morning, we were so tired we just ate our breakfast, grabbed our already-made lunches in the brown paper bags, threw on our green parkas, woolen hats, and gloves, and walked out the door still half asleep. But Mom would have none of that on this day. She wanted things to be upbeat at the breakfast table before her big day. She wasn't allowed to eat or drink anything.

"Now, while I'm away, I want you to make sure you help your father," she explained. "Maureen and Kathy, you help with the laundry. Johnny, you fold the clothes and put them away. Danny, you help with the dishes, and Margaret, you sweep the floor. I don't want to come home here to a dirty house with laundry piled up, do you understand? That would make me very unhappy."

That came through loud and clear. One thing we absolutely weren't going to do was make our mother unhappy upon returning from her operation at the hospital.

"Maureen, you are in charge until I get home today," Dad instructed, then looked at his two boys. "And I don't want any horsing around from you two. Do you understand?"

"Yes sir," I replied.

After breakfast, Danny and I went into our room to get dressed in our St. Bede's uniforms.

"You better not goof around while Mom's gone," I ordered Danny, and we stood there a few feet apart, getting dressed.

"Just worry about yourself," he snapped back. "I never start the fights. I just finish them."

"Yeah, on the bottom," I replied, quickly realizing my wisecrack might start a tussle. "Hey, I'm sorry. Forget that. I'm not saying anything or doing anything to cause trouble."

"About time, you broad," Danny jabbed back.

I walked out of the room, grabbed my brown lunch bag, and gave my mom a hug.

"Don't worry, Johnny, I'll be all right," she said, holding me and giving me a kiss of reassurance to let me know everything was fine.

For that moment, as she held me against her, everything in the world was all right again.

<small>Chapter Twenty-nine</small>

A PRAYER FOR HELP

"**D**ear God, please help my mother to be all right. We love her so much! She is such a good person. She prays every day. She helps people any way possible. She is such a good Catholic and believes in You so much. She helps at the church and sings at the Masses. I love my mom, God. Please help her."

I made the Sign of the Cross and rose from the kneeler in the first row of the dark and empty church that Friday afternoon in April of 1971. This was the same row in which I had sat during my First Communion; the same row I sat in the day I was waiting for my altar boy initiation. As I turned to leave the aisle, I stopped and looked up at Jesus on that familiar cross. I just hoped He would help.

It was 6:00 P.M. that Friday when Dad led all five of us down the dimly lit corridor on the sixth floor of Little Company of Mary Hospital, the cancer ward. I couldn't help but notice all of the religious statues and pictures that were placed in the reception area and along the walls as we walked toward our mother's room at the end of the hall. The large bright room was divided into two, with Mom on the right side and another woman on the left. A white partition separated the large corner room, and it gave both patients plenty of privacy.

When we entered, Mom smiled. In unison, it seemed, we all lunged toward her for a hug, but were stopped by Dad's very strong Popeye-like right arm. Mom had an intravenous tube attached to her left arm, and Dad saved us from creating a medical emergency.

"Wait!" he said firmly. "You have to be careful. Now, one at a time—and be careful."

Margaret, the youngest, gave Mom a big hug and didn't want to let go. She seemed to be shaken by the sight of her mother sitting in a hospital bed with tubes attached to her. We all were a bit jarred. Margaret started to cry. Dad lifted her up to hold her as Danny, then Kathy, Maureen, and I each gave our mother a hug and kiss.

"Hey, everything is all right, Margaret," Mom explained as Margaret sat on Dad's lap at the foot of the bed. "The doctors took the bad lump out of me and now I just have to get better."

Margaret smiled under her tears.

"We got you some chocolate mints, Mom, because we know how much you like them," Maureen said as she placed the small rectangular Fannie May box on the nightstand.

"Thanks, Maureen, but I won't be able to eat those for a while. Why don't you kids have them?"

As the mints were passed around the room, I wasn't convinced that Mom's smile conveyed her true condition.

"Mom, how do you feel?" I asked.

"They have me on pain medication, so it doesn't hurt that much right now. I'll be fine in a few days."

Just then, the stout Dr. Fitzgerald entered the room holding a chart. A black stethoscope hung over the front of his doctor's smock. Dr. Fitzgerald had been our family physician ever since I could remember. He took care of all of us, and we liked him because every time we had an appointment with him, he always gave us a Tootsie Roll Pop sucker when we were finished. For kids, that made it all worthwhile.

"Bernie, I need to speak to you and Terry alone," he said to my father, with a tone in his voice that didn't sound good.

It got Mom's attention, as her eyes grew wide with concern. Dad just stared at the doctor, wondering if something was wrong.

"Maureen, take the kids down to the reception area," Dad said, handing Margaret to me. "I'll be down in a few minutes. Kids, give your mom a kiss goodbye. We will probably leave when I'm done talking with Dr. Fitzgerald."

As each of us gave Mom a kiss, she couldn't hold it back anymore. She began to cry.

"I'm okay, kids," she said. "I'll see you tomorrow, right?" Then we all started to cry. We hated seeing our mother cry. God, why couldn't everything be okay, I prayed in silence.

As I walked back down that dim corridor, somehow I knew something bad was happening. We sat on the long padded benches along the wall in the circular reception area with the nurses' station in the middle. A few minutes later Dr. Fitzgerald emerged from the hallway. He waved to us and continued around the corner to the elevators.

We sat there staring at that corridor for what seemed like an eternity, waiting for Dad to come out. About fifteen minutes later, we saw him wiping his eyes as he walked down the hall. He approached the nurse at the desk and muttered something I couldn't hear well enough to understand.

"C'mon, kids, let's go," he said.

"What's wrong, Dad?" asked Kathy.

"Nothing. Mom is fine. She will have to stay in the hospital a few days longer than we thought. They just want to be sure they do everything to take care of her properly. It's okay."

Silence filled the small elevator packed with six Ruanes riding down to the lobby, with only the murmur of the elevator filling our ears. Dad sniffled a few times, which bothered me. Something else was wrong.

The walk across California Avenue to the parking lot seemed to take forever. We just wanted to know what was going on with Mom. But we didn't want to ask Dad. He was upset enough.

When we arrived home, Dad told everyone to get into their pajamas and go straight to bed. After Danny, Margaret, and Kathy had fallen asleep, Dad woke me up and called me out to the kitchen table where Maureen was already sitting.

"Look, you two are the oldest, so you are going to have to help," explained Dad in a somber tone. "Your mother is going to be all right, but the lump they took out was sent to a lab and it is malignant."

I'm sure a puzzled look crossed my face. What did that mean?

"She had breast cancer and it was spreading. They think they got all of it out, but they can't be certain. Dr. Fitzgerald said she now has to begin a series of chemo-therapy treatments to make sure they kill all of it. He said it's not going to be easy for her. She's going to be tired a lot. She is not going to feel normal. She's probably going to be irritable, not herself. So we have to continue taking care of the house and help your mother. Can you help me with that?"

Maureen and I nodded, but we were both a little stunned at the news. As a kid, that term "breast cancer" sounds bad. But at that time, I had no conception how devastating the illness could be to a person's mind and body. I knew Mom had a lump in her chest and they took it out with an operation. That didn't sound scary.

Kathy had an operation to take out her tonsils. Dad had an operation to remove kidney stones. Operations were just something they did at the hospital to take stuff out of you that didn't belong there. But a breast cancer operation was not that simple.

Over the next few days, Dad would either bring Maureen or myself up to the hospital to visit Mom and leave the other one home to watch Danny and Margaret. They were too young and it was too emotional for everyone involved. Poor Margaret was only six years old and she really missed her mother. Danny was only nine. Kathy, twelve, had the choice of staying home or going to the hospital to visit. She went a few times, but I think it depressed her so she only went with Dad about half the time.

The news of the malignancy may have gotten my mother's spirits down for a short time, but she was a fighter and rebounded quickly. When we visited her that Saturday afternoon, she had already prepared herself mentally for the battle and was ready to go. Seeing her spirits return reassured us.

The next Friday, Dad had Maureen join him to pick up Mom from Little Company of Mary, just one week after the operation. Dr. Fitzgerald was pleased with her progress and optimistic that her attitude and strong will would get her through the treatments just fine.

I ran home from school that day as fast as my legs would carry me. I did not see our blue Chevy in front of the house. Were they home? Dad probably parked the car in the garage, so as not to attract attention. The front door was open, so I knew someone must be home. I bolted inside the door, dropped my books on Dad's armchair, and walked quickly into my mother and father's bedroom. There they were. Mom was sitting up in bed, smiling, with Maureen sitting at the foot of the bed and Dad standing on the other side.

I lunged at Mom, giving her a big hug.

"Johnny!" she said, taken aback by my burst of energy. "Easy now." She wrapped her arms around me. The world felt right again.

I could hear Danny coming through the front door.

"I'm home! Where is everyone?" he shouted.

"In here," Dad bellowed. "We're in the bedroom."

Danny came tearing around the corner.

"Mom!"

He jumped on the bed next to me.

"Out of my way, broadly," he said to me, giving Mom a big hug.

She kissed his forehead, so happy to see him again.

Margaret and Kathy appeared a few seconds later and the same scene was repeated, except Margaret didn't want to let go of her mommy. I don't think she wanted her to leave the house again; none of us did.

During the next few days, Mom gained more strength and began to work her way into her normal lifestyle, taking care of all of us. We argued with her about it, but while we were at school, she moved right back into washing the clothes, cooking the meals, and cleaning the house. I'm sure it must have kept her mind off her condition and gave a sense of normalcy to her day.

And as the days passed, life seemed slowly to return to normal. Mom was singing again, which for us meant everything was back to normal. The hills were alive with the sound of music, and so was our home as Mom belted out her favorite show tunes.

As I knelt in church serving 10:00 A.M. Mass that first week of May, I prayed to God that things could go back to the way they were before her operation. I wanted that happy, normal life we all enjoyed so much. I wanted to sit in front of the television set and watch *The Dean Martin Show* and *Twelve O'Clock High* with my mother in one armchair, my father in the other, as my brother and sisters sat behind me on the couch. That was happiness to me. We were all together, a happy family, enjoying life.

It's funny how the mind works, but with Mom home and things seemingly back to normal—at least for a short while—I started to feel the weight of the pain that had saturated my heart and mind fall off. I started to feel happy again. Kneeling on the altar during Mass three days a week, my thoughts were dominated by my mother. And I would look up at the cross to Jesus for the strength to get through it.

But I knew the cure for me. Each day I got home, I did my chores, hugged my mom, and shot right back out the door with my Spalding basketball in hand. I dribbled all the way down to the St. Bede's Church parking lot and shot hoops for at least an hour. Marty, Mike, and Eddie always knew I would be there, and that usually resulted in a game of two-on-two a few times a week.

On Wednesday morning, May 5, we all trudged off to school knowing Mom would go in for her first treatment. When I returned from school that day, she was sleeping.

"You have to be quiet when Mom is sleeping," I told my brother in a stern tone. "She is going to be tired when she gets back from the hospital."

My brother just looked at me and leaped off the couch to start the daily wrestling match. I picked him up and hauled him through the front door.

"Look, Danny, I'm not kidding about this!" I hollered. "When Mom is sleeping, you have to be quiet in the house."

Danny was angry. Oh great!

"Danny, I'm not trying to be mean, but you have to understand, okay?"

I felt terrible. He was just a little boy and his mother was sick.

"C'mon, broadly, let's go shoot hoops."

I rarely invited Danny to shoot with me, so the invitation elated him. We took turns dribbling the ball, passing it back and forth as we ran down the street toward St. Bede's parking lot. Although Danny was only nine, he was a pretty tall kid, only a few inches shorter than me at the time. He could shoot at the ten-foot basket with no problem, which was remarkable for his age, I thought. He was a good athlete and we had a fun time playing games of "horse" that day.

Each Wednesday morning for the next four weeks, Mom would go in for her treatment. And each Wednesday afternoon, we would find her lying in bed when we returned home from school. On the other days, she seemed fine. One afternoon after arriving home from school, she called us into her room. With all five of us on her bed, she wanted to warn us about an upcoming event so we were prepared. I'm sure she was most concerned about the younger ones and wanted to be sure she didn't shock any of us, especially Margaret and Danny.

"This medicine they are giving me helps me," she explained, as she reached into a large white box and took out a Styrofoam head with a wig on it. "But the treatments will make me lose my hair for a short time. So I am going to have to wear a wig for a few months until all of my hair grows back."

Kathy had trouble understanding this, as did the rest of us.

"Why would you lose your hair, Mom? Are you sure it will come back?"

"Yes, this is normal for patients who go through this type of therapy," Mom said. "So I didn't want you to be surprised when you saw me without my hair or with a wig on. Do you understand?"

We each nodded, but this hair thing didn't sit well with me. Why would she lose all of her hair? Throughout May, Mom continued to go for her chemotherapy treatments. We started to notice clumps of hair in the girls' bathroom and the bathtub. I think all of us would check Mom's hair to see if it looked any different. She had so much of it, we never really saw the drastic change. By May 15, Mom decided it was time either to wear her wig or a head garment. Mom chose to wear her green head garment on most days, and that's the most vivid memory I have of her during that difficult time.

I was serving Mass almost every day by this point. I wanted to be at church, praying. I prayed to Jesus for my mother. I knew the Mass so well, I could serve it with my eyes closed, so I was able to focus on prayer throughout most of the service.

Mom finished her treatments on Wednesday, May 26, and Dad decided this was worth a celebration for the family on Thursday when Mom was feeling better. We rarely went out to dinner as a family, so when we did, it was special. And dinner out for the Ruanes usually meant Vito & Nick's Pizzeria, a neighborhood favorite.

Vito & Nick's is a small Italian restaurant on the 8400 block of South Pulaski Avenue with red-and-white-checkered tablecloths on the left and a long bar on the right. White Italian lights, the kind people use to decorate Christmas trees, were hung on the paneling above the bar, I guess to give the place a festive look. Either way, we loved their pizza, and the price was right, so it was the perfect place for any family celebration.

May was the home stretch to summer and what we hoped would be a break in our lives after so much turmoil since Christmas. Mom had to go into the hospital for one more set of tests that would confirm all of the cancer was out of her. Her appointment was scheduled three days after my final day of school at St. Bede's.

I ran home from school quickly that day to get the good news from Mom first. To my surprise, she had not arrived home. Danny, Kathy, and Margaret came running through the front door minutes later. We all ate our snacks, thinking Mom would be walking through the door any minute. Soon Danny began to get antsy and went next door to play with his friend, Buddy Butz. Margaret and Kathy were determined to be there when Mom returned. They parked themselves on the couch in the front room, watching *Lassie* on WGN-TV.

I grabbed my basketball from the garage and thought about running down to the parking lot to shoot, but halfway down the block I decided to turn around. I was going to be there when Mom got home. I just sat on the front porch steps dribbling the ball in front of me and thinking about everything—Mom, school, my upcoming graduation. Around 3:45 P.M., I spotted Maureen walking briskly down Kostner from 87th Street, where the bus dropped her off.

"Is Mom not home yet?" she asked.

"It should be any time now," I replied, then spotted our Chevy coming down Kostner.

"She's home! Mom's home!" I yelped and ran up the steps quickly and opened the front door, yelling in to my two sisters, "Mom's home!"

Margaret and Kathy came flying out the front door and down the steps, joining Maureen and me as we waited by the curb. We backed up a few steps as the car approached. Then we saw it. Dad was driving. Mom was in the passenger side and she didn't look well.

The closer they got, the clearer we could see their faces. Mom's face was red. She was crying. Oh no, now what?

Dad stepped out of the driver's side first.

"Kids, get inside," he directed, pointing his finger at the front door.

"What's wrong?" asked Kathy.

"Just get inside. I'll talk to you there."

"Is Mom all right?" I asked.

"Get inside!" Dad hollered. "Now!"

We walked quickly up the three steps and into the front door. I walked to the picture window. The girls sat on the couch. I watched Dad help Mom out of the car. She was very upset. Dad held her in his right arm and walked her up the three steps and into the front door. There she was, crying terribly. Mom and Dad didn't say a word. He just kept walking with her to their bedroom, then closed the door.

"Kathy, go get Danny," Maureen ordered.

Kathy, who was starting to cry herself, ran out the front door. We could hear her yelling our brother's name as she ran across the front lawn. Like the day Mom found out she was going to have an operation, there we were, sitting again in the front room, waiting to find out what was happening. What could they tell Mom that would upset her so much? She had to be okay. She had the lump removed. She did the chemotherapy. What else could she do?

Kathy and Danny came back through the front door a few minutes later. Waiting on the couch, we all turned our heads as we heard the doorknob from the bedroom turn. The door swung open and my father stepped out. He closed the door behind him. Now my dad was crying. My dad never cried—just that one time at the hospital. C'mon, God, I thought. What's going on here? Dad walked past us wiping his eyes with the white hanky he always carried in his pants pocket.

I didn't see him walk down the steps, so I peaked around the corner and saw him standing on the porch, leaning against the white metal railing. I was going to be a man about this. I looked at my brother and sisters, then decided to walk out the front door. I stopped just outside the door and looked at my dad. He didn't look up when I approached.

"They didn't get it all," he said.

"What?" I said, seeing my sister Maureen appear at the door behind me.

"The X-rays showed there is still more of the cancer in her chest. They have to do another operation."

I was stunned. This wasn't over. It was just starting again. My poor mom! How would she get through this? This was a crushing blow to her morale. She thought she was done with the operating room, done with chemotherapy, done with cancer.

I walked back through the front door, past Maureen, and up to my mother's bedroom door.

"Mom, can I come in?" I asked, knocking lightly.

"I'm okay," she cried.

I opened her door to find her sitting on her bed, saying the rosary. Tears were pouring down her cheeks. There were no white clouds to be seen out her bedroom window on this day, just gray sky.

"Mom, you're going to be all right," I said, trying to give her some hope, some positive feedback. "You did it once. You can do it again. I know you can."

I put my arms around my mother, whose tears fell down onto my right arm.

"I'm so sorry, Johnny. I'm so sorry!" she said as her head slid onto my chest.

I was sure things were not right in the world on this day.

Chapter Thirty

A FAREWELL TO ST. BEDE'S

Friday, May 28, 1971, my last day at St. Bede's Grammar School, was a joyous day to be sure. When I arrived at school, my eighth-grade class was giddy with the thought of not having to come back to this school where most of us had spent our formative youth, going to the same building, same old classrooms, same desks, same cloakrooms, same washrooms—everything was the same. We were ready for a change of scenery.

It would be a short day. Arrive at 8:00 A.M., clean out our desk, hand in our books, and at some point receive our final report card and go home. Class was scheduled to be dismissed at 11:00 A.M. This was for eighth-graders only. The other students had another week left before their summer vacation would begin.

As Sister Pelagia called out each student's name, one by one my classmates got up to get their final report card. John Harey, one of the class clowns, raised both his arms in victory after receiving his orange paper-sleeved report card. Sister Pelagia could no longer punish him for his bad conduct, and Harey reveled in that knowledge. He was finished. If she tried to punish him for his display of accomplishment, he wouldn't listen. She couldn't tell him to stay after school to clap erasers or clean the blackboard. No, John Harey wouldn't listen. He had his final document. He would just leave. All the students watched as he danced back to his desk and exclaimed, "I am out of here!"

"Not yet, you're not," Sister Pelagia snapped. "You have two practices next week before graduation on Friday. So sit down and behave or you won't be receiving your diploma. Do you understand?"

Harey just laughed and sat down.

Dave Dazzo was next. Here was a kid who had caused her terrible stress over the past school year. I thought it would be fitting if, after she handed Dazzo his report card, she stood up and danced, raising her arms in the air and shouting "He's out of here!"

The other students filed up one at a time, respectfully receiving the report card and pulling out the folded document from the sleeve to see their grades as they returned to their desks. Mark Leko, who was just a few seats away from me, was probably the smartest kid in class. When he received his report card, he didn't have to check it. He knew he had straight A's. I knew he had straight A's. Everyone in class knew he had straight A's. He was the tall boy with the sandy blond hair and black-rimmed glasses. He looked smart. He was smart. And a nice kid as well.

I was sitting waiting for Sister to call my name, but I could see she was all out of report cards.

"John Ruane, would you please see me after class is dismissed."

Everyone turned and looked at me. I could feel the flush of the blood fill my face. A buzzing filled my head. What happened? Why didn't I get a report card? The kids were looking at me like I had done something wrong. They must have been wondering why I didn't get my report card as well.

"I have enjoyed teaching most of you this year," Sister Pelagia said, wrapping up our time with her. "And I hope you will all go on to have success in high school, college, and beyond. Class dismissed!"

She barely got "dismissed" out of her mouth, when the shouts and cheers rang through the room; several boys ran out of the classroom door and straight to the exit. The girls grouped together with their friends and talked as they made their way out the door. I just watched, wondering why the one day I looked forward to celebrating was now being ruined.

"What happened?" Leko asked me.

I just shrugged my shoulders, trying to hold back the tears. I waited for all of the kids to leave before approaching the teacher.

"John, I was told this morning that I am unable to give you your report card until your parents make the final tuition payment," she explained in the nicest manner possible. "Your mother is at the rectory now meeting with Father Griffin and would like you to meet her there. I'm sorry."

I just stood there, stunned. There was no holding back the tears. I was embarrassed. I felt like the world's biggest criminal being sent to face the Grand Jury.

I knew I had to avoid all of the kids celebrating just outside the exit doors near the gym. As I poked my head out of the classroom, I could see them, they were happy. They were done, even John Harey and Dave Dazzo. But I wasn't. My parents couldn't afford to pay the final tuition payment. Of course they couldn't. My mother had just been operated on for breast cancer, and the hospital bills were huge. My dad was trying to take care of my mother, five kids, and go to work every day for the city of Chicago's Water Department, digging ditches and laying water pipes—a very tough, physical job.

I walked down the hall away from the gym exit where all the happy kids were standing. I put my head down so no one could see me and quickly made my way through the corridors to the farthest exit, which let me out in front of the rectory. As I exited, I looked to make sure no one in my grade was around. Quickly, I ran across the street and rang the bell of the rectory door. What would they say to me? I had no idea what to expect.

An unfamiliar lady answered and led me to Father Griffin's office, knocking on the closed door.

"Yes," Father Griffin's familiar voice bellowed.

"I have the Ruane boy here," she said, and a few seconds later the door opened, revealing Mom sitting in front of Father Griffin's desk. She was crying. In an instant, I forgot my embarrassment. All I could think about was Father Griffin making my mother cry. This was the woman who gave her heart and soul to this church and that priest. And when times got tough for the Ruane family, Father Griffin turned his back on us and wouldn't let me graduate.

I ran over and gave my mother a hug, then glared up at the heartless priest.

"We are done here," said the man whom I had assisted at Mass for four straight years. He handed my mother the report card, and she looked relieved.

"Thank you, Father Griffin," she said, wiping her eyes with a white tissue.

How could she talk to this man with respect? All she wanted was to correct the situation and stay in his good graces. I couldn't understand her.

"We will get the money to you as soon as possible," she said, working to gain her composure as she stood to leave.

"I know you will, Mrs. Ruane," he said, sounding like we had better get him every cent of the thirty-five dollars we owed.

"We have been aware of your health problems for some time now and will pray for your recovery and good news on Monday," he continued, revealing he indeed had known about her health problems and upcoming exam.

"Thank you so much, Father, that means a lot to me," Mom said, so happy to have the pastor's prayers.

Mom took my hand as we walked out the door into the bright sunshine. Kids in my grade were still hanging around the school, so happy to be done. Well, now I was done too.

"Are you okay, Mom?" I asked hoping she wasn't too upset.

"Yes, Johnny. We weren't able to pay the tuition this month and Father Griffin just wanted to make sure we could take care of it later," she said, justifying his position.

I never could understand or forgive Griffin's money-focused actions. How could a pastor of a Catholic church make a woman seven weeks out of the hospital after a cancer operation, followed by chemotherapy, come crawling to him crying and begging to please let her boy have his report card?

I guess our family's record over a decade meant nothing—pitching in to help start the church, supporting every plea for more money in the Sunday collection, singing at the Masses and my altar boy service. Damn it, we need your money and we need it now, was Father Griffin's attitude. I thought about asking him if Jesus would hold a struggling family's feet to the fire. Or would He overturn the table in the pastor's office and call him a hypocrite? I knew the answer to that question, even at fourteen years old.

My mother never saw the apparent heartlessness of Father Griffin's action. The priests were always right in her eyes. She was a product of Resurrection Parish, where she and many of her friends had planned to become nuns. The priest was a holy and reverent fixture in her neighborhood while she was growing up on the West Side of Chicago during the Great Depression. As a parishioner of St. Bede's, she was a loyal, devoted, and committed Catholic. The only time she would ever let Father Griffin down was when cancer got in her way. She would apologize, promise the money, anything to stay in his good graces—that is all that mattered to her.

It's probably better that my mother didn't have a full perspective on Father Griffin or the financial situation of the church. According to the Chicago Archdiocese tax records, in 1965 St. Bede's was pulling in $159,388 in contributions, plus donations of $170,922 to the parish building fund. By 1971, the parish was taking in $376,356 in parish donations. Each year, Father Griffin was able to pay an additional $103,000 against the principal of the mortgage on the church, which cost the parish a total of $700,000 to build. Each year, the church had a surplus. In 1965, it was $63,000. On June 30, 1969, the surplus funds on deposit with the Chancery totaled $130,942—a tremendous amount of money back then. He was doing a great job running a business but a lousy job being a priest. His focus was money, and he lost sight of the poor souls he was supposed to be saving because of his devotion to parish solvency.

Griffin's apparent obsession with money was the most frequent complaint heard from St. Bede's parishioners during the 1960s. All too often during the homily, instead of talking about the Gospel, Father Griffin would use this time to call on everyone in the parish to donate more money. He would cite the costs to run the school, the mortgage on the church, utilities and maintenance costs, and so on. These appeals came just a few years after my parents—and many other parishioners—had forked over a good deal of money to help build the church. And the people in this parish were hard-working, blue-collar, middle-class families—many of whom worked for the city of Chicago, just like my dad. No one was wealthy.

Christmas and Easter were always Griffin's best and longest appeals. He knew that twice-a-year Catholics needed to hear his call for more money.

"I know how busy all of you are, and the demands of raising your families is very difficult," he would say during the homily on Christmas and Easter. "I would like to see all of you attend Mass each Sunday, as the Ten Commandments require. But if that is impossible and you are unable to make the commitment of time, please show God your commitment to his church through your donation."

This ploy must have worked because it seems I heard that same sermon annually during Mass on the two holiest days of the year. Once I became an altar boy and was actually up there with Father Griffin during Christmas Mass of 1968, I watched the faces of those in the pews as he delivered the talk. Some listened, some looked bored, others just looked down into their hymn books, not really interested in hearing it once again. But in this appeal, he was really going to get their attention.

"If we aren't able to raise the funds needed to cover our expenses, I'm afraid the Archdiocese will have to consider other options for our church and school."

The heads popped up from the hymn books at this statement. Other options, what does that mean? Oh, it was clear now, and all eyes in the church were wide and looking at Father Griffin. As he turned away from the pulpit, I could see a slight smile cross his face. He had gotten to his audience and he knew it. A few seconds later, Mr. Chubs and his crew, carrying the long straw-handled collection baskets, descended on the gathering. As they shot the baskets down each pew, it looked like a jackpot for Father Griffin.

When the collection had finished, I ventured back into the altar boys' room to get an extra paten for Communion and could hear the jubilant ushers in the sacristy. I peaked around the corner and could see Father McInerney standing at the table as Mr. Chubs and crew poured their collection baskets into one very large straw basket sitting in the center of the large table in the middle of the room.

"Oh, he did it good this year!" Mr. Chubs exclaimed. "Did you see their faces?"

The priest couldn't wait to start counting the money. He couldn't be bothered with reliving Father Griffin's threatening fund-raising speech. No, he was busy licking his index fingers to count the loot. I had never gone back during this part of the Mass and wondered if this occurred every Sunday.

As Mom and I walked down Kostner that sunny Friday with report card in hand, she swung my arm back and forth, just as she had done when I was six years old and the world seemed friendlier. For a few minutes, she was relieved, smiling and happy that God had given her another month to pay the tuition and remain a good Catholic.

Chapter Thirty-one

THE CELEBRATION

A lone string of white Italian lights hanging across the ceiling at Vito & Nick's restaurant began to blink that Saturday evening as the six of us sat waiting for our table, while the music from the rock group Chicago played in the background. We each were seated on red, padded stools at a counter running along the length of the window. The see-through plastic shade in front of us protected our eyes from the bright setting sun, keeping the restaurant atmosphere as dark as always.

My graduation ceremony had taken place the day before at St. Bede's Church, and Dad wanted to have some type of celebration for my big day. He didn't want me to feel slighted because of the family troubles. I appreciated his consideration for my accomplishment, but none of us felt like celebrating. Our mother was back in the hospital recovering from what we were told was another successful operation.

Only a few months earlier, Dr. Fitzgerald assisted the surgeon who removed cancerous cells from her left breast. The stout, gray-haired Irish physician, whom Mom literally trusted with her life, followed with aggressive treatments of chemotherapy. She was scheduled to begin radiation, but the X-rays taken during her exam five days earlier showed a spot on her breast. This time Dr. Fitzgerald said it would require a mastectomy. They had to be sure to get it all, or it would spread.

On Wednesday, June 2, Mom was back in the operating room at Little Company of Mary, but this time with a different surgeon. The procedure went longer than expected.

"We have your table ready for you now," the Vito & Nick's hostess said as she walked the six Ruanes to the long table covered by a red-and-white-checkered tablecloth.

No one talked about Mom that evening, but she was all I could think about. No one said much of anything. I just sat there looking at all the happy people in the restaurant, while listening to the horn section of the group Chicago fill the room with one of their hits, "Only the Beginning."

I wished Dad had picked somewhere else to have a graduation celebration. We all had been sitting in this same restaurant just one week earlier, celebrating Mom's final chemotherapy treatment. She was so happy that night. That was a reason to celebrate. If her first operation had been a success, all seven of us would have been clinking our Pepsi glasses, talking about how great it is for me finally to be out of St. Bede's.

I would have reminisced to Mom about my fourth-grade teacher, Miss Darlene Lausus, and how she always said "Hmmm" after every sentence. And how a group of wiseguy boys would say "hmmm" right along with her, creating a chorus of "hmmms." Or the all-too-scary-looking Mrs. Consentino and her drawn-on eyebrows and the nightmares I would have about her. Or Sister Pelagia and the horrible way Dave Dazzo and his gang taunted her.

I would reminisce about the beautiful Miss Pasco and the wonderful crush I had on her in fifth grade. I would praise Mrs. Lemmonier, such a nice lady and good teacher, who had to deal with the paste-eating, paper-tearing Phillip Barton. God bless her for her patience.

I would toast Sister Mary, my second-grade nun who had such a kind face. Her positive encouragement really helped me do well in 1963. I never would forget her stoic reaction to the news over the loudspeaker that President Kennedy had been shot. The always-upbeat Sister Linda would be toasted for teaching her seventh-graders how to stand with our left leg forward and right hand on right hip to look cool. The school could have used about ten Sister Lindas.

Father Richard would be highlighted for sparking so much interest in the Mass for all of those kids who found it boring until he showed up and introduced the Sunday guitar service.

I would forget the often-inebriated Father McInerney and the times I couldn't help thinking about him when I passed the rectory on garbage day, only to see a garbage can filled with liquor bottles and beer cans.

And, of course, I would stand at the table, raise my Pepsi glass high, and hail the holy Father Griffin with his John Wayne walk and penchant for asking parishioners for money nearly every Sunday to show their Christianity.

The two large pizzas arrived at our table and, out of habit, Danny grabbed three pieces of the thin cheese pizza the moment the round platter was put down. For the first time that I could remember, however, no one else grabbed for the next piece. We just sat there looking at it. As Danny stuffed his face with the first piece, his eyes looked up to see the rest of us watching him. He slowly pulled the slice of pizza back from his mouth and looked at us a bit embarrassed. Dad quickly broke that awkward moment by holding up his glass.

"Let's all toast Johnny for graduating from St. Bede's. Congratulations, Johnny!" he said as five other glasses were raised, then clinked together to symbolize the happy moment. "Now come on, kids, everyone eat. Let's go. Your mother's going to be just fine."

We forced ourselves to eat that evening, but if this was to be a true celebration, Mom had to be there.

"Dad, can we go see Mom tonight?" I pleaded with him. "That would be the best gift you could give me."

Dad just looked at me, knowing full well that Mom was not in great shape, emotionally or physically. It had only been three days since the mastectomy. He had been up to see her each day, allowing only Maureen to join him.

"Okay, we'll go when we are finished here," he said to an instant roar of approval from his five children, now smiling a little for the first time all night. "I'll go call her to let her know we are coming."

As Dad left to find the pay phone, I could feel the burst of energy at the thought of getting to see Mom for the first time since the operation. Dad had told us that it was not an easy surgery, but she came out strong. Mom was a fighter.

When Dad returned to the table, he already had the restaurant bill in hand.

"Are we ready?" he asked, knowing there wasn't much visiting time left at the hospital.

As we entered Little Company of Mary, Dad worked to prepare us.

"Now listen, because you need to understand Mom is going to look sleepy, groggy. She is on pain medication to help her recover. Margaret and Danny, I want you to see your mommy, but I think it would be a good idea if you visited for only a few minutes, okay?"

Margaret and Danny just nodded, probably feeling a bit nervous and uncertain.

"Seeing you kids will make her so happy, so be sure you give her a big hug and kiss. But be careful of the wires and tubes, okay?"

Everyone nodded.

Once again we found ourselves on the sixth floor, the cancer ward. Dad had us wait in the reception area. We watched him disappear down the long corridor on the opposite side, as we sat and watched the nurses answer phones, fill out charts, and direct visitors to the correct rooms. A few minutes later, Dad emerged and waved for us to follow him. Instantly, the five of us popped up and marched down the hall. Mom's room once again was at the end of the hallway, with a large glass window that gave her plenty of sunlight. We walked into her room at seven-thirty, which gave us only thirty minutes until visiting time ended.

As excited as we were to see her is as stunned as we felt when we saw her. Her face was puffy, her eyes watery. She was groggy and weak. She could barely smile, but smile she did when she saw all of us standing in front of her. Margaret slowly leaned forward and kissed her mommy on the cheek.

"Oh Margaret, I missed you," Mom said.

"I missed you too, Mom," Margaret said as she hugged her gently.

A parade of hugs and kisses followed, and it seemed to give Mom a burst of energy that I knew wouldn't last. But for a few moments, she was with her family and happy again. It had to be so lonely in that hospital by herself, lying there in pain all day and night.

After about five minutes, Dad picked up Margaret to take her and Danny back to the reception area, but they would have none of it.

"We want to stay, Dad," said Danny, then in unison with Margaret begged, "Please!"

Dad gave in and they sat along the ledge near the windowsill as we told Mom about my graduation, Vito & Nick's, and how much we all missed her.

"Dr. Fitzgerald said I am going to be all right this time," she said in a gravelly, muffled tone because of the medication she had been given. "I am supposed to go home Wednesday."

"Wednesday!" Kathy said excitedly. "I'm going with Dad to pick up Mom."

"Me too!" blurted Danny.

"Now don't get carried away, kids," Dad said, holding his hands up to settle us down. "We'll see when it's time, okay?"

Maureen gave Mom a sip of orange juice.

As I looked at my mom, I wanted to tell her how much I wished she had been at my graduation ceremony. I sat at her bedside praying that this would be the end of her medical problems and we could get our lives back to normal.

My prayer would not be answered. The worst was still ahead for Mom and all of us.

Before going to St. Bede's that Friday evening, Dad drove me to Marty Durk's house for pictures. This could have been our last big moment as best friends, and his dad wanted to record the two boys together in our blue caps and gowns.

At church later, Marty had been given a special assignment as lectern, a great honor to him and a testament to his oratorical skills. Seeing him up there on the altar made his parents, sisters, and best buddy very proud of him. I was seated in the tenth row next to my basketball teammate Mike Roar, a kid I was glad to have known during my time at St. Bede's. It was too bad the eighth grade wasn't filled with kids like Mike.

My father, three sisters, and brother were seated in the pews to the left of the altar. When I glanced over toward them, I could see my dad waving and smiling while Kathy held the Kodak camera up and a light flashed in front of her. I knew Dad was trying to put on a good face. The five of them sat there looking depleted, empty, which is exactly how I felt.

Unlike my First Holy Communion and Confirmation, I barely paid attention. All I could think about was Mom lying in a darkened hospital room, alone, in pain. I had asked Dad if I could skip the graduation, so we all could go visit her, but he wouldn't even consider it. He wanted to see his son receive his diploma from the school he had worked so hard to put me through. In Ireland, he only received a seventh-grade education, so he appreciated this graduation more than anyone.

About ten minutes into the Mass, the air-conditioning in the church kicked on, which blew directly onto the large purple banner set on the right side of the altar, behind where Marty and the other reader, Jennie Maples, were seated. The banner was held up by two poles, running up close to the ceiling. The air pouring out of the vents caused the banner to sway. Marty had just finished the first reading and was turning to return to his seat when the banner began to descend right toward him.

"Look out!" yelled several of those in the front pews.

Marty reacted quickly, grabbed Jennie, and yanked her out of the way, sparing the pretty brunette from injury. It was without question Marty's greatest moment at St. Bede's, and he received grateful applause for his heroic act.

When the main event of the graduation, the diploma ceremony, finally took place after Holy Communion, I could see how happy the other kids in my class felt.

It really was a major accomplishment. Sister Rita and Father Griffin stood at the foot of the altar calling out our names. As they handed each graduate the rolled-up paper scroll, cameras flashed as each family recorded the moment.

Dave Dazzo was in the pew in front of me, and I could see his parents' wide smiles at the sight of their young bully graduating. When Dazzo stepped out of his pew to walk to the front of the altar, his father scurried to a spot along the altar rail close to him to record this momentous occasion.

"Smile, Shooter!" the football coach ordered, his voice carrying all the way to the back of the church.

When it was my turn, I couldn't even look at the pastor.

"Congratulations," Sister Rita said, handing me the certificate.

"Thank you, Sister Rita," I responded politely, shaking her hand as a camera flashed just to my left, causing me to blink.

My sister Kathy was kneeling a few feet away, holding the camera and smiling. She darted back to the pew and I could see my family sitting and smiling. Dad clasped his hands together signifying a victory. At least for a few minutes, they all looked happy.

The next day, Saturday, I walked into St. Bede's around noon to check the schedule. This was to be my final week as an altar boy. Before I entered the glass doors to the darkened church, I stopped and walked to the large wooden board to take one last look at the brass nameplates of the soldiers from our parish who had served in Vietnam. I was familiar with so many of the soldiers' names because I had gone to school with their younger brothers or sisters. They were all just kids, only four to five years older than me, and now they were fighting in jungles thousands of miles away. And some had red stars next to them, killed in action.

Sure, my family was struggling to come to grips with my mother's battle against cancer, but obviously we weren't alone when it came to confrontations with seemingly uncontrollable challenges.

Every time I saw that board, it reminded me of how many families have to face life's battles on so many different fronts. How horrible it must have been for the parents to deal with the possible loss of their sons. Those boys were just getting started in life, just like me, and now some were gone. In five years, that might be my name on that board. I only knew one answer; the same answer my mother relied on. "Put your faith in God," she always told me.

I walked through those familiar glass doors one more time and down the main aisle, turned left at the altar rail, and followed it around through the double doors. The altar boys' room was empty and quiet. I looked at the white paper with the altar boys' Mass schedule, which my friend Eddie had taped to the cabinet door. My name was three from the top, just as it had been all year. But next to it, there were no Masses scheduled. I looked down the list to see if the other eighth-grade boys had been assigned Masses. There's Phillip, no Masses. Marty, nothing. Mike Hannon, blank. I guess we were all done.

I walked over to the closet and took out my altar boy vestments to take them home for good. I searched through the closet, which was packed with hanging vestments. A new group of altar boys was being trained, so there were an unusually large number of garments hanging in the closet. After a few minutes of pulling and tugging to see the names on the yellow masking tape across the back of the white surplices, I found mine and pulled hard on the metal hanger to pry it loose from the closet.

I held it up in front of me and just looked at it. I had been through so many experiences wearing that holy uniform. Once I walked out that door and down the steps, that was it—I was no longer an altar boy. I never really had considered what it would feel like to lose that aspect of my identity. I was proud of being an altar boy; proud to serve God on the altar.

I turned to take one last look at the room. There was the brown church pew placed against the wall next to the closet that we sat on waiting for Mass to begin. There was the wine bottle; the same brand that Tim Rink introduced to all new altar boys. I picked up one of the cruets and thought about how many times I had poured water and wine into a priest's chalice with it. I looked into the priests' room. The safe was closed and the long table empty; no large basket of money with ushers rifling through to count the collection.

I swung the black and white vestment over my right shoulder, holding the metal hanger with my right index finger, and walked toward the plastic accordionlike doors for one more look at the altar. The second I crossed through the door, I could feel the emptiness of the massive church surround me while I strained my ears in the silence. I made my way to the front of the altar and looked up at the cross. I placed my garment down on the red rug and knelt at the top of the steps. This was the spot where I tried to fake my way through my first Latin prayer with Father Griffin.

I placed my hands together in prayer, pointing toward Heaven, and said the Our Father one last time on those steps. I prayed for my mother, asking God to please help her fully recover from the operation and rid her of the cancer for good. I prayed for my father, for my brother and sisters. I prayed that God would help us through this difficult time. I prayed for the boys who died in Vietnam and their families.

As I finished my prayer, I glanced over at the kneelers on which I had been stationed for the past four years. I walked over to the corner kneeler with the golden bells set on the rug next to it. The church was so dark and quiet that when I reached down with my left hand and lifted the bells, the light chiming shot through the church, bouncing off the walls. I shook the bells one last time and filled the entire church with that familiar ring. This time I didn't have to watch Father Griffin's face to determine when the appropriate time was to stop ringing the bells.

"Mr. Ruane!" a voice boomed out from the other side of the altar, startling me. I put the bells down and stood up to see Father Griffin looking none too pleased.

"May I ask what you are doing?" he said in a stern tone.

"I was just ringing the bells . . ."

"I can see that! But why are you doing that?" he barked.

I knew I was finished with him; I would never have to serve Mass for him again or deal with him, for that matter. I could feel a warm rush fill my face as fast as the anger came up from my heart into my throat and out of my mouth.

"I'm ringing the bells for the last time," I said, my voice filled with anger.

I struggled to keep my composure. My mother wouldn't want me to be disrespectful.

"I served my last Mass today."

Father Griffin just looked at me, perhaps realizing he had pushed me too far.

"I see. . . . Well, that's fine."

He quickly turned and walked down the altar steps, making his way down the main aisle. His appearance had changed since I first watched him walk down that aisle eight years earlier. His hair was gray and his face reflected the strain of managing such a large parish. But his posture was still perfect, with head tilted slightly to the right, his left hand against his stomach as his right arm swung with each long step, producing the dignified gait we all knew well. He was Father John Wayne.

As he disappeared, I knelt back down and said one more Our Father, asking God to help Father Griffin become a better spiritual leader. He should get plenty of credit for starting the parish in 1953 and building it up to one of the largest parishes in the Chicago area, with more than 2,300 families and 1,900 children attending the grammar school. That was a great accomplishment that no one can deny. It took a great commitment, a lot of hard work and dedication. When he died in the fall of 1975, he left the church debt free.

As I reflect on my days at St. Bede's, I am eternally grateful that I was given the opportunity to serve on God's altar. I know it made me a better Catholic and a better person. It placed a moral template within me that never would be broken. Like everyone, my moral fiber may have suffered a few chips and cracks along the way, but the experience of being an altar boy cemented the direction I would follow the rest of my life.

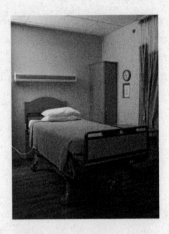

Chapter Thirty-two

OAK FOREST HOSPITAL

It was a sunny Friday morning, June 27, 1975. I stood on the side of the old metal bed at Oak Forest Hospital looking down at my mother, praying that she would come out of the coma she had been in for more than a week. She looked gray and gaunt—so bad. The familiar green cloth head garment covered the graying strands of hair remaining. It was so hard to look at her in that condition. She had been in the fight for her life and was losing.

I wish I had known. At eighteen, I thought she had been moved from Little Company of Mary to Oak Forest Hospital during the first week of June because Dad couldn't afford to keep her at the Catholic hospital any longer. I prayed every day and night that God would save my mother. "Thy Will be done," I prayed directly from the Lord's Prayer. I had complete faith in God's mercy for someone so devout.

She was three and a half years past her mastectomy, and the accepted "cured marker" for breast cancer was five years. Mom never saw it coming. On March 27, 1975, when she went in for her annual exam, the tests showed the cancer had returned. But this time it was in her spine. This was devastating! Home from school that Thursday afternoon, I watched Mom break down crying. She was angry and sad; totally frustrated. Why did the cancer come back? Was this a death sentence?

Did she have the courage and energy to fight it again? She sat in the worn brown armchair in the corner of the living room smoking a Kent, crying. I had to help somehow.

"You'll be all right, Mom," I encouraged her. "You did it before. You can get through it."

"I don't know, Johnny," she cried, turning her head away from me, her eyes glazed, pretending to look out the front window. "I just don't know."

When Dad arrived home from work an hour later, she called him into their bedroom to give him the bad news. About ten minutes later, Dad walked out of the room, his eyes red and shoulders slumped. As bad as things were, he knew they were just about to get a great deal worse.

The spinal cord was too risky for an operation. The doctors would have to attack with medicine, chemotherapy, and zap it during the same time period with radiation. This would be intense therapy that would take its toll on Mom's body and spirit. There would be side effects. The cancer was spreading quickly, and it was the only chance she had to survive.

Maureen was away at nursing school. The rest of us sat in the living room that evening. We traded looks as we listened to the muffled sounds of Mom and Dad talking in the middle bedroom. There were cries of "What am I going to do?" There was sobbing. There were long periods of silence. Our parents were faced with a life-threatening situation that would affect all of us. I tried to think of something I could do to help. But what?

When we awoke the next morning, Mom's attitude had changed, at least for the time being. She was ready to go to war. We had a family meeting at the kitchen table, just as we had had almost four years earlier. Our parents knew we would be in this war with them, and they needed to get us ready for the battle.

"It's going to be a lot harder than the first time," Mom said. "The therapy will be more intense. I won't feel well most of the time, and I want each of you to help your dad out around here."

Over the next six weeks, she went to the hospital twice a week for treatments. As before, when she returned home, she lay down on her queen-sized bed, trying to recuperate. We had been around that block before, so we knew once she was finished with it, she would be okay again. As the weeks went on, she lost her hair and started wearing a green head garment. I hated that thing. It represented cancer to me. She became thinner. Her face lost its color. She sat in the armchair, looking sick and smoking a cigarette.

Unlike the first fight, Mom didn't have the energy to do housework this time. At this age, we each had daily chores and we picked up all of Mom's normal duties.

Dad took care of all the cooking, except on weekends when Maureen came home from nursing school, which was a great help to him. Kathy helped out with the laundry. I folded and put away all the clean clothes and made sure all of the bedrooms were cleaned, with beds made. Danny and Margaret helped with the kitchen, washing the dishes, making their beds, and staying out of Dad's way. That was the biggest help. Keep the house organized and clean and stay out of Dad's way. He didn't need any fights or arguments from his kids. He didn't have to say a thing. We could see he had the weight of the world on his shoulders.

One Saturday in early May, my girlfriend Charlotte Danhoff, whom I had been dating for nearly a year, had come by our house for pictures before departing for the St. Laurence High School senior prom at the Congress Hotel on South Michigan Avenue. I first laid eyes on Char on July 2, 1974, at Ford City Cinema, where I worked as an usher and she as a candy girl. I found her very attractive, with long brown hair, beautiful face, big brown eyes, olive skin, and an eye-catching figure. I was even more taken by her great personality and sense of humor. But most important, she was without question the nicest, kindest girl I had ever met. Only a few weeks after I started to date her, I knew she was the one for me. Char was special.

Even though Mom felt horrible, she was upbeat and friendly to Char, making us believe she really was okay. Mom snapped the photos as we posed in the living room, Dad sitting on the couch with his arm around Margaret. Dad was the one who didn't look well. The stress of Mom's sickness and financial pressures had taken their toll on him. How he got up for work every day to dig ditches and lay pipes at the age of forty-nine was beyond my teenage comprehension. It must have been the work ethic developed in the bogs of Ireland and the realization he had to provide for his family.

One morning before leaving for school, I noticed Dad was completely pale, looking very sick. I tried to talk him out of going to work, but he wouldn't consider it.

"I have to go," he said. "I have to pay the bills. I can't miss."

"Can't you call in sick?" I begged to no avail.

It was during this time period that Dad's brother visited us. My uncle Johnny, who was known as Brother Robert of the Patrician Brothers, had finished his teaching assignment at Loyola near Los Angeles and was returning to Ireland. In the few days he spent with us, he helped lift Mom's spirits considerably. He also noticed something that I completely missed. Mom was losing her sight, and her hearing had become very good.

"Usually when a person loses one of their senses, one of the other senses will increase," he explained one afternoon during lunch at the Berghoff Restaurant in the Loop. He was right. Mom was going blind.

On Thursday, May 22, Margaret had just gotten home from school when Mom started spitting up blood. An ambulance arrived a short time later to rush her to the emergency room at Little Company of Mary. Her treatments had taken a toll and she was bleeding internally. Dr. Fitzgerald had her admitted to the hospital, where they would alter the treatment in an attempt to save her. The only ones who seemed to know the seriousness of the situation were my father and older sister. The rest of us thought she was just going back into the hospital as she did in 1971.

We were back on the sixth floor again visiting Mom, who was given that same end room with the two beds. For two weeks, we marched up to the sixth floor and helped Mom take sips of 7-Up through a red-striped straw or feed her red and green Jell-O with a white plastic hospital spoon. She didn't look good and was almost completely blind.

She would be okay, though. I would pray every night, "Thy Will be done." God won't let me down. I was convinced the Almighty would bring my mom back to health. I didn't know how, but I knew God would help her. I had complete faith.

On Monday, June 16, we learned that Mom was being moved over to the larger Oak Forest Hospital at 159th Street and Cicero Avenue. This was not an environment to which we were accustomed or appreciated. Little Company had a warm and caring religious atmosphere, decorated with statues of the Virgin Mary, crosses on the walls, and other religious objects placed along the hallways, rooms, and waiting areas.

Walking through the halls at Oak Forest Hospital was depressing, with the light green walls desperate for a coat of paint, old people being wheelchaired around, and the smell of bad food in the air.

"Dad, we can't let Mom stay here," I pleaded. He just looked at me. He didn't want her there either, but he could do nothing about it.

Mom was lying there, her eyes open, but blind. She couldn't see her new surroundings, a blessing. Dad talked with the nurses who updated him on her condition, while Maureen, Kathy, Danny, Margaret, and I stood there looking at the mother we loved so very much. This place was cold and dark, as forbidding as a public bus station.

Back at home that night, I sat on the top bunk bed praying for hours, repeating Hail Mary after Hail Mary after Our Father and emphasizing "Thy Will be done." God would save her, I was absolutely certain.

Dad received a phone call from the hospital around six o'clock on Thursday, June 26, just after dinner. I was in the kitchen clearing off the table and overheard him talking. He hung the phone up on the wall and looked dejected, leaning his forehead against the wall next to the phone. After a few seconds, he must have realized I was standing in the kitchen, and he turned toward me.

"That was Dr. Fitzgerald. Your mother has gone into a coma."

"A coma?" I said, not quite sure what that meant.

"She's unconscious. It's like she is asleep."

"She'll come out of it, though, right?"

Dad again just looked at me, frustrated. A few minutes later, he left for the hospital alone. We were already asleep when he returned. The next morning I asked him about visiting Mom. Dad told me it would be a good idea for me to visit the next day.

So there I stood on Friday morning, June 27, 1975, overlooking my mother, who lay there with her eyes closed, in a deep sleep.

"Mom, I'm here," I said, watching to see if there was any reaction.

None.

"Can you hear me, Mom?"

Nothing.

I just looked at her.

There were beds all along the wall with very old people in them, invalid ninety-year-olds. Why was my mother here? This was the place they sent people to die, but I didn't know it. I couldn't consider it, wouldn't consider it. My mother was going to be okay, right? "God's Will be done." And He would never let my mother die at forty-six years old.

I had to be sure Mom knew I loved her. We were not the kind of family to express our love openly for one another, to say directly "I love you" at night before going to bed, or when leaving for school. We just didn't do it. Yes, we all knew we loved each other, but I stood there so frustrated that I had never actually said it to Mom.

I looked at her gray, gaunt face with the green head garment and thin gray hairs coming out the side, wishing I had told Mom a million times how much I loved her. I wanted to tell her how much I appreciated everything she had done for me, taking care of all of us, cooking the meals, cleaning our clothes, making sure I did what I was supposed to do. Loving us!

She went out and bought all of those Christmas presents every year, stacking them under the tree, so her kids would have a nice Christmas. She and Dad didn't have much money, but they weren't going to let their kids down. That always meant so much to me. They gave up everything for us. They put us through Catholic schools when they couldn't afford it, made sure we had good clothes, lived in a nice house in a nice neighborhood. They were the model for good parents, sacrificing everything for their kids. They were the model for good Catholic parents, completely unselfish, the example of Jesus.

"Mom, can you hear me?" I pleaded, hoping she would open her eyes.

She didn't.

I leaned in toward her, praying she could hear me.

"Mom, I just want you to know that . . . I love you very much. I love you, Mom."

She never moved, never reacted. I have been told people in comas sometimes know what is going on around them and can hear what is being said to them. They are absorbing it but can't respond. It's like being in a dream. I just hoped and prayed Mom heard me. I watched her for a few more minutes, then prayed the Our Father and Hail Mary.

"Please, God, please, God, I beg You," I said in a whisper over my mother. "Please help my mother to be okay again. We all love her so much. She is such a good person. Please, God!"

I left the hospital about eleven o'clock and drove north down Cicero Avenue in my used green 1967 Plymouth Fury, thinking only of my mother lying there alone in a coma. I prayed all the way home, Our Fathers followed by Hail Marys. I was so upset, I began talking out loud. "Thy Will be done! Thy Will be done!" I repeated, trying to convince God as I drove home. When I reached Kostner, I spotted Dad's 1973 silver LeSabre parked in front of the house. He had come home early to visit Mom in the hospital and asked me if I would pick up Maureen from Michael Reese Hospital while he got cleaned up. He wanted my older sister to join him.

Dad let me use his car to pick her up. On the drive home down the Stevenson Expressway, I told her about my morning with Mom.

"She didn't open her eyes at all," I said.

"She's in a coma," Maureen replied.

"I know, but how long will it last? When will she come out of it?"

"It's different with every person. She may come out of it today, she may never . . . the doctors just never know."

"She's going to be all right," I said. "She's going to come out of it."

I could feel Maureen in the passenger seat just looking at me, and I wondered if she knew something I didn't know.

When Dad and Maureen left that afternoon for Oak Forest Hospital, I went back to work on the painting project I had started a few days earlier, hoping to take my mind off my morning visit. Two hours later, I was on the top rung of Dad's wooden ladder, halfway down the gangway, scraping the gutters just above Mom's room when I saw Dad's LeSabre pull up in front of the house. I stood holding the gutter and watched Maureen step out of the passenger seat. She looked distraught, and she walked with slumped shoulders toward the house. Dad looked even worse.

I hustled down the ladder to the side of the porch where Dad stood, resting his hands on the corner of the white railing above the sidewalk in the gangway.

"Your mother has died," he said, his eyes filled with tears.

I just looked at him feeling completely stunned.

"What? What happened?" I gasped. A buzz filled my head, and I lost my breath for a moment.

"We had only been there a few minutes and she . . . she died."

It hit me like the hardest punch I had ever been hit with in my life. I was furious!

"God," I said, swinging my fists wildly at nothing, but maybe at God. "Thy Will be done. God!"

I bent over resting my hands on my knees, crushed. I stood up trying to catch my breath and swung my right fist hard through the air.

"Please! God!"

Dad walked into the house, not knowing what else to do or say. His reaction was very different from mine. He must have known she would die.

I sat down on the porch steps looking at the grass, feeling like I was sitting in the worst nightmare of my entire life. And there was no escape. There was nothing I could do. My mother was gone. God had let her die. I stood up and swung my fist through the air again, then sat back down holding my head with my hands.

The world had lost a truly good person who had grown up during the Great Depression and had lost her mother young. She could have been a nun or professional singer, but she chose to get married and raise a family of five and sing in God's church.

A two-day wake at McInerney Funeral Home drew large crowds of friends and family. Looking at Mom in the golden brown casket was difficult; it didn't even look like her.

"Mom, I know you are in Heaven," I prayed silently on the kneeler, looking at her powder-covered, madeup face, the familiar black wig covering her head. "You shouldn't have died so young. I miss you. We all miss you. Someday we will all be together again."

I didn't cry. I couldn't cry. I was still too angry. I looked at Mom wishing I could do something to bring her back to life. I made the Sign of the Cross, stood, and touched her cold hands, which were folded over her stomach.

"I love you, Mom," I said, looking at her, hoping that she had heard me at the hospital.

For two days, we stood to the left of Mom's casket greeting hundreds of people. Dad kept up a strong front, but I knew he was really hurting inside. He spent a good deal of time talking with his uncle Bill Naughton and later his aunt Ellen, uncle Jack Naughton's wife—the family that met him when he came over from Ireland. They were his last link to Ireland. His uncle Jack, who visited his homestead in Ireland and took responsibility for Dad in America, had died of leukemia in 1968. His uncle Tommy Naughton, with whom Dad had earned his first American wages tending his uncle's bar, had died in 1969—I served the Mass. His cousin Mick Naughton, the fellow with whom he came over from Ireland in 1948, had died young of a heart attack in 1956. His uncle Bill was really the only one left. This is not what he envisioned when he came to America.

The funeral at St. Bede's was the most difficult part of the experience. I hadn't cried at all up until that point. I thought I would be angry forever. But when that familiar pipe organ rang out the introduction to "Let There Be Peace on Earth," Mom's favorite song, a flood of tears poured down my face. I couldn't stop. I bent over in the pew and struggled to catch my breath. My sisters, brother, father—anyone who knew my mother—couldn't contain the emotions. That song was our mother.

Father Jeremiah Duggan, the new associate pastor, led the Mass. Father Griffin was not there. I learned later that he was fighting for his own life, also battling cancer. Father Duggan barely knew Mom, but he must have been told a great deal about her, as he recounted her contributions to the church as both a parishioner and cantor.

Looking out the back window of the limousine, we could see the funeral procession of cars was at least a mile long. We turned right off 87th Street and into St. Mary's Cemetery parking lot next to the yellow-bricked chapel just off the road. They directed us into the chapel, where Father Duggan led the large gathering in prayers, repeating Hail Mary after Hail Mary, just as he had done at the funeral home the previous two evenings. This is where we said goodbye to Mom. We each took our last look at the casket and walked out the door toward the cemetery.

Dad had picked out two gravesites about fifteen feet behind the statue of St. Paul, just outside the chapel. He paid $250 for each and another $100 for Mom's flat gravestone with an Irish cross in the right corner and rosary beads wrapped around the crucifix. The inscription on the stone read, "Therese Ruane, Mother, 1928 to 1975."

That didn't begin to tell the story.

Chapter Thirty-three

A BROKEN
HEART

O ur home was filled with silence throughout the summer of '76. There was
nothing more deafening than the silence left by Mom's passing. She was gone,
and we all could feel it. Dad knew this silence from the loss of his own mother in
Ireland. He looked so unhappy, depressed.

Every time I thought about that day Mom passed, anger filled me again. I wished
I could do something to bring her back. This was the year we learned the lesson
that when someone passes on, we had to keep going, keep living. We were told
time would heal our pain. Well, time was moving too slow, and the pain seemed
never ending.

For the next year, I stayed as busy as possible. By the fall of 1976, I was attending Mayor Daley Junior College and playing on a championship hockey team,
while working in the dispatch office at United Parcel Service on Jefferson Street
and spending all of my off time with my girlfriend, Char.

I could feel my mind and body beginning to move ahead from the despair. I
was attending college, playing hockey, making good money, and I had a great girlfriend, whom I loved very much and was serious about marrying. I was so serious
about her that in July of 1976, I drove south down I-55 to Bolingbrook and a brand-

new monster mall called Old Chicago to purchase a $1,200 marquis diamond ring at one of the jewelry stores. A few days later, I found myself with Char in Grant Park for the Fourth of July celebration, watching Mitch Miller and his orchestra perform at the Petrillo Band Shell. As the sun set, we walked over to Buckingham Fountain, to view the colorful water display shooting into the starlit sky. It was a beautiful night.

Standing with Char along the rail around the fountain, I dropped down to one knee, took her hand, and asked her to marry me. A big smile crossed her face and tears of joy poured down her cheeks as I slipped the silver band with the quarter-carat diamond on to her left hand. With the famous fountain's light mist falling on us, we kissed to seal our engagement with no date set—just the hope that someday we would be married.

Life seemed to be back on track until one Friday evening, October 8 of 1976, when Marty Burns from the personnel department at UPS walked into the dispatchers' office to tell me I had an urgent call from my sister Maureen. He asked me to follow him upstairs to his office, where I could return the call and have some privacy. I couldn't imagine what was happening. Why was Maureen calling? Why did Marty believe I needed privacy?

"Dad had chest pains and went to the emergency room," Maureen said with panic in her voice. "They diagnosed it as heart failure and have admitted him."

Stunned, I felt dazed as I sat back in the brown swivel chair. Dad was certainly depressed, but there was never any indication that he was having a health problem. And this was very serious, heart failure.

"I'll be right home," I said, and stood up quickly. "Marty, can you let the people in dispatch know I had to leave. It's an emergency."

Marty nodded.

"Good luck. Let us know if there is anything else we can do."

I drove home that night in my 1966 Mustang and turned on the radio, only to hear the first few notes from the song "Don't Fear the Reaper." I quickly turned it off.

The next morning, all five of us visited Dad on the third floor of the all-too-familiar Little Company of Mary Hospital. I thought I wouldn't see that orange-brick building for many years. Dad was dressed in a white hospital gown and had an IV in his arm. He looked to be in good spirits.

"Dr. Fitzgerald says I just have to get my weight down a bit, don't eat salt, and drink a lot of water," he informed us, smiling and happy to see his kids, especially Kathy, who had just returned home during her college break.

Dad was kept in the hospital five days, when they decided he was well enough to send home. It was easy to see he had lost a good deal of weight and looked better than he had in years. He was thinner, and the stress was off his face. Maybe the trip to the emergency room was a blessing in disguise.

It was just before three o'clock on Thursday, October 14, when I arrived at Little Company of Mary to pick up Dad in my very small and very used Mustang. This wasn't the best car for him to be riding in, but he endured the cramped trip home, which took about fifteen minutes.

"Dad, I just want you to know something," I said, looking out of my smudged windshield as I drove north down California. "I know I said this to you once before, but I just want you to know that I love you very much and I appreciate everything you have done for us."

Dad turned and smiled.

"Thanks, Johnny," he said. "I'm not going anywhere."

"I know, but I just wanted to make sure. . . ."

Once home, it was hard for Dad to sit still. He really tried to be a good patient, listening to Dr. Fitzgerald's orders to rest, but he was always so active. On Friday, he realized the family had not celebrated my twentieth birthday and announced that on Saturday we would all go to Stump's Pub, a great steak restaurant located at 111th Street and Southwest Highway. We had only been there once before as a family because of the expense, but Dad really wanted to make my birthday a special occasion.

Unlike our celebrations at Vito & Nick's over the years, Stump's had a much different ambience—a nicer, more expensive feel to it. We all ordered steak, even Dad, who had the butt steak, medium rare, which may not have been the best choice coming out of the hospital. The six of us really had a great time together that night, and somehow it was apparent that maybe we were all turning the corner on our sadness and heading in the right direction. Dad talked about how he planned to go back to work on Monday, which was too ambitious, but he assured us that he was fine.

When we arrived home that evening, he told us that he was going to go out for a few hours to see some friends. He had been confined to the hospital and home for more than a week, so we understood. I went to bed around eleven o'clock and Dad still had not returned.

The next morning I was sound asleep at approximately seven o'clock, when I felt something disturbing, and I opened my eyes, startled to see my sister Maureen standing over me, holding my shoulders to shake me awake.

"Johnny, Johnny, wake up!" she said, crying. "Daddy's dead!"

"What?"

"Daddy died! He's lying in his bed. I found him there. He's dead!" she cried.

I shot up out of my bed and ran down to the back bedroom. The lights were already on and there was Dad in his white T-shirt and shorts, lying there on his back, eyes closed, lifeless. I touched his arm, which was cold. I just stood there over him for what seemed like hours, staring in disbelief. This couldn't be happening.

"He was fine last night," I said, feeling both shocked and numb. "He was fine!"

"I heard a noise in the middle of the night, like a loud moan," Maureen said. "That's the sound a person makes just before they die."

Unlike Mom's death, Dad's passing left me completely dumbstruck. It came out of nowhere. Poor Margaret was only twelve. Danny was about to turn fifteen. Kathy was eighteen. I had just turned twenty. Maureen's twenty-first birthday was a week away.

Only seventeen months after Mom's funeral, the five Ruane children were back at McInerney Funeral Home for Dad's wake in the same large room, and the same spot, in which Mom had been viewed. Maureen now took the lead, making the arrangements for the wake and burial. I was in charge of keeping the others organized. Under these circumstances, Maureen and I had to focus on our responsibilities before we could think about mourning the loss of our father.

Like Mom's wake, Dad's two days at the funeral home were filled with shaking hands for hours with those who knew him. And he knew a lot of people. There were friends from the music business, folks from the neighborhood, city workers, the Irish of Chicago, and so many relatives including his good friend Jim Conoboy, the man who introduced him to Mom. It was incredible to see the multitude of friends, so many of whom expressed their great affection for our mother and father. The room was packed from four o'clock until it closed at nine, with people reminiscing about Dad and the good times they had with him.

Father Jeremiah Duggan once again presided over the funeral at St. Bede's as I prayed for my father and mother. I was numbed by the experience, and I lost all of my energy and motivation. The only good thing was that Mom and Dad were together again in Heaven. He was never the same after she died.

The doctors listed the cause of death as a heart attack, but I knew better. Dad died of a broken heart. When you spend twenty-two years with a person, raising five kids, struggling to make ends meet each month, it creates a bond that can't be broken.

Dad's funeral was the first time I had been back to St. Bede's since Mom's funeral. I had no intention of coming back once this ritual was over. I sat in the first pew on the right with my brother and three sisters, looking over at the American flag draped over the coffin, honoring my dad's service in the military. I looked up at that cross wondering why God had to take him so early, so young—50 years old. I watched my brother and three sisters kneeling, praying, and crying. I kneeled down next to Margaret and made the Sign of the Cross.

I didn't have anything else to say, to pray. I was so filled with disappointment, so shocked by the unexpected early departure of Dad. I made another Sign of the Cross and sat back in my pew feeling frustrated. The tears began to flow down my cheeks. I was beat.

Again I found myself in a limo looking out the back window and the two-mile line of cars in the funeral procession to St. Mary's Cemetery. Father Duggan led the prayers once again in the yellow-brick chapel, Hail Mary after Hail Mary after Our Fathers. As the military veterans folded the American flag, we could hear the firing of the guns outside for the twenty-one-gun salute. One of the army vets presented the triangular folded flag to Maureen and me as we stood to the side of the casket.

The five of us walked out of the chapel to the gravesite, which had a green tarp over the newly dug burial plot for Dad, next to the still noticeably fresh covered mound of earth where Mom was resting. Maureen selected an Irish cross for Dad's flat gravestone, which read, "Bernard Joseph Ruane, Father, 1926 to 1976."

As with Mom, it didn't begin to tell the story.

In the spring of 1977, when things looked bleak and life seemed worthless, Malachy Mannion, Mike Reilly, Thomas McAuliffe, and Pat Hennessey were among a group of wonderful people who organized a benefit for the five Ruane children, calling on the South Side Irish of Chicago to help. The benefit was held in St. Bede's Church basement in May of 1977, drew two thousand people, and raised enough money to pay off Mom and Dad's medical bills as well as the mortgage on our house. It also allowed me to continue attending college. If that money had not been raised, I would have been forced to quit school and take the job with the Chicago Water Department that Dad's co-worker, Rich Famaghetti, had offered. The people who organized that benefit were angels. The people who attended it saints. And the five Ruanes were blessed to have two parents that inspired so many people to step forward and help.

Maureen and I became the legal guardians for Danny and Margaret, while Kathy continued attending college in Iowa. Char was a major help to us during this time period, helping to cook the meals and do the laundry. She and I postponed our wedding plans until Margaret and Danny were older.

There had been a void in our home after my mother's departure. With my father gone, it felt like we didn't belong there anymore. It was Mom and Dad's house. The happy house we once all shared and enjoyed was only a memory to us. All seven of us sitting in the living room on Thursday evenings, eating Mom's chocolate brownies and watching *The Dean Martin Show* was such a warm and wonderful time. We were all so happy together.

I never could have those times back again, but I would cherish them forever. I missed my mom and dad so much back then.

And after thirty years, I miss them just as much today. It still hurts.

I love you, Mom and Dad.

Chapter Thirty-four

RETURN TO CHURCH

C hristmas 1986.
　　My wife, Char, and I are standing in the middle pews along the west wall at St. Bede's Church. I am holding our beautiful five-month-old daughter, Megan, in my right arm listening to the organ play the "Hallelujah" before the priest steps to the lectern to read the Gospel. I don't know this tall, thin, dark-haired priest, Father Norbert Maday. I had struggled with my religious commitment for more than a decade. This was one of the few times I had attended Mass since Father Jeremiah Duggan had married Char and me in this same church on April 3, 1982.

Getting married at St. Bede's and having Megan baptized there were always a given. But now we had a child and we wanted so desperately to raise her properly, as we had been raised. That's when I was forced to make a major decision: to face my faith head on and review the decisions I had made about my religion. It was easy to avoid this confrontation up until the moment Megan entered the world. But now I was a parent and had a huge responsibility to meet.

I asked myself some hard questions to come to terms with my life as well as the new life my wife and I would be guiding over the next two decades. Did I believe in one God Almighty, maker of Heaven and Earth? Absolutely. Did I believe in Jesus Christ and the sacrifice He made for all people? Yes, and I never doubted it for a second. Did I believe the Catholic Church was a good institution evolving directly from Jesus and His Apostles? Yes, and I had been studying this more during that time period to make sure I had a much better understanding and knowledge of religious history. Was there any other religion I would consider? No. I believed in the teachings of the Roman Catholic Church.

There really wasn't a choice. I was raised Catholic and provided with a good moral base. At thirty-one, I had experienced enough of life to appreciate the goodness and moral direction apparent in most Catholics I had known.

Char had also been raised in the Catholic Church, attending St. Albert the Great. Just as I had considered becoming a priest, she had given serious thought to becoming a nun. We were both on the same moral page of life, and it had been learned from our parents at home, and as students at Catholic schools and churches. Growing up I felt very close to God, praying every day. God provided strength, understanding, and comfort.

Over the time that I stopped attending church regularly, my faith became less focused, but I never stopped believing in God or the work Jesus did on Earth, the example He set. I was certainly a lapsed Catholic, bitter that my mother and father were taken from us so young. I came to realize that my plea to God when my mother was fighting for her life, "Thy Will be done," was not "My will be done." It meant accepting God's determination of the fate of my mother and father, as difficult as that is to do. And if God decided to take them early, I had to learn to accept that decision.

I'm certainly not alone with this dilemma. People all over the world go through this same conflict every day. Think of all of the men killed in wars, victims of earthquakes, floods, random shootings, airplane crashes, 9/11. How do loved ones and family members deal with that trauma? How do they justify their belief in a good God when He takes their loved ones? That's the challenge for all of us.

To return to the Church, I had to accept God's will over my wishes. It is one of the most difficult lessons of my life, repeated over and over again on different levels. I can pray, I can ask for God's help, but ultimately the outcomes in life are up to the Lord. Once I reached that level of acceptance, I was able to return to the Church as a dedicated and committed Catholic. I thank God for the blessing of children that forced me to face that decision and my rebirth into the Catholic Church.

On a bright, sunny Sunday morning in September of 2006, I am standing with my wife, Char, in the fifth row at St. Peter Chanel Church in Roswell, Georgia. Our four children—Megan, twenty, Sean, sixteen, and identical twins, Maggie and Kelly, eleven—stand between us, holding up their green hardcover songbooks, singing the entrance hymn with the 250 other parishioners at the 9:00 A.M. Mass in this growing parish in a northern suburb of Atlanta.

We watch the Rev. Frank McNamee at the back of a procession led by four altar servers, a deacon, and lector as they make their way down the main aisle while the voices of the singing parishioners fill the church. Unlike the garments I once wore at St. Bede's, these altar servers wear the white surplice over red cassocks.

At this time, St. Peter Chanel is a five-year-old annex building for the new church, which is expected to be built in the next few years—once all the money is raised. The annex serves its purpose well, and I think to most observers it may look like a full-fledged church. There are twenty-five rows of comfortable, high-backed green cloth chairs facing the altar, which looks similar to most altars, just smaller. Two long steps lead up to a platform, with the standard altar in the center and golden tabernacle behind it. The altar "servers," as they are referred to now because girls are included, sit on a red padded bench against the back wall, directly across from the high-backed throne-style priest's chair.

On this Sunday, we watch our pastor, Father Frank, as he is most often referred to, make his way up to the altar, where he stops in front of his thronelike chair, turns toward us, and continues singing with the congregation. At the end of the hymn, he leads us in making the Sign of the Cross, "In the name of the Father and the Son and the Holy Spirit."

The gathering reverently replies, "Amen."

Father Frank raises up his hands and says with a strong Irish brogue, "Good morning!"

"Good morning, Father!"

My wife and I are strong supporters of Father Frank. He is an Irish priest from the same area of the Emerald Isle as my father, Galway. He is in his midthirties, of medium height and build, with a full head of graying locks cut conservatively. His heavy beard is clean-shaven, revealing a rosy complexion. He wears a large pair of thick eyeglasses that makes it apparent he has poor eyesight.

As we watch Father Frank on this Sunday, or on any other Sunday, it is clear he is a bundle of energy. The entire time he stands on the altar, he is fidgeting, looking from right to left and shuffling his feet as he says Mass. He is a good man! A very good man! He is the kind of priest I wish I had the honor of serving as an altar boy. Priests in the 1960s like Father Richard blazed the new religious trail for priests like Father Frank. Thank God!

Our experience in Father Frank's parish, as well as a few other parishes over the past two decades, has solidified our belief that there are Catholic Churches in this world led by good priests providing proper moral direction for their parishioners. Unfortunately, the current reputation of the Catholic Church is focused on the negative acts of a small percentage of men who have used the Church and abused their position to hurt children, some of whom were altar boys.

Those reports have not turned us against the Church. They have made us more careful and selective, trying to be certain that we are involved in a parish led by a good moral leader. That is why we feel so lucky to be parishioners at St. Peter Chanel with Father Frank leading the flock.

And we continue to follow the philosophy and tradition passed down by my parents. All four of our children attend Catholic schools, where the religious environment is ever-present and all-school Masses a regularly scheduled activity. God is in their lives on a daily basis, and for that we are most thankful.

I remember watching my daughter Megan when she was in the children's choir at St. Michael's Church in Orland Park, Illinois, in the fall of 1994. She stood among twenty other third-graders, singing her heart out on the steps of the altar while the parishioners watched. There is nothing more beautiful than a children's choir, and I could not hold back tears as I watched her beautiful face singing in God's house. What a wonderful moment!

But as I scanned across all those angelic faces that day, a thought occurred to me. All of those boys and girls were pure, untainted children with a positive and hopeful view of the world. Over the next ten years, their minds, bodies, and souls would be taken in various directions based on the guidance each was receiving from their parents, teachers, priests, coaches, relatives, neighbors, and friends.

In a decade, all of those kids are of college age, and I wonder if the challenges, pitfalls, and temptations in life have ripped the angelic wings from their backs. Or did their Catholic faith help guide them through the temptations and peer pressures they faced? What if they were to be assembled at twenty-eight years old, or thirty-eight? The point is, as parents we have a responsibility to raise our children with the best moral direction we can provide, because the journey through life is difficult enough for all of us. Having no sense of moral direction just makes the journey that much harder, leaving the faithless lost and confused.

My parents worked very hard to make certain their five children were raised in the Catholic faith. And although it wasn't perfect then, and perhaps some believe less perfect now, it is a religion I truly believe takes most of its followers in the right direction—despite the criminal and degrading acts of some. The key for Catholics today is knowing the individual priests of their church because, in effect, they are their church.

The message given to us by God through Jesus Christ and His Apostles is a good one. Some human beings are always going to find a way to take advantage of a good thing and perhaps even destroy it. But after two thousand years, the Catholic Church, with all of its turmoil in history, still stands. The message lives because the message is good and true, and the Messenger was sent from Heaven.

None of us ever will live up totally to the example of Jesus, but all of us must continue to work toward Heaven. As Catholics, we are taught about the mystery of faith. And as an adult, I have read many books to educate myself about the Bible, Jesus, and the Catholic Church to try and diminish that mystery. My studies have given me a better understanding of each of those subjects, but nonetheless, my faith is still a mystery.

Given all of the questions and conflicting stories in the Bible, I have come to the conclusion that the Gospels and New Testament provide a roadmap for moral direction. I want to be a good and honest person, living a good life and doing good to honor God. And like any person, that is a difficult thing to accomplish. But I keep trying. Sometimes I succeed, sometimes I fail. But I never give up.

I am the product of two good parents and a mother who believed strongly in God and the Catholic Church. They didn't have all the answers either, but they did have a pretty good idea of right and wrong. Because of them, my brother, three sisters, and I all turned out to be decent people, good Catholics. If I can do as well for my kids, I will be happy. That is why we are sitting in St. Peter Chanel Church, watching Father Frank begin the Mass. It's the house of God and the faith I want my children to maintain in their lives.

Chapter Thirty-five

MONUMENT OF
LOVE

The sky was overcast with a threat of rain on Saturday, July 28, 2004. Maureen, Danny, Kathy, Margaret, and I were back in the front pews of St. Bede's Church with our families. Nearly thirty years after losing our mother and father, we decided to honor them with a more impressive grave monument at St. Mary's Cemetery that would provide a more detailed account of their lives and the contribution they made to the world.

Father Marion Soprych, the associate pastor, honored our request to dedicate the 8:00 A.M. Mass to our parents, allowing me to read a memorial essay on the altar about the lives of the two people who meant so much to us. This is the eulogy that should have been given at their funerals, but we were all too young and distraught to even think about such a thing. I stood behind the new, small metal lectern that had replaced the large wooden one I knew from my altar boy days. Looking out at those familiar pews, I was surprised to see the church had a fairly good-sized congregation, mostly elderly parishioners, some of whom I recognized as friends and neighbors of my parents.

The five of us were there to honor our parents in their church and bring proper closure to their lives. Being able to state their history on the altar of that magnificent sanctuary along with their sacrifice and efforts for their five children and church felt like the appropriate conclusion for their time living on South Kostner.

After Mass, Father James Hyland, who was a priest at St. Bede's in the 1980s, was kind enough to meet us at the cemetery to bless the new monument and perform an appropriate Catholic dedication. My brother, three sisters, and I stood with praying hands in front of the large black inscribed stone monument, surrounded by our spouses and the sixteen children we brought into this world. As the priest spoke, I couldn't help but think about how happy my parents would be knowing their five children were able to overcome the adversity of their early departures and live happy lives as practicing Catholics.

Maureen spent twelve years as an oncology nurse in the cancer unit at the University of Chicago's Billings Hospital. She married Tom Gibbons, a lawyer, and has four children: Tracy, Austin, Claire, and Paul. After having her first child, she elected to stay home to raise her children in their home in the southwest suburbs. They are parishioners at Our Lady of the Woods Parish.

Kathy graduated from Illinois State University, married Tom Savory, a construction worker, and has three children: Colleen, Ben, and Martha. She is in a management position at Northwestern Hospital in Chicago, where she has worked for more than twenty-four years. They live in a closeknit Catholic community, about two miles from our old home on South Kostner and are members of Most Holy Redeemer Parish.

Danny graduated from DePaul University with a physics degree, married Shari Klutcharch, a grammar-school teacher who spent time teaching at St. Bede's, and they have three children: Kasie, Karlie, and Michael. Danny later earned a master's degree in marketing from St. Xavier University, where he was No. 1 in his class. He has worked for West Shore Pipeline as an engineer for the past fifteen years and covers high-school sports for the *Chicago Sun-Times* as a side job. They belong to St. Terrence Parish.

Margaret graduated from Northern Illinois University, married Mike Sedlak, an investment analyst, and has two children: Brian and Marilyn. Margaret worked in the information technology department for Tellabs before becoming a homemaker to stay home and raise her children. They are members of St. Francis of Assisi Parish.

I graduated from Chicago State University with a degree in English and landed a job at the *Chicago Sun-Times* and later moved into public relations. I have been running my own agency for more than twelve years, while writing books and plays and coaching kids in several sports on the side. Char worked at Chicago Title and Trust guiding new homebuyers through the closing process before becoming a full-time homemaker for the past decade, raising four very active and beautiful children.

Between the five Ruanes from South Kostner in Chicago, we have brought sixteen Catholic children into the world, none of whom has had the opportunity to meet two of the best people God ever put on this earth, our parents.